Jim Thorpe

Jim Thorpe
A Biography

WILLIAM A. COOK

McFarland & Company, Inc., Publishers
Jefferson, North Carolina, and London

LIBRARY OF CONGRESS CATALOGUING-IN-PUBLICATION DATA

Cook, William A.
    Jim Thorpe : a biography / William A. Cook.
        p.   cm.
    Includes bibliographical references and index.

    ISBN 978-0-7864-6355-8
    softcover : 50# alkaline paper ∞

    1. Thorpe, Jim, 1887–1953.   2. Athletes — United States —
Biography.   3. Indian athletes — United States — Biography.
I. Title.
    GV697.T5C66   2011   796'.092 — dc23   [B]   2011021908

BRITISH LIBRARY CATALOGUING DATA ARE AVAILABLE

On the cover: Jim Thorpe at the 1912 Summer Olympics in
Sweden, in his Canton Bulldogs football uniform, and in
spring training with the New York Giants in 1918

Manufactured in the United States of America

McFarland & Company, Inc., Publishers
Box 611, Jefferson, North Carolina 28640
www.mcfarlandpub.com

For Andrea Teitelbaum
A lovely lady in so many ways

Table of Contents

Introduction

Not too long ago, whenever the question of who was the greatest athlete of the twentieth century occurred in casual conversation, the name of Jim Thorpe would quickly be introduced into the dialogue. But today, in the second decade of the twenty-first century, Thorpe's star seems to flicker more than shine. In fact, there are at least a couple of generations of Americans who have no idea who Jim Thorpe was or what he accomplished in the world of sports.

Among some informed observers, the theory has prevailed for several decades that Jim Thorpe was intentionally maligned by his legions of critics and contemporaries. Also it has been alleged that various historians and writers have manufactured negative facts and incidents and falsely attributed them to Thorpe, which has resulted in harming his legacy. Therefore, to separate fact from fiction, it is time to tell Thorpe's story again.

Jim Thorpe was a gifted athlete and excelled in every sport in which he participated. When it was a game, it just came easy to Thorpe. The better the competition, the better he performed. When Thorpe won gold medals in the pentathlon and decathlon in the 1912 Olympic Games in Stockholm, setting a record that would stand for two decades, it prompted Sweden's King Gustav V to proclaim "You, sir, are the greatest athlete in the word." Perhaps at that time, Jim Thorpe was indeed just that.

At the time of the 1912 Olympic Games, Thorpe was already a legendary All-American football player and track star at The Carlisle Indian School. A few years later he would become a pioneering professional football player with the Canton Bulldogs. Then he would become one of the founders of the National Football League. Also he played professional football for a paltry salary when the game was in its infancy and unbelievably rough and tumble play prevailed by today's standards.

Despite the historical criticism of his ability on the baseball diamond — that he couldn't hit a curve ball — Jim Thorpe played major league baseball for six seasons with the New York Giants, Cincinnati Reds and Boston Braves, and played several other seasons with highly competitive Triple A clubs in the minor leagues. Also it is only fair to point out that Thorpe played professional baseball in the "deadball era" preventing him from using his overwhelming power to hit home runs. He was also a tenacious wrestler, excellent lacrosse player, a very good bowler and a good golfer.

But as life is more than games, it was life outside of his familiar comfort zone in the stadium where Thorpe had problems excelling. For Jim Thorpe the troubles began when he was arbitrarily stripped of his Olympic medals in early 1913 by the A.A.U. and the American Olympic Committee, for committing the sin of having played minor league baseball for $15 a month during the summer while a student at The Carlisle Indian School. At that time, such summer activity was common among collegiate athletes. Thorpe got caught because he played under his correct name rather than use an alias, and it's impossible to think that following his 1912 Olympic achievements and the enormous fame which followed, there would be any place in the world for Jim Thorpe to hide. He had become a household name and his picture was in every newspaper around the globe.

Jim Thorpe was born in the Indian Territory before it was joined with the Territory of Oklahoma and admitted to the Union as the State of Oklahoma. The U.S. 7th Cavalry's massacre of the Sioux and Lakota at Wounded Knee in South Dakota occurred when Thorpe was two years old. He grew up in the Native American culture of the late nineteenth century and was confronted with the existing racism of the time. Nonetheless, while his life story does bring to light many events surrounding the history and plight of the Native American experience of that time, the life of Jim Thorpe is not just an Indian story. In fact, Jim Thorpe was not even a full-blooded Indian, but rather an ethnic mixture of Sac and Fox, Pottawatomie, Irish and French.

As an adult Thorpe's stardom more often than not trumped his ethnicity on the playing field. But in society at large, he was held to a different standard than his white contemporaries. Married three times, he had a penchant for the heavy consumption of alcohol, was aloof, had wanderlust and made many bad business decisions that left him nearly financially destitute throughout much of his life. Thorpe's frailties were regarded by his critics as indigenous to his Native American background. Still, there was nothing complex about the personality of Jim Thorpe—what you saw was what you got. He was a star athlete who chose not to act like one.

Throughout it all, the good times and bad times, Thorpe had a perpetual twinkle in his eye. He was a man with a huge sense of humor and was always ready to unleash a practical joke on an unsuspecting bystander. His achievements in football were so large and legendary that when he was recalling events in later years, it was nearly impossible to determine if he was stretching the facts or not. In 1951, replying to a question posed by a wide-eyed fan about the longest punt he ever made, Thorpe stated rather nonchalantly, 90 yards, when he played for the Canton Bulldogs. But he couldn't remember who the opposing team was.

Jim Thorpe cared deeply about his family and others he came to know throughout his tumultuous life. Perhaps his greatest fault was that he trusted those involved with his life way too much. Those he trusted so often harbored ulterior motives while guiding his most important life and business decisions. The reality about Jim Thorpe was that he was a victim of circumstances more than a man of great physical character lacking moral character, as his critics would suggest.

Although Thorpe was indifferent to his celebrity, never read his fan mail and turned down hundreds of offers to use his name, others viewed him as a cash cow. Almost from the time Thorpe became a national star on the gridiron scene at The Carlisle Indian School in 1909, until the day he died in 1953 at Lomita, California, outside Los Angeles, someone was attempting to profit from his athletic fame. Glenn "Pop" Warner, his coach at Carlisle, profited from his association with Thorpe; John McGraw of the New York Giants profited from his association with him; so did George Halas and the other founders of the National Football League, Hollywood profited from him, the Olympic Games profited from him. In fact, the attempt to profit from Jim Thorpe's athletic fame continues posthumously to this very day.

In an attempt to cash in on Jim Thorpe's fame, in 1954 a deal was worked out by Thorpe's third wife Patricia and the former Pennsylvania towns of Mauch Chunk and East Mauch Chunk, located between Harrisburg and Gettysburg. The two towns merged to become The Borough of Jim Thorpe, Pennsylvania, and then became Thorpe's burial site. However the town has never really seen a windfall in tourism resulting from his burial within its borders.

Nonetheless Jim Thorpe is still not permitted to rest in peace in his $17,000 mausoleum located on a quite hillside just outside of town. In a further appalling affront to his legacy, in June, 2010, Thorpe's oldest son Jack (by his second marriage), filed suit attempting to exhume his father's body from its final resting place and return it to tribal control in Oklahoma. The outcome of that suit was not known when I completed the manuscript.

In this work, I have attempted to fairly and accurately chronicle the life and times of Jim Thorpe, both on the athletic field and in his personal affairs. Most of the previous works done on Thorpe tend to emphasize his Olympic glory and college football heroics. However, one of the areas of his life which

I have attempted to expand upon and provide broader detail and analysis of is his major league baseball career. Not enough has been written about this phase of Thorpe's life. In previous works, his baseball experience is either dismissed entirely or quickly gone over in a superficial chapter, relegated to nonessential status in his total story. The truth is Thorpe was dedicated to making it in the big leagues. However, he was not taken seriously by those responsible for managing his career or those in the media who wrote about it. In many ways, Thorpe had become a tourist attraction in a big league uniform long before becoming a tourist attraction lying interred in a mausoleum at Old Mauch Chunk, Pennsylvania.

Thorpe's passion for and participation in baseball deserves as much attention in telling his story as does his participation in track and football. Nonetheless it is impossible to ignore Thorpe's glory on the gridiron and his achievements in the Olympic Games. So in order to understand the Thorpe story completely, first the reader needs to know who the man was and where he came from and how the world around him molded him into the man he became. Then it is necessary to chronicle his involvement in the three sports of baseball, football and track concurrently, as I have done here.

To tell the complete story of Jim Thorpe, it is necessary to follow him from his lofty position at the peak of the mountain in American sports heroism to his slow mudslide down the side of that mountain into the pit of obscurity. It is still appalling to consider that in just 20 years, two decades, Jim Thorpe went from being the most celebrated athlete in the world for his achievements in the 1912 Olympics Games in Stockholm, to not having enough money to purchase a ticket to view the 1932 Olympic Games in Los Angeles.

In writing this account of Jim Thorpe's life, I should like to acknowledge the following organizations that opened their archival material to me and thereby provided a wide variety of information that assisted my attempt to gain a broad understanding of the man. They are the Cumberland County Historical Society, Carlisle Pennsylvania, Pro Football Hall of Fame, Canton, Ohio, and the National Baseball Hall of Fame and Museum Library, Cooperstown, New York.

1

Ancestors

The Fox were fierce warriors and fought against the Sioux, the Illinois and the French. During the early and mid–eighteenth century, the French kept up a campaign of harassment against the Fox that by 1730 had reduced the tribe to a mere handful. The Sac and remaining Fox Indians were separate tribes closely related to the Algonquins linguistically. But the two tribes were allies and they met in Wisconsin and joined to become one powerful tribe of 6,500. Following a war against the Illinois in 1765, the united tribes of Sac and Fox moved into the Illinois territory. Then in 1804 the Sac and Fox Indians were tricked by the U.S. Government into ceding their vast tribal lands in northwestern Illinois and by treaty moved west of the Mississippi River. Although many refused to go, by 1831 most of the Sac and Fox had crossed the Mississippi into Iowa.

The Black Hawk War of 1831 was named after their leader, Chief Black Hawk. At the age of 15, Black Hawk had distinguished himself in battle. At 17 years old he led a Sac and Fox war party against the Osage and took his first scalp. By the time he reached 19 years old he had led his tribesmen against an equal number of Cherokee and killed half of them. Black Hawk was also a great athlete who was the best runner, jumper, swimmer and wrestler in the tribe.

In May 1832, Black Hawk, with 450 warriors and 1,500 women and children, returned to Illinois to reclaim their tribal homeland attacking frontier settlements. Governor John Reynolds called for Illinois volunteers to assist federal troops in repelling the invasion. One such volunteer was Abraham Lincoln. Lincoln was chosen by his fellow volunteers as the militia captain of the force of volunteers from the New Salem area. However, Lincoln was to see practically no military action in the conflict.

The conflict came to a conclusion on July 21, 1832, when federal troops caught up with Black Hawk's band at the Battle of Wisconsin Heights. On August 8, Black Hawk surrendered. Then a desperate race ensued by Black Hawk's band toward the Mississippi which culminated with the tribe's destruction on the river's banks by the U.S. Army and Illinois militia.

Chief Black Hawk spent his last years living on a reservation at Fort Des Moines. It was there that Jim Thorpe's Irish grandfather settled among the Indians and married one of Chief Black Hawk's granddaughters. The two had a son they named Hiram. He was Jim Thorpe's father.

Jim Thorpe was said to have had a remarkable resemblance to his great-grandfather Black Hawk and was extremely proud of the genetic connection. "I am no more proud of my career as an athlete than I am of the fact that I am a direct descendant of that noble warrior,"[1] remarked Thorpe.

However, in his later years Jim Thorpe would say with a soft smile that he was not an FBI (full-blooded Indian). Thorpe's ethnic heritage was actually five-eighths Indian. His father Hiram Thorpe was half–Irish and half–Sac and Fox. His mother Charlotte was three-quarters Pottawatomie and Kick-apoo and one-quarter French. She was a devote Roman Catholic and raised her children accordingly.

But throughout his life, Jim Thorpe expressed as much pride in his Irish heritage as he did in his Indian heritage. Also Thorpe felt that it was because of his ¼ Irish heritage that he could not handle the "firewater."

Thorpe's half–Irish father Hiram was an adventurer, blacksmith, hunter, trapper and trader. He was a big man, six feet two and 230 pounds, and was considered the best wrestler in the county. Hiram married at least five Indian women and fathered more than 20 children.

Hiram Thorpe lived peacefully on the reservation growing up, marring and starting a family. But when government officials on the reservation at Fort Des Moines began to interfere with Indian prerogatives, Hiram made plans to leave. When his wife died, he left Jim Thorpe's half-sister Mary and half-brother Frank, in a school on the reservation and set out for Indian Territory in Oklahoma. Soon after arriving in the Indian Territory, Hiram married Char-lotte View, a 220-pound woman who was Thorpe's mother. The two gave birth to a son they named George, who was seven years older than Jim Thorpe.

Hiram Thorpe and his family lived on land granted for use by the Indians as a result of the General Allotment Act of 1887. However, they never owned the land. The Thorpes' ranch consisted of 160 acres and they raised hogs, cattle and horses and a few crops. According to Jim Thorpe's son Jack, the cabin was built on top of a ridge, because the Sac and Fox people always built their houses on a ridge to get the wind.

On May 28, 1888, James Francis Thorpe and his twin brother Charlie were born in a one-room log cabin built by his father from hickory and cot-tonwood trees on the North Canadian River in Prague, Oklahoma. Prague was a trading point for most of the Indians in South Central Oklahoma, not far from Shawnee. There is some historical argument about the year of Jim

Thorpe's birth. The *Baseball Encyclopedia* lists it as 1887. But according to Thorpe, his papers from the Indian Nations listed his birth year as 1888. Regardless, Jim and Charlie were healthy, robust babies each weighing ten pounds.

It was not difficult to tell Jim and Charlie apart. According to Thorpe, Charlie had dark copper skin. As for himself, he had the physique and facial expression of a Native American, but he had lighter skin coloring and a strong Irish jaw that gave him a slightly different appearance. Charlie was Jim's constant playmate until he died of spinal meningitis at the age of eight.

Soon after Jim's birth his mother looked out of the window and saw the sun shining brightly on the path to the cabin. Following the Indian custom of naming the child after the first sight the mother sees after giving birth, Charlotte gave Jim Thorpe the Indian name of Wa-Tho-Huck, which translated means "Bright Path."

2

The Road to Carlisle

Following the Revolutionary War, the question of how to deal with the Indian problem during white westward expansion and settlement had been constantly in the foreground of American domestic policy. President Thomas Jefferson created the reservation system and declared that all native peoples should be moved by force if necessary beyond the Mississippi River. But decade by decade the boundary for Indian lands just kept getting smaller.

Eleven months after the Thorpe twins were born in the Indian Territory of Prague, Oklahoma, the United States Government opened up two million acres of Oklahoma to settlement by white people. On April 22, 1889, 50,000 men and women, nursing mothers, businessmen, laborers, farmers, hobos and thieves from every state in the Union, who became known as "the Boomers," rushed to the western border of Oklahoma in the anticipation of free land. All that was required to stake a claim for 160 acres was to drive a pointed stake into the ground. Within 24 hours claims for all two million acres had been staked. Armed U.S. Cavalry attempted to keep order, but chaos reigned. Overnight new towns such as Oklahoma City and Guthrie were born.

Until this time, most of Oklahoma had been deemed by the U.S. Government as Indian Territory. Since the early 1800s the Osage, Wichita, Kiowa and Comanche Indians had been living there. Between 1820 and 1840 five other tribes from the southeastern United States, the Cherokee, Choctaw, Creek, Chickasaw and Seminole Indians, known as the "Five Civilized Tribes," were relocated into the Indian Territory.

The Indian Territory served as the destination for the United States government's policy of Indian Removal from the east coast and southern areas. The policy was carried out vigorously by President Andrew Jackson following passage of the Indian Removal Act of 1830. After following the "trail of tears," from the southeast, the "Five Civilized" tribes settled in, set up towns such as Tulsa, Tahlequah and Muskogee, built homes, planted crops and established their own governments and schools.

Many of the Indians from the "Five Civilized" tribes who had become planters owned slaves. Some had previously owned slaves and brought them with them on the "trail of tears." Subsequently many of the tribes fought on the side of the Confederacy during the Civil War. As retribution, the U.S. government had already taken away the western half of Oklahoma from the "Five Civilized" tribes, but it remained Indian Territory. Then in 1889, the Indian Territory was opened to settlement after the U.S. Government felt intense pressure from whites. During the administration of President Benjamin Harrison, three million acres of Oklahoma land was forcibly purchased from the Indians.

At that time, except in a few big cities in the eastern United States with diverse populations, the white, Protestant work ethic and its three components of education, hard work and thrift was the dominant culture for most of American society. However, for the 250,000 Indians in North America, a different philosophy prevailed.

Robert Ornstein, PhD., is a psychologist, educator and writer who taught at the University of California Medical Center and Stanford University. His pioneering research on the bilateral specialization of the brain has done much to advance the understanding of how people think. Ornstein offers a rather esoteric definition of the differences in white and Indian cultural thought. Ornstein believes whites or Anglos are predominantly concerned with materialism in their thinking, thereby relying nearly wholly on the rational, intellectual function of the human brain's left cerebral hemisphere. Therefore, from their arrival on the North American continent whites "have viewed the land as a vast treasure house of inanimate nature to be plundered at will."[1] On the other hand, the Indians, going back to pre–Columbian times, "were geared to the brain's right hemisphere, which controls intuitional and spiritual perceptions, reflecting their holistic orientation in space and time."[2]

If one accepts Ornstein's explanation, it would follow that, to most whites of the late nineteenth century, the "Five Civilized" tribes' form of civilization was a half-baked loaf. Some of the skepticism of whites toward the prevailing standard of civilization among the tribes was fueled in part by a stereotype perpetuated by the habits of the Indians themselves. Eastern whites often viewed the typical Indians of the western planes as lazy, content to bask in the sun while the squaws did most of the work.

Although a competent and elaborate system of schools was established in the Indian Territory to educate the Indians, many of them seemed to prefer the traditional communism and spiritualism inherit in tribal life. They remained indifferent to their relationship to the changing world around them. Furthermore the U.S. Bureau of Indian Affairs was constantly attempting to insert itself in every aspect of tribal life, causing the Indians to be suspicious of the government's motives, keep them at arm's length and reject the white man's obsession with materialism.

When Jim Thorpe was three years old, the family moved one mile up the river to a new cabin that was larger with two rooms. There his two sisters, Mary and Adeline, and brother Eddie were born. Thorpe grew up Western and Indian. Oklahoma would not join the Union as the 46th state until 1907. Also the oil boom had not yet taken place in Oklahoma, and oil wells had not yet fouled the streams. The woods were still wide open and all the Thorpes became self-reliant, skilled hunters, tracking game by sign and running their coon hounds. Jim was a dead shot with a rifle and bagged his first deer at age ten. However, he was taught by his father Hiram to kill only what was needed for food. There were plenty of wild horses and by the age of 15 Thorpe had learned to rope and ride wild ponies. His passion was to work with new and unbroken colts that were born each year. Later Thorpe would say saddling and riding unbroken colts made him strong and alert.

The Thorpe farm, thanks to an additional allotment from the government, now consisted of two tracts of 160 acres, and the daily chores were considerable. Jim's major task was to feed all the livestock. In the evenings, when all the chores were done, the Thorpe family sat down to dinner and Hiram led them in prayer. He instilled in his children a sense of gratitude for all the beautiful things that God had created. Prior to their meal, they drank water because it was the substance of life. Then they gave thanks to God for the food they were about to eat.

Usually on Saturday afternoons all the men from the nearby village would gather in front of the Thorpes' cabin. Sometimes their families brought food for an impromptu feast later that evening. Then all the men would compete with one another in various sports such as running, wrestling, horseback riding, and high and broad jumping. Thorpe said that his father was always the undisputed champion in these games.

In 1894, Jim and Charlie began their schooling at the Sac and Fox reservation school near Tecumseh about 23 miles away from where the family lived. They only came home on holidays and in the summer. The school was adequate academically and strict in discipline. Some of the Indian students could not speak or understand English, so it took considerable time to complete lessons. On many occasions students were subjected to corporal punishment when they could not spell a simple word.

Jim had a hard time adjusting from the start. His mind wandered from the blackboard to the woods. Charlie's attention span was stronger and he was the better student. However, it was at the reservation school where Jim first experienced baseball. His older brother George instructed him in the game. Like white students of the time all over the west, the Indian students would choose up teams and, lacking diamonds, play games out in a field. They called it prairie baseball.

The bond between the twins was very strong and they did everything together. When Charlie died during their third year in school, Jim, now eight years old, suddenly became withdrawn, a loner and homesick. Terribly despondent in 1898, just before the end of his fourth year at the school, Thorpe decided to run away from the school and walked the 23-mile distance home. However, upon arrival his mother frowned and his father Hiram scolded him with swaggering western bravado, telling Jim that he had to get right back on the horse that had thrown him. Hiram immediately returned Jim to the school by walking him the 23 miles back.

That summer, Hiram, knowing how deeply Jim felt the loss of Charlie, allowed him to accompany him on a major hunting trip for the first time. Hiram Thorpe was filled with boundless energy and it was a very difficult task for Jim, ten years old, to keep up with him as he sometimes covered more than 30 miles a day. Thorpe was to remark that on one occasion when they did not have enough horses to carry their entire kill, his father slung a deer over each shoulder and carried them home, a distance of 20 miles.

When the fall came Jim returned to school. However, still unable to adjust without Charlie, he ran away again. Once again, Hiram took him back. Jim immediately ran away again, this time using a short-cut to reach home in 18 miles and before his father arrived. Now Hiram Thorpe was livid. He vowed to send Jim so far away to school that it would be impossible for him to run away again. During the summer Hiram had made the acquaintance of a recruiter from the Haskell Institute just south of Lawrence, Kansas, an Indian school ran by the U.S. government. At the time, it had more than a thousand Indian children enrolled from more than ninety tribes.

On September 18, 1898, young Jim Thorpe was enrolled in Haskell. Haskell had adopted the military school type of training that was in use at the Carlisle Indian School at Carlisle, Pennsylvania. So the Indian students wore uniforms, marched and were discouraged from holding on to tribal ways.

It was at Haskell that young Jim Thorpe saw his first football game. An Indian on the Haskell team by the name of Chauncey Archiquette, a big 200-pound fullback, became his idol and Jim tried to emulate him. Archiquette took a liking to Thorpe and made a leather football for him stuffed with rags. Too young to play football, Thorpe organized a team among his classmates. They would practice on the Haskell athletic field when the football team was not using it. He said that even then he played in the backfield because of his speed. Thorpe and his classmates also played baseball and basketball. Furthermore Thorpe began to watch the track team and began jumping a fence over and over as if it were a hurdle. Nonetheless, Thorpe was not happy with his educational experience at Haskell, and his truancy continued.

In 1900, Thorpe learned of a letter that his father sent to Haskell officials stating that he had been shot in a hunting accident. The letter included train fare for Thorpe to come home to Oklahoma. However, the school officials concealed the letter from Thorpe. When he learned about the letter from a classmate who had seen it, Thorpe decided to run away from Haskell. So he hopped a freight train, hoping that it was headed south, only to discover that it was headed in the wrong direction. During the night he jumped off and began walking the 270 miles home. It took him weeks to get there and when he finally arrived at home, he discovered that his father had lost a lot of weight but was out of danger.

This time he was not scorned for leaving school and was welcomed back home. However, a few weeks later, his mother died of blood poisoning and was buried at the Sacred Heart Mission in Sacred Heart, Oklahoma. A few weeks later, Thorpe and his brother George were beaten brutally by a deeply grief-ridden Hiram. After Hiram had gone into Shawnee on business, Jim and George went fishing and neglected to feed the livestock. When Hiram returned, he found his herd scattered about the farm and lost control.

While Jim remarked later that he deserved the beating, he didn't feel like taking it. Without having even a penny in his pockets, he decided to leave home and set out for the Panhandle country of Texas. Jim Thorpe was just 13 years old and he was determined, according to tribal custom, to prove himself a man. After finding work fixing fences and taming wild horses, he stayed there a year. He saved enough money to buy a team of horses. His self-esteem restored, Jim went back to his father's home with the horses and was welcomed back.

The next three years Thorpe helped his brother George care for their younger siblings Mary, Adeline and Eddie, who was three. Jim also made another attempt at getting an education and attended a public school in Garden Grove about three miles from his family home. There were no sports at the school and it was all book work. However, according to Thorpe, although he never liked books, he was happy, he had his horse to ride, the woods to hunt in and the stream to swim and fish. By now Thorpe had acquired a reputation as a rather shiftless youth, lacking in ambition. His predominant trait was a huge sense of humor. At the school, if a prank was perpetrated, it was certain Jim was mixed up in it.

There are two common accounts of how Jim Thorpe became enrolled at the Carlisle Indian School. Thorpe never acknowledged if one or the other was true. One story is that, sometime in early 1904, Alex Crain, a government agent working around Wewoka, Oklahoma, discovered Jim Thorpe after speaking with George Washington, a legendary football player at Haskell, who had known Jim while he was enrolled there. Crain became convinced of Thorpe's enormous potential as an athlete and believed he would be a good fit for Pop Warner and Carlisle.

By 1904 no explanation of the Carlisle Indians football team was necessary. The squad was already famous coast-to-coast. Thorpe had already demonstrated some prowess in baseball through his pitching and baserunning abilities, playing on an organized team in Prague sponsored by Ensley Barbour, proprietor of the only movie house in town. Also when participating in the Indian games of medicine ball and lacrosse, he showed some very high promise. The teams he played on always seemed to win. It seemed that inside of Jim Thorpe there was some latent ability. But at that time, he had not been pushed to show his overall potential. In fact, he didn't care for athletics one way or the other.

So according to this account, Crain approached Hiram Thorpe and convinced him to enroll Jim at Carlisle. Thorpe's older brothers had attended Carlisle, so it didn't take much convincing for him to agree, and he signed an application blank to enroll Jim in the school. According to Hiram, Jim was getting worse every day and "I wanted him to go and make something of him Self for he cannot do it hear."[3] (The spelling is the elder Thorpe's.) Furthermore, legend has it that Hiram was also convinced of Jim's athletic potential and wanted him to show other races what an Indian could do.

The other account of how Jim Thorpe was enrolled in Carlisle suggests that it was simply happenstance, that Alex Crain had no particular knowledge of Thorpe's potential athletic prowess and was simply traveling through his Oklahoma territory on a fundamental exercise of his duties for the Bureau of Indian Affairs. Acting in an official capacity, Crain asked Hiram Thorpe if he cared to enroll his son. So the fact that Thorpe's name appeared on the Carlisle application blank rather than a neighboring Indian youth's was simply the luck of the draw.

Regardless of which story is true, on February 4, 1904, Jim Thorpe, 15 years old, got off the train at Carlisle, Pennsylvania and reluctantly entered the Carlisle Indian School. He had only a basic knowledge of letters from his learning at the reservation schools, weighed just 115 pounds and didn't even remotely resemble an athlete, much less a world-class athlete. A little over two months later, on April 24, Hiram died from blood poisoning. Jim was unable to return home for his father's funeral. Hiram Thorpe was buried in the community cemetery in a prairie near the Garden Grove school house.

The Carlisle Indian School was founded on November 1, 1879, by former U.S. Army Lieutenant Richard Henry Pratt. Pratt had been born at Rushford, New York, December 6, 1840, and grown up in Logansport, Indiana. Serving in the Army of the Cumberland during the Civil War, he had fought in the battles of Shiloh, Nashville, Pittsburg Landing and Chickamauga. Following the war he returned to Indiana and entered the hardware business. However, in 1867 he re-entered the Army as a Second Lieutenant in the Tenth U.S. Cavalry and was assigned to duty in Texas, the Indian Territory of Oklahoma and at Ft. Sill after it was staked out in 1869 by Major General Philip H. Sheridan.

Ft. Sill was used as a base of operations in campaigns to stop hostile tribes from raiding border settlements in Texas and Kansas. After being promoted to First Lieutenant, Pratt commanded a unit of "buffalo soldiers" (African American Cavalry) against Indian tribes in campaigns of 1868-69 and the Red River War in 1874-75. In part, Pratt's assignment was to keep the Kiowa, Cheyenne and other sometimes hostile tribes on reservations. It was while in service with soldiers of color during these campaigns that Pratt began to express a sense of fairness toward the races.

In late 1875, Lieutenant Pratt was detailed to Fort Marion, St. Augustine, Florida, to oversee Indian prisoners of war. It was there that he was first successful in his attempts to educate Indians. Pratt established a school and also sent Indians out on labor details. Both endeavors brought Indians into contact with white civilization. Many of the Indians quickly adapted, wanted to stay and some even sought to have their wives and children sent to Florida. However, the government opposed the request and made plans to return them to reservations upon their release.

Sympathetic to the plight of the Indian, Pratt sought to expand his Indian educational experiment and was sent to organize an Indian Branch of the Hampton Normal and Agricultural Institute in Virginia. Up until this time Hampton had been a school established for the exclusive education of Negroes. Nonetheless, in the fall of 1878, Lieutenant Pratt was sent to Dakota to select Indian students for Hampton. Soon after he brought 49 Indians to Hampton and was ordered to remain with them while they adjusted to their environment.

According to Pratt, "When we begin to give our Indians the same chances of development and association as a real part of our American family, which we force on foreign immigrants and all our other folks, they will quickly become like the rest of us. The Indian problem originated with and is perpetuated by us, and the Indian is in no sense to blame."[4]

After three months at Hampton, Pratt reported to the Secretary of War that his task had been completed and requested that he be returned to his regiment. But the U.S. government had been impressed with Pratt's ability to educate and socialize Indians. So he was encouraged by the Secretary of War and the Secretary of the Interior to continue with such efforts.

Based upon his observations at Hampton, Pratt felt it would benefit the Indian and African American students if they were separated, because the two groups had different needs. Pratt felt that as the eight million African Americans already spoke English and had lived and worked among whites for 200 years, they were familiar with their dominant culture norms. The Indians, who spoke very little or no English, would require a more intense socialization process. Furthermore as deeper prejudice existed in white society towards African Americans, their integration into the body politic was a far different and more difficult task than that of the Indians. In short, Pratt theorized that, by separating Indian students, who were fewer in number, from African American students in the educational process, he was putting them on the "fast track" to assimilation in white society.

In 1878, at the suggestion of the Secretary of War and Secretary of the Interior, a special clause was inserted into the Army Appropriation Bill, authorizing the detail of an officer of the army, not to be above the rank of Captain, to oversee Indian education at Carlisle. General William Tecumseh Sherman, commander of the army, and General Winfield Scott Hancock, commander of the Department of the Atlantic where the Carlisle Barracks were located, both agreed and Lieutenant Pratt was detailed as the superintendent and granted permission to convert part of the U.S. Army's underutilized 6th Cavalry Barracks in Carlisle, Pennsylvania, into an Indian school. While the Indian education project at Carlisle had been launched, a formal bill for authorization of funds would not be approved by Congress and become law until July 31, 1882.

The Carlisle Barracks had an interesting history. During the Revolutionary War, Carlisle, in a location remote from military operations, was used by the colonial government as both a recruiting station and a POW camp. After two British regiments were captured by General Montgomery in Canada in the spring of 1776, prisoners were sent to Lancaster and then some were sent on to Carlisle. Later in the year, after these prisoners were exchanged, Hessians captured by General George Washington at Trenton were sent to Carlisle. On the night of July 1, 1863, the barracks were ordered burned by Confederate General Fitzhugh Lee on his way to the Battle of Gettysburg. The barracks were rebuilt in 1865 and used as a school for cavalry and a depot for U.S. stores, until this operation was transferred to St. Louis in 1872. At the time Captain Pratt suggested it for the site of the Indian school, it was unoccupied.

In 1879 the first 82 Indian children and young adults arrived in Carlisle. They ranged in age from ten to 25 years old. Some were recruited by Pratt from the Lakota tribes' Rosebud and Pine Ridge reservations in the Dakota Territory. In fact, Pratt went to the Dakota Territory and met personally with Rosebud Chief Spotted Tail Milk and Pine Ridge Chief Red Cloud. Spotted Tail gave Pratt five of his own children to enroll in Carlisle. A few weeks later more Indian students arrived who were members of the Kiowa, Comanche and Cheyenne tribes that were U.S. Government prisoners from the Red River War that Pratt had been engaged in. They had been transported from Leavenworth to Florida.

Although the teachers had been hand-picked by Pratt, hired and were ready to start expediting the educational process, the Bureau of Indian Affairs considered Carlisle a low priority and failed to provide the necessary supplies and equipment for the school. As a consequence, for months the first students had no beds and slept on the floor wrapped in their blankets. Pratt had also hired a barber to cut the arriving students' long hair. It was this tonsorial requirement that would be the first cultural disconnect between the school and its students. To the Lakota, cutting their hair was symbolic of mourning when someone had died. Consequently, pained wailing could be heard throughout many of those first nights.

There would be other cultural clashes in the immediate days following. One involved the issuing of army clothing in order to get the Indian students used to wearing the white man's clothes. Immediately many of the Indian children cut off the legs of the trousers at the hip, laying the upper part aside and using the legs as leggings. To remediate the situation, Lieutenant Pratt assembled the students and explained to them that the clothes which had been issued were property of the U.S. Army and belonged to the U.S. government. Therefore, as it was not their personal property, it should not be mutilated. It was only loaned to them so that they might present an appearance consistent with that of the people that they would now come in contact with each day. Dressing like the white man would eliminate barriers to acceptance for them.

The Carlisle Indian School was, by definition, a non-reservation school with modern buildings. However, Carlisle was not a college, but rather a vocational school with no grades higher than the 12th. The Carlisle Indian School was the white man's academic equivalent of a high school. Jim Thorpe had wanted to study electricity at Carlisle but it wasn't offered.

There were separate two-story dormitories for boys and girls. The students were awakened each morning at 6:00 A.M. by a bugle call, and taps were at 9:00 P.M. each evening. Breakfast was at 7:00 A.M., served in a large dining room. The school day was split between academics and industrial and home keeping education. Half of the day the students' classes included such subjects as English, math, history, drawing and composition. For the boys, the other half of the day consisted of training in the trades of carpentry, tailoring, tinsmithing, shoemaking and blacksmithing. The girls were taught in homemaking skills such as cooking, sewing, baking and laundering.

There was a strict quasi-military code of conduct to be followed at Carlisle. The students marched to and from their classes. Speaking their native language, or any other language than English, could result in a beating or having their mouth washed out with lye soap. Running away from the school would result in lock-up in one of the six cramped cells in the guard house built by Hessian prisoners during the Revolutionary War. Students could also be subjected to hard labor for various infractions. However, there was also a form of democratic justice that existed at Carlisle. Some punishments for rules broken were determined by a panel of the student's peers.

Every other Saturday the students who were on good behavior were permitted to enter the town of Carlisle. The boys and girls went on alternating weeks. On Sunday, they were all permitted to attend the church of their own faith. While the boys were permitted to attend on their own, it was necessary for the girls to have a chaperone. On Sunday evenings there would be a common religious service held in the school's auditorium. Speakers from the town of various faiths would be invited to lead the service.

Following Superintendent Pratt's philosophy that old tribal ways needed to be broken, the mission of Carlisle was to educate the Indian students and provide them with life skills that would assist them in avoiding a return their old tribal ways of living. To enhance the socialization of the Indian students, Pratt implemented an "outing system" through which Carlisle students each summer were placed in homes or on farms in the surrounding area to help them become better acquainted with white people and develop their work ethic. When students completed their education at Carlisle they were expected to go forward as American citizens and assimilate into white society.

Pratt's assimilation plan had its critics. One of the most vocal was Congressman Marcus Aurelius Smith of the Arizona Territory. According to Smith, "There is as much hope of educating the Apache as there is of educating the rattlesnake on which he feeds."[5]

Another critic, Gertrude Bonnin, aka Zitkala-Sa, was a famous Indian author and artist who had at one time taught at Carlisle. Bonnin objected to the forceful Christian indoctrination of the Indian students, the military-type discipline and limiting their education to vocational training. It was her belief that Carlisle was a "miserable state of cultural dislocation"[6] that created lasting problems for the children when they went home.

Between 1878 and 1918, 8,858 male and female Indian students would pass through the Carlisle Indian School, including Jim Thorpe. To the majority of Indians in the United States, Carlisle was their university. They considered it the highest honor that their children attended the school. Notwithstanding the historical arguments, pro and con, in regard to the forced socialization of the Indians in the Carlisle program, it is a fact that the overwhelming majority of Indian students who passed through the school, when so few other opportunities existed for them, emerged to live independent and productive lives, or became leaders upon their return to their tribes. Jim Thorpe became an American icon.

Lieutenant Richard Henry Pratt opened the Carlisle Indian School only two years after Colonel George A. Custer and 264 soldiers of the 7th U.S. Cavalry were killed in Montana by bands of Lakota and Cheyenne in the Battle of the Little Big Horn in the Sioux Indian War. The success of Carlisle is amazing when it is considered that Pratt's efforts in establishing a formal system of education for Indians were occurring at a time when relations between the tribes and the U.S. government were still extremely fragile. For his efforts in starting the school, in 1883, Richard Henry Pratt would be promoted to Captain.

3

The Rise of the Carlisle Athletic Program

The first Indian to play major league baseball was James Madison Toy, a first baseman in 1887 for the Cleveland Spiders of the American Association. Later he was a catcher in 1890 for the Brooklyn club of the same circuit. Toy, who was from Beaver Falls, Pennsylvania, was part Sioux. However, Toy's major league career was shortened due to an injury. Catching in a game for Brooklyn, Toy was struck in the groin by a pitched ball that bounced off the corner of home plate. The injury resulted in intermittent periods of pain for Toy so severe that it required supervised therapy with doses of morphine. Unable to play ball anymore, Toy returned to Beaver Falls and worked as a stove molder until his death on March 13, 1919.

Baseball had been one of the first sports organized at the Carlisle Indian School. But in 1897 when Louis Sockalexis, a Penobscot Indian from Maine, began playing for the Cleveland Spiders in the National League, interest in baseball soared among students on the Carlisle campus. This led Superintendent Pratt to have concerns that baseball could be disruptive to the school's summer outing system. He was sure a lot of Carlisle team players would choose to pursue playing professional baseball during the summer where they could make $50 to $150 a month, rather than $5 working on a farm, and have a lot more fun doing it.

The first baseball star to emerge from Carlisle was the great Charles "Chief" Bender. He attended Carlisle a decade prior to Jim Thorpe's entry into the school. At 5 feet 11 and 140 pounds, Bender hardly seemed athletic. Still he played football, although he hated it and hated practice too. Used as a reserve end, he was far from a standout.

But baseball was another matter; Chief Bender could pitch with authority. He began pitching batting practice for Carlisle. But by 1902, he had grown to six foot two, 185 pounds and was pitching in the American League for Connie Mack and the Philadelphia Athletics. In all, Bender would pitch major league ball for 16 years, finishing with a record of 210–127, including a no-hitter against Cleveland in 1910, and pitch in five World Series for the Athletics. In 1953, Chief Bender was elected to the National Baseball Hall of Fame. With Bender on the mound, Connie Mack became the first major league manager to win three World Series (1910, 1911, and 1913). Mack stated that Bender was his favorite pitcher because he never let him down in a crisis.

A teammate of Bender's on the Athletics in 1904 was Lou Bruce, a half–Iroquois and half–Scotch outfielder from St. Regis, New York. Bruce played in 30 games for Connie Mack with a batting average of .267 in 101 at-bats. Following his days on the diamond, Bruce became a Methodist preacher.

Besides Chief Bender, other Carlisle baseball team players who would precede Jim Thorpe to the major leagues included: Frank Jude, a Chippewa from Libby, Minnesota, who played one year with the Cincinnati Reds in 1906; Charles Roy, who pitched in seven games for the Philadelphia Phillies in 1906; Louis LeRoy, who pitched for the New York Highlanders in 1905-1906 and the Boston Red Sox 1910; and Mike Balenti, who played two years in the major leagues, Cincinnati Reds 1911 and St. Louis Browns 1913.

Jim Thorpe, who would play parts of six years in the major leagues (1913–1915, 1917–1919) with the New York Giants, Cincinnati Reds and Boston Braves, and George Johnson, who pitched for the Cincinnati Reds in 1913-1914 and the Kansas City team in the Federal League in 1914-1915, would be the last Carlisle players to make it to the major leagues.

Although for a small school Carlisle had more than its share of players going on to the big leagues, the baseball program was never a huge success, and in 15 years of existence (1895–1909) the team had but five winning seasons, achieving only a .466 winning percentage. But the slow demise of the baseball program at Carlisle was con-current with the rise of its popular football and track programs and the hiring of Coach Glenn Scobey "Pop" Warner in 1899.

Charles "Chief" Bender (Sports Story Reprints).   The genesis of college football is generally accepted as November 6, 1869, when Rutgers defeated Princeton 6–4. The game is considered to be the first intercollegiate football game. The following year, in 1870, Columbia began its football program. Both Harvard and Yale were quick to follow. Over the next two decades football programs were started at colleges all over the United States, including Michigan (1879), Army (1890) and Illinois (1890). By the turn of the twentieth century, football programs had been established in nearly every major college across the country as the sport became thoroughly entrenched in American culture.

In 1876, the same year that the National League was founded in professional baseball, Princeton initiated the calling of a convention that resulted in the founding of the Intercollegiate Football Association. The modern game of football was starting to evolve. By 1879 scrimmage downs instead of the rugby scrum was introduced into the game. Then in 1880, Yale succeeded in getting the number of players on the field reduced from 15 to 11. Later in the 1880s the wedge appeared and interference or blocking became a part of the game.

The wedge, or flying wedge, would eventually become outlawed. The play occurred as the quarterback took the ball from the center and then the rest of the team lined up on each side of him and drove down the field until he was tackled or scored. In 1888 tackling below the waist was legalized, which forced a sweeping change in offensive formations in order to protect the ball carrier.

By 1894 there were considerable changes in the rules of the game. The wedge, which had proved to be the cause of so many injuries, was outlawed. The game time was reduced from 90 to 70 minutes, tackling of an opponent who didn't have the ball was prohibited, and a kickoff had to travel ten yards to be in play. Finally a third official, a linesman, was added to the officials' team of the referee and umpire

On New Year's Day in 1902, the first Rose Bowl game was played as Michigan defeated Stanford 49–0 before a crowd of 8,000. The game produced a gate of $6,000. Still the game of football would continue to evolve for the next couple of decades. The ball used in the teens and into the early twenties would resemble the shape of a pumpkin, and the goal posts were placed right on the goal line.

At Carlisle, the military oriented superintendent William Henry Pratt preferred drills and marching for his students to athletics. But he also believed sports instilled character in students. Pratt was concerned about injuries to his students, particularly from the rough and tumble brand of football played at the time. Equipment was scarce. There were some very light helmets, but only a few players chose to use them. Players' thighs were protected by strips of bamboo.

Pratt was also concerned about the dignity of his students and how his Indian athletes would compete with whites. Nonetheless, in 1886, Pratt purchased uniforms for the Carlisle teams, built a gymnasium and authorized both a baseball and a football program to be started at Carlisle.

It didn't take long for Pratt's worst fears to become a reality when a student by the name of Stacy Matlock, a Pawnee, suffered a broken leg in the Carlisle vs. Dickinson game in 1892. Consequently, Pratt discontinued football. But after listening to passionate pleas from 30 of the school's students, Pratt allowed the football program to start again in 1893. However, he insisted on certain conditions. One was that the Carlisle boys play fair at all times. Second, acting like an early version of Branch Rickey counseling Jackie Robinson before signing him to a big league contract, Pratt was adamant that his players should turn the other cheek. His Indians should not slug any opposing white player, even if they had been slugged. It was Pratt's belief that by not returning a punch the Indian players could set an example for the white race. Pratt emphasized his belief that, by following his code of conduct on the field, the team could become the most famous in the country.

In a few short years, the Carlisle Indians would become a major power on the gridiron, playing against the most formidable college teams of the era. But the athletic ability of the Carlisle players would have far more to do with the football program's success than their self-control or sense of fair play. However, as Carlisle was not a college or university, its football team was not eligible for recognition as a champion and not eligible to play in any league or conference. This circumstance usually led the football analysts and critics of the time to rank Carlisle lower than the team deserved in the national rankings and polls.

What is less known is that, while the Carlisle football team was working on becoming a national sensation in the 1890s, the Carlisle band had already achieved such a lofty status. The 30-piece band was led by Indian student Dennis Wheelock, an accomplished cornet player, who also wrote and arranged music for the band. For years the band had been giving sold-out concerts on the East coast, and had played at the 1893 Chicago World's Fair to rave reviews. In fact, the management of the World's Fair was so impressed with the Carlisle band that they accepted a concert performed in Festival Hall as payment for admission fees to the Fair grounds for the 150 other Carlisle students who had traveled to Chicago for the event.

With the Carlisle athletic department up and running, Superintendent Pratt wanted a successful sports program, and he believed that through football lay the path of least resistance to achieving his goal. So in 1896 the Carlisle football program began in earnest. After soundly defeating Dickinson College, 28–6 and Duquesne A.C., 18–0 in the first two games, the Indians would finish the season with a record of 5–5–0. While they would also defeat Cincinnati, 28–0, Penn State, 48–5 and Wisconsin, 18–8, losses came at the hands of Princeton, 22–6, Yale, 12–0, Harvard, 4–0, Penn, 21–0 and Brown, 24–12. However, Carlisle had demonstrated that it was now capable of competing with powerful Ivy League teams.

The Carlisle vs. Wisconsin game played on December 19, 1896, in Chicago, is arguably considered the first football game played at night under electric lights. The game had been arranged by the Chicago Press Club and came with a controversial connection to the proposed contest. The Carlisle football season had officially ended with the Brown game on November 26. However, following their great performance in the 1896 season, Carlisle had suddenly become a national curiosity. Now the Chicago Press Club was making a substantial financial offer for the Indians to come out west and play the powerful Wisconsin Badgers under the electric lights. Superintendent Pratt weighed the pros and cons in regard to his government funded school playing an extra game for the sake of profit. In the end, Pratt decided that, since the athletic programs were self-supporting and not funded by the government, he would ignore the controversy and gave his thumbs up.

Upon arrival in Chicago, the Carlisle team and contingency, numbering 45, was met by representatives of the Press Club and lodged in the Palmer House, one of the finest hotels in the city. The game was played in the Chicago Coliseum before a crowd of 15,000 and consisted of two 35-minute halves of play. *The Indian Helper,* the Carlisle Indian School weekly newsletter, described the game as "hotly contested resulting in a victory for us 18–8. Never was fairer and more thorough officiating done. Mr. Wren (Harvard) who officiated as referee and Mr. Gould (Amherst) who acted as umpire deserve great praise for their just decisions at critical moments."[1] There is a historical side-note to this contest in that it was the first known football game to be played in the West in which some players wore helmet headgear.

But historical debate prevails on whether or not the Carlisle vs. Wisconsin game in 1896 was actually the first football game played under electric lights. Others that lay claim to the title include the Mansfield Normal vs. Wyoming Seminary game, played in September 1892, at the Great Mansfield Fair in Pennsylvania. The game ended in a 0–0 tie at halftime due to the poor quality of the lighting. Another claimant for the title is the Kanaweola Athletic Club of Elmira vs. Philadelphia Athletics game which took place November 21, 1902, in Elmira, New York. The Athletics, organized and managed by Connie

Mack, were an early attempt at forming a professional football team. The Athletics won the game, 39–0.

In 1897, the Carlisle Indians finished with a 6–4 record and once again lost to every Ivy League team they faced, Princeton, 18–0, Yale, 24–9, Penn, 20–10 and Brown, 18–14. But along the way they had beaten Cincinnati again, 10–0, blown out Pennsylvania College, 84–0, and trounced Dickinson, 36–0 and Bloomsburg Normal, 26–0. Also the Indians made a return trip to Chicago to play under the lights again and this time defeated Illinois, 23–6.

The 1898 Carlisle football squad finished the season with a 5–4 record. However, while the Indians continued to loose all the Ivy League teams on their schedule, the games with Yale, 18–5 and Harvard, 11–5, had been close. Furthermore Carlisle finished the season with a win over Illinois, 11–0. Between 1896 and 1898 the Carlisle football program had achieved a record of 17–12 and Superintendent Pratt was praising his players' efforts and the manner in which they were representing the school. "My boys have gone into the football craze lately and have even been so ambitious as to make arrangements to play with several prominent college teams, and I am sure they will give these teams hard contests,"[2] said Pratt. While Pratt expressed pride in his boys, the fact was, he wanted more—a lot more.

So in 1899 Pratt recruited Cornell coach Glenn Scobey "Pop" Warner to come to Carlisle and take over the football program. He agreed to pay him a salary of $1,200 a year. Pop Warner's Cornell squad had played Carlisle in the 1898 season and won the game, 23–6, although the outcome was controversial. First of all, the Cornell players had freely slugged the Carlisle players in the game. The Indians, following the edict of Superintendent Pratt, did not return any punches. Furthermore their protests fell upon the deaf ears of the umpire. Second, the umpire seemed quite biased toward Cornell. On two occasions the Indians took the ball across the goal line for touchdowns only to have them called back for no apparent reason and the ball turned over to Cornell. The officiating was so bad that it prompted Indians captain Frank Hudson to refer to the umpire as the 12th member of the Cornell Team. According to an article in the *Indian Helper,* October 14, 1898, "Irregular playing was resorted to by Cornell throughout the game. They were heavier players as a team than the Indians, and had not a suspicion of a reason for their conduct which was far from creditable. This sentiment was even voiced by many residents of Ithaca."[3] However Warner liked what he had seen in the Indians and believed with better coaching they could win a lot more games. So he accepted the Carlisle post and eventually he would run the athletic department.

Warner had played varsity football at Cornell 1892–1894. He played left guard and was made captain of the 1894 squad. Warner was nicknamed "Pop" by his Cornell teammates because at 25 years old, he was older than most of his teammates. He graduated with an LL.B degree in 1894 and accepted his first coaching job at Iowa State College. In 1895 he accepted the head coaching position at the University of Georgia. In 1897, he returned to Cornell as head coach and by 1897 Warner's squad was using the T-formation. At Carlisle, Pop Warner would serve two terms as head coach (1899–1903 and 1907–1914).

While the big colleges like Minnesota, Yale, Syracuse and others had a several thousand students for coaches to select players from, at Carlisle Pop Warner had only about 250 students from which to select players to fill-out his squad. Most of the Carlisle football players were between 18 and 27 years old. Although some of them were in their early 20s, academically they were in the third grade.

When Warner arrived on the Carlisle campus and met his players, he told Pratt that it was impossible to make a football team out of such a bunch of skinny boys. However Pratt was adamant in assuring Warner that because his boys spent the summer months participating in his outing program on Pennsylvania Dutch farms, they built themselves up physically by working for the frugal farmers who believed in getting their money's worth.

Warner was also faced with the challenge of uniting players from various tribes into a cohesive unit. Among other techniques, he used emotive condi-

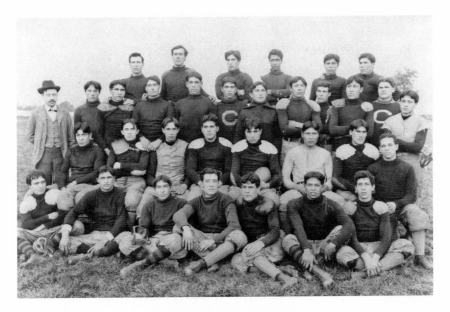

Carlisle Indians 1899.

tioning to arouse the passion of his Indian players. He told them football gave them an opportunity to compete on an even playing field with whites — beat them at their own game. When the Indians were ahead by a large score, Warner pushed them to keep playing hard, just as they did when they were behind. Furthermore, while most major college football teams of the time had assistant coaches, Pop Warner coached the Carlisle Indians by himself. Only on occasion would someone be appointed to help him a bit.

It all seemed to work and immediately Warner demonstrated that he could make the Carlisle football program a huge success. In Warner's first year as coach, on November 30, 1899, the Indians beat Columbia, 45–0 on their way to a 9–2 season and national recognition.

One of the innovations that Warner introduced at Carlisle that year was putting offensive backs in a sort of sprinter's starting position, supporting their body weight with one or both hands, instead of the customary position of the time for backs, standing with feet apart and hands resting on their knees. The result was that his offensive backs were able to use their speed better and got away quicker. Soon it was used everywhere in college football. Pop Warner's playbook consisted of only about 20 plays. But no one knew what the next play would be except the quarterback and Warner. The plays were called at the line.

Warner was fortunate that to begin his tenure at Carlisle, he inherited such a superior player in quarterback Frank Hudson, who was capable of drop-kicking the ball with either foot. Hudson would be selected in 1899 as a Third Team Walter Camp All-American.

Warner also inherited Jimmy Johnson, who notwithstanding Jim Thorpe would become arguably the best football player that Carlisle ever produced. Jimmy Johnson only stood 5 feet, seven inches and weighed 138 pounds, but he was a natural leader. Johnson was a Stockbridge Indian from Edgertown, Wisconsin. He came to Carlisle in 1899 and by 1902 was the starting quarterback on Warner's eleven.

Johnson's most memorable game was against Northwestern in 1903. After the first ten games of the 1903 season, Carlisle had a record of 7–2–1, having lost to Princeton, 11–0 and Harvard, 12–11. The game against Virginia ended in a 6–6 tie.

Coming into the game against Carlisle, Northwestern had a record of 10–0–2, having been tied by the University of Chicago and Notre Dame. In Chicago, Northwestern games had become so popular that they were moved from Evanston to the White Sox ball park at 39th Street. When the two teams met on Thanksgiving Day, Jimmy Johnson led Carlisle to a 28–0 victory over Northwestern, handing them their only defeat of the season.

However, Jimmy Johnson is probably more famous for his hidden ball play in the Indians' 12–11 loss to Harvard a few weeks earlier on October 31. Harvard was the most respected football team in college football at the time, and a fierce rivalry had developed between the Indians and the Crimson. At halftime Carlisle was leading, 5–0. On the opening kickoff of the second half, Jimmy Johnson received the ball and the rest of the Indians formed a semicircle wall around him. Albert Exendine pulled up the back of Charles Dillon's jersey and Johnson placed the ball under it. Then everyone but Dillon hunched over as if they were carrying the ball. Dillon, who was six feet tall and could run the 100-yard dash in 10 seconds, proceeded to run straight up field swinging his arms while other Carlisle players were being tackled without the ball.

The Harvard fans in the stands could clearly see the ball stuffed in Dillon's jersey. They pointed at Dillon and yelled for the Harvard defense to tackle him. As Dillon approached the goal line, he was confronted by Harvard's captain, Carl Marshall, playing safety. Dillon spread out his arms as if he was going to throw a block on Marshall, who simply side-stepped him. Dillon raced into the end zone for the score. He had run 103 yards for the score (the field was 110 yards at that time). Harvard was outraged and protested, but Pop Warner had warned officials about the play. Nonetheless, Harvard, down by the score of 11–0, fought back hard and won the game, 12–11, and would see that the hidden ball play was never used again.

Pop Warner hadn't invented the hidden ball play. It was John Heisman, head coach at Alabama Polytechnic Institute (now Auburn), who used the play in games against Vanderbilt and Georgia, when Warner was the head coach (1895-1896). Warner first used the hidden ball play against Penn State when he was coaching at Cornell.

However, Warner began to implement other changes in the game at Carlisle that became standards for all teams, such as the single wing formation, crouching start for backs and flying body blocks. Also, he would pull guards and tackles out of the line to lead interference.

Jimmy Johnson was named a Walter Camp First Team All-American in 1903. He had been named a Third Team All-American in 1901. After leaving Carlisle, Johnson enrolled in Northwestern Dental School. Although the dental school had a football team of its own, it was legal at the time for a university or college to use graduate students who had played four years at another school. Therefore the next two years, Johnson played quarterback at Northwestern, helping the team to a 16–4–1 record. The four games that Northwestern lost in the 1904 and 1905 seasons occurred when Johnson was out with injuries. After finishing dental school at Northwestern, Johnson took up practice in San Juan, Puerto Rico, made about $5,000 a year, and later fought in World War One.

Following the 1903-1904 academic year, Colonel Richard Henry Pratt was forced out as superintendent of the Carlisle Indian School. So he retired from the Army. During his tenure at Carlisle, Pratt had continued to rise through the ranks, having been promoted to Major in 1898, Lieutenant Colonel in 1901, Colonel in 1903, and finally Brigadier General in April 1904, a year after retiring from the Army.

The reason for Pratt's forced departure from the school he had founded was ideological. Francis E. Leupp, the commissioner of Indian Affairs in the administration of President Theodore Roosevelt, was knowledgeable about Indian tribal culture and had previously worked for the Indian Rights Association. His philosophy in regard to educating the Indians was vastly different from that of Pratt. First, Leupp felt that Indian art was capable of standing on its own and deserved preservation. It was not necessary to completely wipe it out in order to re-socialize the Indians. In describing the method of teaching art at Carlisle, Leupp remarked, "The Art Department at Carlisle had been engaged in teaching Indian children, whose own mothers were masters of decorative design, to paint pansies on plush pillows and forget-me-nots on picture frames. It was not the fault of Carlisle that the standard of art in America should resemble the counter of a department store; it was the fault of our whole civilization."[4]

Leupp looked upon the silversmith work of the Navajos with awe. He felt that to ignore such advanced skills by the Carlisle teachers was reprehensible. He felt teaching the Indians to make jewelry and gewgaws at Carlisle was a waste of time and effort. It would be far better to use the Indians' inherent skills and start to produce marketable goods that could be sold in white communities such as butter knives, napkin rings, salt shakers and trays.

Furthermore Leupp favored a system of providing more localized education for Indians and closing boarding schools that were located far from the student's reservation. In essence, Leupp wanted to make Carlisle an advanced environment for learning that occurred after the Indians' primary education had been completed nearer their reservations. His attitude toward Indian education was in diametric opposition to the core beliefs of Pratt, who believed that to successfully educate the Indians, they needed to break clean with the cultural norms of the reservation and totally adopt white culture as a model for day-to-day living.

Pratt was succeeded as superintendent by Captain William A. Mercer. Although Mercer would place a much heavier emphasis on athletics at the school, even making them compulsory, Pop Warner decided to return to Cornell and departed the Carlisle campus on July 8, 1904. In his first tenure of five years as head football coach at Carlisle, Warner had brought the program into national prominence and achieved a record of 39–18–3.

However, also during Warner's tenure the demise of the Carlisle baseball program had begun. Superintendent Pratt had taken notice of how football enhanced the school's national reputation as well as his personal reputation. In addition, Pratt had enjoyed taking the road trips with the team. Although in 1901 Warner had hired former major league player Harry Taylor (1890-1891 Louisville, American Association; 1892 Louisville, National League; 1893 Baltimore, National League) to coach the baseball team, the Indians barely had a winning season in 1901 (12–11–1) and a losing season in 1902 (5–11).

So Warner announced his expectations that the track team should be stronger than ever in the 1903 season, with more meets to participate in. Warner stated that "since track and field seem more adapted to the Indians than baseball and it is almost impossible in the limited time for practice to have successful teams in both of these branches of sport, it has been decided that track athletes will have preference over baseball, and all our energies will be devoted to the former."[5] For the baseball program at Carlisle it was the beginning of the end.

Furthermore Warner explained how the track athletes missed baseball practice for track practice, then missed baseball games for track meets. The reality was that a double standard existed at Carlisle in the practice of rewarding track athletes for superior performances (i.e., first place finishes), while the baseball players got nothing. Track athletes were showered with watches, jerseys, and other gifts when they excelled; there was no reward for baseball players in hitting a home run or being the winning pitcher. Mose Blumenthal, a local booster who owned a clothing store in downtown Carlisle, was only too happy to provide any Indian track team member or football player with a new suit of clothes and overcoat. In addition, both the track team members and the football players were housed in a separate dormitory and ate a diet provided at a training table, consisting of huge portions of rare steak, eggs, potatoes and milk. The baseball players dined in the student mess.

The bottom line was that Pop Warner as a coach was spread thin, and de-emphasizing baseball in the spring permitted him to concentrate his efforts where his primary interest lay, in coaching track and recruiting football players. Eventually the baseball team was left to the team captain to manage, or the occasional short-term temporary coaches like Harry Taylor. Nonetheless, the demise of baseball at Carlisle had begun, although the program would struggle on for acceptance in the Carlisle athletic department through its final season in 1909.

When Glenn Pop Warner returned to Cornell in the fall of 1904, Ed Rogers, the son of a Minnesota pioneer backwoods lumberman and a Chippewa Indian mother, became head coach of the Indians football team. Rogers was a former

Carlisle student who had played end at Carlisle (1896–1898). Rogers also played college football at Minnesota and was the team captain in 1903 when the Gophers had an 11–0–1 record.

Rogers took the Indians to a surprising 9–2 season in 1904, losing only to Harvard, 12–0 and Penn, 18–0. The Indians beat Virginia, 29–14 and Ohio State, 23–0. In one game Carlisle was leading Albright College 100–0 when the game was called ten minutes into the second half. Following the 1904 season, Rogers returned to Minnesota and began practicing law in Minneapolis. In 1968, Ed Rogers was inducted in the College Football Hall of Fame.

In 1905 the Carlisle Indians were coached by George Woodruff, who had played college football at Yale with Amos Alonzo Stagg. Woodruff had coached at Penn, 1892–1901, winning national championships in 1894, 1895 and 1897. Prior to coming to Carlisle, Woodruff had been the coach at Illinois in 1904. Under Woodruff the Indians compiled a 10–4–0 record. Two of the Carlisle loses were to local athletic clubs rather than college teams — the hard hitting Massillon A.C., 8–4 and Canton A. C., 8–0. In between these two games in Ohio, Carlisle defeated Cincinnati, 34–5.

Frank Jude, the Carlisle baseball great, also played football for the Indians as a substitute end. At the time, Army was emerging as a powerhouse in football, having lost only two games in 1904 (Harvard, 4–0 and Princeton, 12–6). In the 1905 Carlisle vs. Army game played at West Point, Jude recovered a fumble and ran 65 yards for a touchdown that won the game for Carlisle, 6–5 (touchdowns were only five points by the rules of the time). Quarterback Frank Mount Pleasant kicked the extra point, although this task was usually performed by Jude, who would kick a phenomenal 32 out of 34 successful attempts at a point after touchdown during the season. The tenth-ranked Carlisle Indians concluded the 1905 season with a 76–0 trouncing of Georgetown in Washington, D.C., with Frank Jude kicking seven of seven points after touchdowns.

When George Woodruff left after the 1905 season, he was replaced as coach by former Carlisle great Bemus Pierce. A huge tackle for the time at six foot one and 225 pounds, Pierce had become Carlisle's first All-American selected to Walter Camp's 1896 2nd team. In the 1906 season Pierce would coach Carlisle to a 9–3–0 season.

4

Pop Warner Meets Jim Thorpe

On May 28, 1904, Jim Thorpe turned 16 years old. He had been enrolled at Carlisle for only four months and his father had been deceased for a little over a month. At the end of the school year in June, in accordance with Captain Pratt's Indian outing system, Thorpe left Carlisle to work in the home of a white man at a nominal wage and become immersed in the dominant culture norms of the Protestant work ethic. He would only return to Carlisle to continue his education three years later, in 1907. However, Thorpe would later say that he was anxious for the experience.

On June 17, 1904, Jim Thorpe began his outing experience working in the home of A. E. Bucholtz, a Pennsylvania Dutch farmer in Summerdale, Pennsylvania. He was in service there for a year. His pay was $5 per month, half of which he was permitted to keep and the other half kept in a trust at the school. His duties were cleaning the house and learning to cook. However, he was not allowed to eat with the family and ate in the kitchen. Nonetheless, there were two children in the home and he taught them all the games he knew.

All of the families used by Carlisle for outing placements were screened by the school, and any type of abuse of a student was very rare. However, in the spring of 1905, Thorpe requested a transfer from the Bucholtz home. He requested the transfer for two reasons. For one, he now had money in the bank and was receiving quarterly annuities from the government. So he felt independent. Furthermore, he didn't like eating in the kitchen. Also Thorpe loathed working indoors. He longed for the outside. His request was granted. He was transferred to work for James L. Cadwallader in Dolington, Pennsylvania, where his principal duties were gardening.

In September 1905 he was transferred to work for Harley Bozarth, who operated a trucking farm near Robbinsville, New Jersey. His wages were now $8 a month, his principal task was to cut asparagus and he was allowed to eat with the family. In the spring of 1907, just before turning 19, Thorpe was transferred to a farm at Yardley, Pennsylvania. He was getting restless.

The Carlisle Indian School had received permission from state authorities in Harrisburg allowing students to attend public schools while in the outing system. There is some question whether any fees due the local school district were paid by the family to whom the student had been assigned, or taken out of wages the student had earned. Nonetheless, Jim Thorpe had continued his studies during his outing experience. At this point, he believed he was ready for the challenge of high school and wanted to return to Carlisle. He had had enough of the outing system and wanted to graduate in 1909 and get on with whatever life had in store for him. So Thorpe left his outing assignment and went back to Carlisle.

After his return to Carlisle on March 9, 1907, he was returned to the farm in Yardley two days later. On April 8, once again Thorpe ran away from his outing assignment and returned to Carlisle. This time he was placed in the guard house. Also the principal insisted that he start school again at the sixth-grade level. The irony is that if Thorpe had been placed in high school at that time, he would have probably graduated from Carlisle by 1909 and never would have achieved the incredible athletic achievements and fame that were in his future.

When Thorpe had completed his punishment and was returned to the school's instruction, the spring athletic season was in progress. He immediately joined the baseball team. Late one afternoon, he and a group of his teammates were crossing the track field to play a twilight game with a campus scrub team. At that time, some of the track team members were practicing the high jump. Thorpe stopped to watch them. According to Thorpe, he watched as they continued to raise the bar higher and higher, until no one could cross it. As the track team members were about to call it a day, suddenly Jim Thorpe asked if he could try it.

There was nothing in Thorpe's physical make-up that would indicate he was different from any other Indian at Carlisle. In fact, Thorpe never considered that he had any more ability in athletics than the average boy of his age. The track boys snickered at Thorpe, dressed in overalls and tennis shoes, as they set the bar up for him. Then to their amazement, he cleared the bar on his first try. Thorpe got up, dusted himself off and continued walking down to the ball field. He didn't know it yet, but he had just jumped 5 feet, 9 inches and set the school record.

A student named Harry Archenbald had been watching as Thorpe made the jump. Immediately he went looking for Coach Warner. In the spring of 1907, Glenn S. "Pop" Warner had also returned to Carlisle and resumed his coaching duties. The next day Pop Warner sent for Thorpe. When Thorpe walked into Warner's office he was still wearing the same clothes as the day before.

"Are those the clothes you had on yesterday when you made that high jump," asked Warner?

Thorpe just nodded affirmatively.

Warner then asked if he had known what he had done. Thorpe replied he hoped it wasn't anything bad.

"Bad! Boy, you've just broken the school record!"

Exuding a huge self-confidence, Thorpe replied that he could have jumped higher in a track suit. Shaking his head, Warner told him to go to the clubhouse and exchange his overalls for a track suit. "You're on the track team now."[1]

So began the most important adult relationship of Jim Thorpe's life, one of supreme trust on Thorpe's part that would guide him on his incredible rise to the pinnacle of stardom in the early twentieth century sports world and one that he would still cling to as he fell from that lofty position with no outstretched arms of Warner's waiting to catch him. Although Pop Warner would eventually demonstrate shallowness in their relationship, Thorpe never stopped praising him. In an interview with a reporter for *Sports World* magazine in 1949, Thorpe was still embracing Pop Warner, stating that he was the only coach he ever had and that no athlete ever had a better one.

Warner recognized the potential of Thorpe and assigned Carlisle football standout and track great Albert Exendine to work with him and be his mentor. Exendine had played three years of football at Carlisle and was the current holder of most of the school's track and field records. While Thorpe participated on the Carlisle track team in the spring of 1907 and distinguished himself with a dominating performance in the season-ending Pennsylvania Junior College Interscholastic Meet, he had not yet demonstrated his full potential. That would come the following year.

The more important aspect of that experience for Jim Thorpe was that he had begun to compete in sports on an organized basis. Now the rather nonchalant and over-confident Thorpe was faced with serious competition. Going forward, in order to compete, he was faced with getting to know himself better. While Albert Exendine had put Thorpe through a rigorous training regimen, he would have to make necessary changes in his attitude about sports. He needed to learn to train on his own, listen to his coach and learn from his mistakes.

Thorpe had also been playing intramural football on the tailoring team (his vocational program), and Frank Newman, one of the teachers who coached his squad, recommended him to Warner for a tryout for the varsity. Up until this time, Thorpe had only put his hands on a real football a few times. The first time Thorpe reported for practice in the fall of 1907, he had a hard time getting a uniform. The trainer, Wallace Denny, an Oneida Indian who later coached for Warner at Stanford, thought Thorpe was too skinny to play football. After some verbal jousting, Denny relented and issued a uniform to Thorpe. However, it was several sizes too large and he looked like a scarecrow.

When Thorpe trotted out on the Indians practice field, his enthusiasm was quashed by Pop Warner, who sent him back to the locker room. He did not want a promising track star getting hurt. Nonetheless day after day, Thorpe continued to press the issue with Warner. Finally Warner relented and Thorpe's actions in his first day of practice literally caused his jaw to drop.

Pop Warner's football practice sessions began with a lot of passing, kicking, and pushing a blocking sled around the field. Although he was 37 years old, during blocking and tackling practice it was not uncommon to see Warner remove the cigarette that constantly hung from his lips and personally demonstrate proper techniques.

Warner also had a drill where he would station the linemen five feet apart all over the field and give the ball to one of the backfield candidates. With the ball in his hands, that backfield candidate was supposed to begin running at one goal and attempt to run the gauntlet of the length of the field, 100 yards to the other goal, while avoiding 50 or 60 players from both the varsity and the scrubs out on the field who were waiting to tackle him. When it was Thorpe's turn, he took the ball, began dodging and sprinting all over the field, knocked a few would-be tacklers to the turf and went all the way. Thorpe gave a repeat performance that afternoon, causing a disbelieving Warner to remark, "He's certainly a wild Indian."[2]

Leon Miller, who later went on to become an associate professor of health and physical education and the head lacrosse coach at CCNY (1933–1960), was Jim Thorpe's teammate on the 1911 and 1912 Carlisle Indians football squad. Speaking about the rigors of the Carlisle football program, Miller said, "Most of the times the games were a breeze as they lasted only for an hour. It was in the scrimmages at the school the fellows fought real hard to try to show up the other fellow as they took the part very seriously. The practice sessions provided many thrills due to the keen rivalries among the players."[3]

Warner assigned Thorpe to the scrubs. For the next two weeks of practice playing against the varsity, running the ball, he broke through the line on several occasions with very little difficulty, prompting Warner to promote him to the varsity. His job would be to sub for Albert Payne, the starting left halfback. Also Pop Warner made some key changes on the squad such as moving standout tackle Albert Exendine to end.

On September 21, the Carlisle Indians opened their 1907 football season right where they had left off before Warner returned to Cornell, with a 40–0 victory over Lebanon Valley. The following week the Indians defeated Villanova, 10–0. That victory was followed on October 2 with a crushing defeat of Susquehanna, 91–0. Penn State was next on the schedule, October 5 at Williamsport, Pennsylvania. Final score: Carlisle 18, Penn State 5. Then the Indians topped Syracuse, 14–6 at Buffalo, and Bucknell, 15–0 in one of the Indians' few home games.

Next on the schedule for the Indians was Pennsylvania at Franklin Field in Philadelphia. Jim Thorpe had sat on the bench for the first three games, finally seeing brief action in the Syracuse and Bucknell games. In the forthcoming Penn game, Pop Warner decided to play Thorpe in the second half of the game. However Thorpe, the ever free spirit, almost blew his chance. When the train carrying the Indians arrived in Philadelphia, Thorpe slipped away from the squad and began to explore the Quaker City. Soon his absence was noticed and a search party formed. He was found well fortified with liquor and locked in his room with the telephone disconnected until it was time to dress for the game.

But Thorpe's big chance came in the Penn game when Albert Payne hurt his knee about five minutes into the first quarter and Thorpe was sent in to replace him. The first time he carried the ball, Thorpe was so excited that he didn't follow his interference and was thrown for a loss. However, the next time Thorpe was given the ball, he ran around end 75 yards for a touchdown. Payne had been hurt so badly that he was sent back to Carlisle. From that time on, Jim Thorpe was the starting Carlisle left halfback. Carlisle won the Penn game, 26–6.

It was also in the Penn game that Pop Warner introduced the passing game as Indians quarterback Frank Mount Pleasant completed 14 passes. Prior to the Carlisle game, Penn had not allowed an opponent to score on them all year.

On November 2, the 7–0 Indians were feeling over-confident as they met a squad of determined Princeton Tigers at the Polo Grounds in New York. The lackluster Indians lost, playing in the rain and on a sloppy field, to Princeton, 16–0. It was Jim Thorpe's first trip to New York. Princeton would be Carlisle's only loss in the 1907 season.

The chastened Indians rebounded in the final three games. First they defeated Harvard, 23–15 at Cambridge. Then the Indians began to prepare for the final two games on their schedule in the midwest. The first game was against Minnesota in Minneapolis. On a cool mid–November morning, 22 members of the team, Pop Warner, assistant coach Jimmie Johnson, Superintendent Mercer, and school physician Dr. Shoemaker left Carlisle in a special railroad car, the "Youngstown bound for Minneapolis." The Minnesota Gophers team was coming off a difficult Western Conference loss to Chicago, 18–12, and had been working hard preparing for the Carlisle game. The coaches drilled the ends in running down the long punts they expected from the Indians, and the players hit hard in their scrimmages. To keep Northrup Field from freezing, each night after practice it was covered with blankets to keep it warm. But when the two teams met on November 16, Carlisle prevailed, 12–10.

Now ahead for the Carlisle Indians was their final contest of the 1907 season, against the undefeated Western Conference champions, the University of Chicago Maroons, coached by the legendary Amos Alonzo Stagg. The Indians began training for the Chicago game at Lake Forest University. Their scrimmages were witnessed by huge crowds. At Marshall Field all seats were sold out for the game and general admission stands were erected at both ends of the field. The University of Chicago campus had recently been hit by a series of smallpox cases among the student body. In fact, E. M. Phelps, quarterback on the freshman squad, had been one of the victims. All members of the varsity were supposed to be vaccinated, but only two actually saw the needle. In preparation for the Indians, Stagg drove his squad to the limit in practice, in particular his lineman, reasoning that if they could keep the Indians from any long gains, Chicago would win the game. However, led by Pete Hauser and Albert Exendine, Carlisle prevailed and the Indians defeated Chicago, 18–4.

The Carlisle Indians finished the 1907 season with a won-loss record of 10–1 and outscored their opponents, 267–62. Walter Camp chose Carlisle end Albert Exendine as a Second Team All-American and Pete Hauser, right halfback, as a Third Team All-American. Later writing in one of his memoirs Coach Pop Warner called his 1907 squad the greatest team he ever developed at Carlisle.

1907 CARLISLE FOOTBALL SCORES

09/21	Carlisle	40	Lebanon Valley	0
09/28	Carlisle	10	Villanova	0
10/02	Carlisle	91	Susquehanna	0
10/05	Carlisle	18	Penn State	5
10/12	Carlisle	14	Syracuse	6
10/19	Carlisle	15	Bucknell	0
10/26	Carlisle	26	Pennsylvania	6
11/02	Carlisle	0	Princeton	16
11/09	Carlisle	23	Harvard	15
11/16	Carlisle	12	Minnesota	10
11/23	Carlisle	18	Chicago	4

However, according to *Chicago Tribune* columnist Walter H. Eckersall, Pop Warner's success was simply a matter of having Indian players who took to the game of football naturally. Eckersall wrote in a column published in the *Tribune* on November 12, 1907, that when an Indian goes to Carlisle he expects to play football. His first ambition is to make the varsity. Furthermore back on the reservation, his tribesmen expect it of him. "The Indian loves football better than any sport his race has known. When the coach tells an Indian player to do anything he never brings life, limb or impossibility into question. He does it. The Indian is always in condition because he likes to be that way, whether he plays football or not. The Indian looks on football as a matter of serious moment and not as a chance to celebrate or spout off pentup enthusiasm."[4]

For Jim Thorpe the 1907 football season had been a year about learning the game of college football, both on offense and defense, and he had excelled. He had made his debut without the fanfare and ballyhoo that was to lie in his future. Following the 1907 football season, with both his parents dead, it seemed to Thorpe there was no reason to go home for a vacation, and he remained on the Carlisle campus.

In the 1907 season well over 100,000 spectators had seen the Carlisle football team play. Huge crowds of 20,000 in Philadelphia, 30,000 in New York, and 25,000 in Chicago had come to see the Indians play. Even the gate for the Syracuse game at Buffalo with 8,000 in the stands had been bountiful. The Carlisle share of the gate for the Chicago game had been $17,000, a huge sum for the time.

For the Carlisle Indian School, gate receipts from the 1907 football season were welcome revenue. Money generated from football paid Pop Warner's salary and went to support the other athletic programs. Revenues from the 1907 football season also provided the funding for a building program on the campus that included a new print shop, an art studio, remodeling in the dining hall and new electrical wiring in the dormitories. In addition, $3,400 was allocated for building a new residential cottage for Pop Warner and his wife on the lower edge of the campus.

Some of the football profits were also passed on to the players in cash bonuses of small amounts of $10 and $15 at a time. But Albert Exendine received a $200 loan. Coach Warner began to have concerns about his practice of paying athletes bonuses, fearing that it might lead to charges of professionalism. So at the end of the following season, he discontinued the practice.

Of course there were critics of the Carlisle football program's success. Some were former employees of the school expressing sour grapes. One such critic was Dr. Carlos Montezuma, the former school physician at Carlisle.

Dr. Montezuma was a full-blooded Apache Indian. In 1871, when he was five years old, Montezuma had been carried off as a captive by a neighboring tribe. He was never to see his mother or father again. A few years later he was purchased for $30 by a traveling artist named Gentile, who happened to be passing through the territory and heard the boy's story. Gentile took the boy to Chicago with him and sent him to school. Slowly but steadily, Montezuma worked his way up through the educational system, paying his way through hard work. In 1889, at the age of 23, he graduated with honors from the Chicago Medical College. Following graduation Dr. Montezuma joined the Indian Bureau of Affairs and eventually came to Carlisle.

Dr. Montezuma, like so many Indians, had been very loyal to Richard Henry Pratt during his tenure as superintendent. On November 24, 1907, the same day as the Carlisle vs. Chicago game, Dr. Montezuma wrote an article for the *Chicago Tribune* complaining that during the past season, for the first time in the history of the school, the majority of players on the Carlisle football team were not students, but rather athletes hand-picked by Pop Warner from different parts of the country. According to Dr. Montezuma, no more than one-third of the team was actually attending class as students. "There is no reason why the Carlisle students should be proud of the success which in 1907 attended the football efforts of a lot of hired outsiders," wrote Montezuma. "As conducted this year the school might just as well have farmed out its football work to anybody who would take the job. The Carlisle football team of 1907 might as well have been called the 'All Around Redmen of the West.'"[5]

Fund raising had fallen off dramatically since Richard Henry Pratt had been forced out as superintendent. Pratt's successor, William A. Mercer, had been somewhat reticent about openly soliciting funds for the school. However, this blind-eye approach of Mercer's to his administrative oversight duties with the football program's revenue left Pop Warner free to determine his own policies in regard to the allocation of the huge gate receipts and game guarantees that the Indians were generating. In less than a decade, some of these practices would be called into question.

But there were already those calling for reform in intercollegiate athletics. For one, multi-millionaire Andrew Carnegie was advocating the elimination of commercialism from college football. Putting his money where his beliefs lay, on Thanksgiving Day, 1907, Carnegie brought the Lehigh University squad to Pittsburgh to play Carnegie Tech and offered free admission to the people of Pittsburgh. According to a spokesman for Carnegie Tech, ending gate receipts would create better football and better college sports of all kinds. The sport would be safer and there would be far fewer injuries to players, because gate receipts made it possible for colleges to hire players to make their teams better. In some cases this induced colleges to hire full-grown men who were pitted against small boys, which resulted in football injuries. In short, Carnegie believed his stand against gate receipts would result in having intercollegiate sports for sports' sake. Expenses for the events could be covered by selling programs.

Captain Mercer resigned as the superintendent of Carlisle in December 1907, citing various health concerns. However, during the fall of 1907, a Federal audit of Carlisle had been taking place which revealed some questionable accounting practices. For one, investigators found that Frank Hudson, the place kicker on the Indians football team, who had taken a job as the school clerk, had embezzled $1,416 from various accounts. As a result Mercer quietly left the school.

Soon after, in April 1908, Moses Friedman was appointed to replace Captain Mercer as superintendent. Moses Friedman had been born in Cincinnati, Ohio, in 1874. He was the son of a Jewish immigrant from Germany. His mother was from a wealthy southern family. A graduate of the University of Cincinnati in 1899, Freidman had taught in the Cincinnati public school system for two years before joining the Indian Service and being assigned teaching duties at the Phoenix Indian School and in the Philippines. Prior to his appointment at Carlisle, he had served as the assistant superintendent of the Haskell Institute in Lawrence, Kansas. Appealing to the reform agenda of the commissioner of Indian Affairs, Francis E. Leupp, under Freidman's tenure, the curriculum of the Carlisle Indian School was broadened to include courses in morals and manners, nature study and native Indian arts.

By now Jim Thorpe was starting to excel in both academics and athletics. He was earning high marks in various subjects such as history, civics, grammar and literature. Likewise his vocational marks in house and carriage painting were good. In the spring of 1908, Thorpe came out again for the Carlisle track team. Pop Warner issued a challenge to Thorpe, telling him if he could jump 5 feet 10½ inches in the high jump, he would take him with the team to the Penn Relays in Philadelphia. Thorpe proceeded to jump 5 feet 11 inches, was taken to the meet, and there jumped 6 feet 1 inch to tie another competitor from Indiana. A flip of a coin would give the first place to Thorpe and his first major track medal. However, his performance in Philadelphia would pale in comparison to what he would accomplish later in the 1908 intercollegiate track season.

On May 14, 1908, Jim Thorpe was noticed nationally for the first time. In a dual meet in which Carlisle defeated Syracuse, Thorpe took first place in both the high and low hurdles and both the high and broad jumps. In addition, in the shot put, he defeated the Orangemen's great shot putter, Thor, who outweighed him by 52 pounds. On the train coming home from the Syracuse meet, Thorpe was sitting and smoking a cigar while talking with Pop Warner. Thorpe told Warner that he really didn't like track and he preferred to play baseball. He said that there was no money in track. In an interview following Thorpe's death, Warner would say that baseball, not football or track, was his first love.

Nonetheless, Thorpe continued with track and in a meet on May 23, Carlisle defeated Dickinson and Swarthmore. Thorpe set a new record in that meet for the shot put. In addition, he would break the Carlisle record for the 220 hurdles in 26 seconds. Also he won the high jump and both high and low hurdles. Finally on May 30, 1908, at the Pennsylvania Intercollegiate meet in Harrisburg, Jim Thorpe won the high jump with a jump of six feet. Also he took first place in the hammer throw, broad jump, and high and low hurdles. A week later, at the Mid-Atlantic Athletic Association meet in Philadelphia, competing against the best collegiate track stars in the east, Thorpe took first place in five events.

Although Thorpe's performance in the 1908 track season had been spectacular and he had become the star of the Carlisle track team, he was not chosen to participate in the 1908 Olympic Games in London. He did participate in the high jump at the 1908 Eastern Olympic trials, but failed to make the team.

Not really caring about his snub or failure at the Olympic trails, Thorpe joined the Carlisle baseball team that by then was playing their final games of the 1908 season. Thorpe got right into the action and pitched a 1–0 shutout against Albright. At the end of the schedule the Indians finished with a 13–14 record. Then some of the players like William Newashe, Mike Balenti and William Garlow left Carlisle for the summer to play for semi-pro teams. One Carlisle player Joseph Twin was asked by *The Arrow*, Carlisle's school paper, where he was going to play ball that summer. His reply was, "The contracts are coming in from different parts of the country."[6]

Thorpe did not play ball that summer. He went home to Oklahoma and spent time hunting and fishing in his old boyhood haunts, while reflecting on the past and his future. But what Thorpe found in Oklahoma that summer was emptiness; the spell had gone and he became eager to return to Carlisle.

Meanwhile, distance runner Louis Tewanima, Thorpe's teammate and the other star on the Carlisle track team, went to London representing the United States in the IV Olympic Games. Louis Tewanima was a Hopi Indian from Arizona. The Hopis claimed to be the first inhabitants of the New World. It was the fourth world that this tribe claimed to have inhabited. While the claim has been disputed, according to anthropologists, the Hopi's pueblo, or village, of Oraibi in Arizona, about 100 miles north of U.S. Route 66, dates from A.D. 1100 or earlier and is believed to be the oldest continuously occupied settlement in the United States.

When Louis Tewanima enrolled at Carlisle he weighed but 110 pounds. He went to see track coach Pop Warner and asked him for a track suit.

"What for?" asked Warner.

"Me run fast good. All Hopis run fast good,"[7] replied Tewanima.

Louis Tewanima finished in ninth place in the 26-mile marathon race at the IV Olympic Games. The marathon is recalled for the most famous incident of the 1908 Olympic Games. Near the end of the marathon, the first runner to enter the stadium was Dorando Pietri of Italy. As he approached the finish line, he collapsed several times and ran the wrong way. Two officials took the staggering Pietri by the arms and led him to the finish line. After he crossed the line, the judges disqualified him. The first place medal went to the second-place finisher, American Johnny Hayes of the Irish American Athletic Club. However, as Pietri had not been responsible for his disqualification, the next day Queen Alexandria awarded him a gilded silver cup.

By early August 1908, Jim Thorpe had aborted his summer vacation in Oklahoma, returned to Carlisle and begun training for the upcoming football season. Over the winter, changes in college athletic eligibility had been approved, limiting student athletes to four years of eligibility. Consequently, Pop Warner would be losing some key talent for the 1908 season, including Albert Exendine, Frank Mount Pleasant and Antonio Lubo. However, 1908 would be the season in which Jim Thorpe became a football star. Albert Payne, who had lost his left halfback position when he was hurt in the Penn State game the previous season, became the fullback for the Indians and Thorpe started at left halfback.

As usual, Carlisle began the schedule at home with some easy games, defeating Conway Hall, 53–0, Lebanon Valley College, 39–0 and Villanova, 10–0. In the Dickinson game Thorpe established himself as a gridiron force to be reckoned with, scoring five touchdowns from beyond mid-field and throwing a 30-yard pass to Pete Hauser for another in the first half. Then Pop Warner sat Thorpe on the bench for the second half. Carlisle continued on with impressive wins over Penn State, 12–5 at Wilkes-Barre, and Syracuse, 12–0 in Buffalo.

Then came Pennsylvania, led by All-American halfback "Big Bill" Hollenback, who was also a pulverizing tackler on defense. Penn was undefeated and out for revenge after losing to Carlisle, 26–6, the previous season. Furthermore the Indians would have to play the game without several starters that were out with injuries, including Pete Hauser, Fritz Hendricks and Vic Kelley.

The game was witnessed by 26,000 fans at Philadelphia's Franklin Field, and Thorpe would later refer to the 1908 Penn game as the hardest fought game he ever played in. The low-scoring defensive battle began with Penn quarterback A. C. Miller going around the Carlisle end for a ten-yard touchdown run, followed by the point after. The game ended in a 6–6 tie with Thorpe scoring the only Carlisle touchdown, then kicking the extra point. For Penn it would be the only blemish on their near-perfect record in the 1908 season, finishing 11–0–1.

The 1908 Carlisle Indians would finish their football season with a record of 10–2–1, outscoring their opponents, 222–55. Following the tie with Penn the Indians defeated previously unbeaten Navy, 16–6, Pitt, 6–0, St. Louis, 17–0, Nebraska, 37–6 and Denver 8–4. The two defeats that they suffered came at the hands of Harvard, 17–0, and Minnesota, 11–6. During the season, Jim Thorpe established himself not only as a fine broken-field runner, but also as a power runner and kicker. Thorpe's national reputation was growing and Walter Camp selected him as a Third Team All-American.

1908 CARLISLE FOOTBALL SCORES

09/19	Carlisle	53	Conway Hall	0
09/23	Carlisle	39	Lebanon Valley	0
09/26	Carlisle	10	Villanova	0
10/03	Carlisle	12	Penn State	5
10/10	Carlisle	12	Syracuse	0
10/24	Carlisle	6	Pennsylvania	6
10/31	Carlisle	16	Navy	6
11/07	Carlisle	0	Harvard	17
11/14	Carlisle	6	Pittsburgh	0
11/21	Carlisle	6	Minnesota	11
11/26	Carlisle	17	St. Louis	0
12/02	Carlisle	37	Nebraska	6
12/05	Carlisle	8	Denver	4

5

Thorpe Plays Baseball in North Carolina

In the spring of 1909, Pop Warner recruited Eugene Bassford from Fordham University to coach the Carlisle baseball team. But for the third straight year, the Indians had a losing season (11–16). Most observers attributed the losing tradition in baseball at Carlisle to Pop Warner's preference for track as a spring sport. Early in the spring, when Carlisle was playing most of its baseball schedule at home, it was possible for the two-sport athletes to compete in both programs. But as the track season set in, track became the priority and those athletes playing baseball were unavailable for most road games.

This included Jim Thorpe, who was Carlisle's ace on the mound. Following the 1909 track season, when Thorpe was able to concentrate on baseball, he pitched a shutout for the Indians vs. Eastern College at Hagerstown, MD. Pop Warner was aware that Thorpe preferred baseball to track. However, even after Warner taught Thorpe to throw a change-up, he still encouraged him to concentrate on track, develop his skills and compete in every meet. As a result of his competing in track, Thorpe played in only a few games for the Indians in the 1909 baseball season. As a result of competing in track, Thorpe usually missed batting practice. So the 1909 season would be the last year that Thorpe received any instruction on the diamond at Carlisle.

Nonetheless, the 1909 track season would once again be a huge success for Carlisle. In an illustration of both confidence in the Carlisle trackmen and his arrogance, Warner took a five-man track team to Easton, Pennsylvania, to compete against Lafayette in a dual meet. Lafayette coach Harold Anson Bruce came to welcome the Indians as they arrived at the Central Railroad Station. When the train pulled in, Bruce was standing on the platform and noticed a few men get off the end of the train. Then Warner and Thorpe got off the middle of the train. Coach Bruce walked toward Warner and asked, "where's your team?" Warner simply placed his hand on Thorpe's shoulder and said, "Here it is."[1]

Bruce, who would later coach the 1936 Austrian Olympic track team, was very concerned. He anticipated that a tribe of Indians would be traversing about Easton. Bruce had organized a highly publicized and well funded meet and didn't want it to go down as a farce. The meet was also part of the Alumni Day celebration. Furthermore, Pop Warner had insisted on a huge guarantee which forced Bruce to solicit donations from the town merchants. Now he was thinking about what he would do when his team of 46 athletes massacred a small band of Indians.

Unable to contain his anxiety later in the day, Bruce stopped by the hotel where Warner was staying and told him about his efforts to organize the meet. He nearly collapsed when he learned that the Carlisle team consisted of only five athletes. Bruce explained to Warner that there were 14 events in the meet and that he had gone all over the Lehigh Valley to raise the Carlisle guarantee. Warner was having a soft drink and as he pushed the straw over to the other side of his mouth, he pulled out a wad of bills large enough to choke a horse. Then he said, "You don't think you can beat me, do you? Want to make a little bet?" Bruce just stared at Warner intensely, as if he were confronted with a madman. As Bruce turned to walk out the door, Warner blurted out, "Harold, I wish you would run the meet off as fast as possible because we want to catch the 4:46 train out of here tomorrow."[2]

In the end, the farce turned out to be the Lafayette team's inability to compete with Carlisle as the five Indians won the meet 71–31 and caught the 4:46 train to Carlisle. Jim Thorpe competed in nine events and won seven of them. After coming in second in the 100-yard dash, he won the pole vault, high jump, low hurdles, shot put and broad jump. Louis Tewanima won both the mile and two mile runs. Other members of the sparse Carlisle team won a few second and third places.

Later in the 1909 track season Pop Warner took a three-man team of Jim Thorpe, Louis Tewanama and Frank Mount Pleasant to Syracuse and defeated coach Tom Keane's team of over 20 athletes by a margin of one point. In that meet Thorpe won five first places, a second and two thirds.

Because of his athletic achievements in the spring of 1909 at Carlisle, Jim Thorpe was getting noticed in the national press and was recognized as a track star as well as a football star. Back in Oklahoma people were puzzled by Thorpe's rise to prominence. Most who remembered him from the Indian school considered him to be careless, shiftless and lacking in ambition. He had been constantly mixed up in pranks. Although he was usually victorious in most athletic games with other Indian boys, he never demonstrated any extraordinary ability. Perhaps it was because the level of competition he faced back in Oklahoma never tested him to the limits of his abilities. Still, there would remain a notion throughout Thorpe's athletic career that he never did anything better than he had to. Unfortunately for Jim Thorpe, it seemed to stick with him.

With the 1909 track and baseball season over at Carlisle, several athletes including Thorpe, Jessie Youngdeer, Joseph Libby and Stancil "Possum" Powell headed south to play minor league baseball, instead of participating in the school's outing system. It would be this decision that would eventually cost Thorpe his 1912 Olympic medals. Playing professional baseball was new territory for Thorpe. A few years earlier, he had tried to make the Anadarko Indians team in Oklahoma as a pitcher, but was released.

The Carlisle foursome headed for North Carolina, hoping to be picked up by teams in the Eastern Carolina League. Libby and Youngdeer, both outfielders, were immediately signed by Rocky Mount. The team also offered Thorpe $15 a week to play first base, and he jumped at the chance. There were several other college athletes playing minor league ball in North Carolina that summer, but unfortunately, Jim Thorpe agreed to play for a pittance and under his own name.

Historically it has been suggested that Thorpe signed to play ball in North Carolina under his own name simply because he was naive. However, when his athletic career is looked at in a prism that demonstrates a broader sequence of events, it becomes clear that Jim Thorpe really didn't care about the formalities associated with participating at different levels of competition; what he wanted was to be paid for his athletic endeavors. One can search endlessly through the life story of Jim Thorpe for a different explanation and it just never comes to the fore. The fact is that by 1909, Jim Thorpe was already in his mind a professional athlete, and he left Carlisle for no other reason than to play minor league baseball for money.

During the 1909 season Thorpe pitched and played first base for Rocky Mount. He finished the season with a batting average of .254 (35/138). His pitching record was 9–10. Also he demonstrated some unusual speed on the base paths that summer. However at the time stolen base statistics were not kept in the Eastern Carolina League.

	Batting						Fielding			
	G	AB	R	H	SB	BA	PO	A	E	Ave.
1909 Rocky Mount, ECL	44	138	11	35	—	254	91	46	13	.913

Although Thorpe was thrilled about being paid $60 a month to play baseball, he wasn't using his money wisely. He was on his own now and there was no banking program as there was in the Carlisle outing system where the student kept half the pay and the other half was kept in a trust at the school.

So Thorpe began to spend his money on "fire water." It would be the beginning of a habit that would follow him throughout his professional sports career. After a night of heavy drinking in Raleigh, he became disorderly. When the police attempted to arrest him, he refused to be arrested until advised by an umpire. Soon after he paid a fine and was released.

At the conclusion of the 1909 Eastern Carolina League season, Thorpe did not return to Carlisle. Instead he went home to Oklahoma without any money and lived with relatives and tribal friends, anticipating the coming of spring and eager to return to North Carolina and play baseball.

Meanwhile, back at Carlisle no one attempted to make any contact with Jim Thorpe, not coach Pop Warner, not his mentor Albert Exendine or even Superintendent Friedman. It seems incomprehensible that the athletic department of Carlisle, with the 1909 football season fast approaching and a tough schedule at hand, would choose to let a Third Team All-American harvest potatoes in Oklahoma rather than invite him to join them. But that is exactly what transpired.

In the Indians' final game of the 1909 season they defeated St. Louis University, 32–0. The game was played on Thanksgiving Day in Cincinnati. Sitting in the stands that day, watching his former team play, was the ghostly figure of Jim Thorpe. Still without Thorpe, the Carlisle Indians finished their 1909 season with a record of 8–3–1, outscoring their opponents, 243–94.

In January, 1910, baseball was officially discontinued at Carlisle by Pop Warner and his action sanctioned by Superintendent Friedman. The baseball program had come to an end in part because each year a few of Carlisle's promising athletes "not including Jim Thorpe," such as Bill Garlow, James "John" Bender, Charles "Wahoo" Guyon, Joe Guyon, Joseph Twin, Lloyd Nephew, William Newashe, Jesse Youngdeer and Wilson Charles, who did not like working on a farm, were opting out of the summer outing program to play minor league ball and earn $50–$150 a month.

It made no difference to Pop Warner or Moses Friedman that former Carlisle baseball players such as Chief Bender, Frank Jude and Mike Balenti had gone on to play in the major leagues. They advanced the belief that by cutting baseball, they were strengthening academics — students would remain in school. By keeping the students in the outing program in the summer, they were being protected from the corrupt influences of bush league managers. Still, the decision to drop baseball was controversial among the Carlisle students. Carlisle had three baseball teams, and to fill the void left by the loss of baseball, Warner started a lacrosse program.

After anticipating the coming baseball season all winter long, in the spring of 1910 Thorpe quickly left Oklahoma and returned to North Carolina.

He once again signed to play with Rocky Mount. Late in the season his contract was sold to Fayetteville. His time in North Carolina that summer was a mixed bag of mediocre performances on the diamond and civil disobedience off it. Playing in 45 games, he had a won-lost record on the mound of 10–10 and at the plate he hit .242 (31–128). He also had 11 stolen bases.

		Batting					Fielding			
	G	AB	R	H	SB	BA	PO	A	E	Ave.
1910 Rocky Mount, ECL	29	76	11	18	4	.237	8	59	7	.905
1910 Fayetteville, ECL	16	52	6	13	7	.250	129	10	5	.965
Totals	45	128	17	31	11	.242	137	69	12	.945

Among the off-field stunts that Thorpe participated in during his stint in Rocky Mount in the summer of 1910 was challenging the tide in the Atlantic Ocean off the coast at Wrightsville, North Carolina. Arthur Dussault was the catcher for the Rocky Mount club that summer and Thorpe's battery mate and roommate. According to Dussault, the day after Thorpe had pitched and won a doubleheader against Wilmington, the team was honored in a party at Wrightsville Beach. Following the party Thorpe went to bed in his room at Mrs. Cooper's boarding house. At 5:30 A.M., he promptly rose and ran out of the house, down the boardwalk and jumped into the ocean. He drifted with the tide for a while, until he was about a half-mile out to sea, then attempted to come back in. "All of us had been warned not to go swimming that morning," said Dussault. "We could see him from the shore and it was evident that he was struggling to get back. He finally made it at 9 o'clock in the morning. When he came out of the water there was no evidence of exhaustion. He walked back to the room and went to bed."[3] No one ever dared to mention it to him.

On July 1, 1910, Thorpe was traded to Fayetteville for pitcher Del Wilson, who had formerly been in the Cincinnati Reds minor league system. According to Arthur Dussault, Wilson gave the Rocky Mount team more pitching strength and helped them to the league championship that year. Thorpe was only an average pitcher who lost as many games as he won. His arm was too short to be good. However, Dussault also stated that once Thorpe got on base, it was very hard to keep him from scoring. "He ran the bases like a horse and went into bases in a manner that would have broken bones in most players."[4]

At Fayetteville, after Charles Clancy, manager of the Highlanders, saw Thorpe pitch in one game he was not impressed. Of course Thorpe could run and he could throw. Even his hitting seemed to be improving. By now Thorpe had grown to six feet tall and was very strong. So Clancy decided the smart thing to do was to move him to first base where he could use his height and reach to take almost everything without shifting his feet. He seemed to be a natural for first base. In fact, Thorpe's overall performance improved at first base. Playing in 16 games at Fayetteville in the summer of 1910, Thorpe hit for an average of .250 (13/52) and stole 7 bases.

Also that summer at Fayetteville, Thorpe hit a legendary home run that fans said was the longest they had ever seen at the Fair Grounds. The home run was so long that a stake was placed in the ground where the ball landed to memorialize it. However on March 7, 1914, Thorpe's titanic blast at the Fair Grounds was surpassed by 60 feet by a ball hit by Babe Ruth, in his first professional game and second at-bat.

While Thorpe's performance on the ball field was improving during the summer of 1910, his off-field behavior was not. One of his more infamous hijinks that summer occurred on the streets of Fayetteville when he went on a rampage in the early morning hours after consuming copious amounts of liquor. After disposing of a detachment of five local policemen sent to subdue him and depositing one in a barrel, Thorpe continued to show his displeasure by walking up to a plate glass window of a grocery store and butting his head against it. As the shattered glass fell from the frame it opened a nasty gash on his scalp. Thorpe sat down on the curb, bleeding from a head wound, and proceeded to roll a cigarette and smoke it. Soon townsfolk gathered around him and an ambulance was called. However, upon its arrival Thorpe refused assistance. Finally the president of the Fayetteville Highlanders was called. With Thorpe still demurring, the police used a lasso to rope and tie him. Then he was chloroformed and hauled away to the infirmary. Following the 1910 baseball season, Thorpe returned home to Oklahoma again, without any money.

Back at Carlisle in the fall of 1910, Pop Warner and the Indians were experiencing their worst football season since 1901. The 1910 Carlisle squad finished with an 8–6 record, losing to Syracuse, Princeton, Penn, Navy, Brown and even the Harvard Law School team, by a score of 3–0. Pop Warner knew he had a good thing going at Carlisle, good pay, free housing, national notoriety, etc. It was time for him to reach out to Jim Thorpe, who still had two years of eligibility remaining.

For some reason, Thorpe had decided not to return to North Carolina for the 1911 baseball season. Albert Exendine informed Warner that he had seen Thorpe in Oklahoma during the summer of 1911 and that he seemed to be in playing condition.

So Warner sent a letter to Thorpe encouraging him to return to school. Even though Warner was well aware that Thorpe had been playing professional baseball for two years, he still told him that, if he came back to Carlisle, he was sure he could make the United States Olympic team and travel to Stockholm in the summer of 1912. To Thorpe, doing nothing but floundering on the farms of relatives and friends in Oklahoma, the possibility of world fame was an offer he couldn't refuse. He immediately accepted Warner's proposal and returned to Carlisle in time for the 1911 football season.

Although Carlisle had lost four of its starters from the 1910 squad, with Jim Thorpe returning to the Indians backfield, in 1911 they would have a fabulous season, finishing with a record of 11–1. The Carlisle team consisted of 20 players and was not very big in size. The starters were Joel Wheelock, who often alternated with Sam Burd as right end and also filled in a half back, weighed 155 lbs., William "Lonestar" Dietz, right tackle, 176 lbs., Elmer Busch, right guard, 181 lbs., Joe Bergie, center, 187 lbs., Peter Jordan, left guard, 173 lbs., William Newashe, left tackle, 187 lbs., Henry Roberts, left end, 178 lbs., Gus Welch, quarterback, 154 lbs., Alexander Arcasa, right half back, 150 lbs., Jim Thorpe, left half back, 176 lbs., and Stansil "Possum" Powell, fullback, 171 lbs.

While most of the regulars sat out the first two games of the season, Carlisle still came charging out of the gate, defeating Lebanon Valley, 53–0 on September 23 and four days later crushed Muhlenberg, 32–0.

In the third game of the season and on their home field, Carlisle faced a stiff challenge from Dickinson, who held the Indians to a 0–0 score at halftime. However, Carlisle rallied in the second half to defeat Dickinson, 17–0. Jim Thorpe played only part of the game, but still managed an 85-yard touchdown run. It was clear that although Thorpe had been away from the gridiron for two years, he had not lost a step and was the Carlisle squad's biggest scoring threat. Hyman Goldstein, one of the Dickinson players in the 1911 Carlisle game, would later say in an interview in the 1970s that Carlisle was the best team in the country. He also added that his greatest thrill in playing football was holding Carlisle to a zero to zero score at the end of the first half.

Next Carlisle defeated Mount St. Mary's, 46–5, and Georgetown, 28–5 at Washington, D.C.

On October 21, Pittsburgh fell to Carlisle 17–0 before a crowd of 8,000 at Forbes Field in Pittsburgh. Jim Thorpe ran for one touchdown and kicked two field goals. The next day a reporter for the *Pittsburgh Leader* wrote, "To say Thorpe is the whole team would be fifty percent wrong."[7] Thorpe's punting was also spectacular as he averaged 60 yards a kick, booting the ball far over the Pitt players laying back for his punts. Pitt center Polly Galvin was responsible for setting up one of the Indians touchdowns by slugging Carlisle quarterback Welch in the face. The assault was so overt that the officials suspended Galvin from the game and placed the ball inside the ten yard line.

The following week on October 28, Carlisle remained undefeated at 7–0 with a 19–0 victory over Lafayette. Thorpe had once said, "Who can get hurt playing football?" The Lafayette game was played at Easton, Pennsylvania, and in the fourth quarter Thorpe was carried off the field with a badly twisted ankle. But the damage by Thorpe to the Lafayette defense had already been done as he had scored two touchdowns and one field goal prior to being hurt.

Pennsylvania was next on the Carlisle schedule on November 4 at Philadelphia. The week before the Penn game found Thorpe on crutches most of the time. Still, a lame Thorpe played in the game, scored one touchdown and intercepted a couple of passes as the Indians defeated the Quakers, 16–0, to increase their season record to 8–0. With Thorpe hurting, Arcasa, Welch and Powell did the heavy lifting and rushed at will through the Penn line.

On November 11, Carlisle visited Cambridge, Massachusetts, to face powerful Harvard. The Crimson, coached by the legendary Percy Houghton, were the 1910 National Champions. In the previous 13 years, the Indians had only beat Harvard once (1907, 23–15). In 1910, Carlisle had been defeated 3–0 by the Harvard Law School team and had not played the Harvard varsity since 1908 when they were defeated, 17–0. Coming into the Harvard game, Carlisle had outscored its opponents 180–5. Harvard had outscored its opponents 78–14.

In the 1911 game Carlisle would not face an all-varsity Crimson team, and the game began with Harvard placing mostly substitutes on the field. Only five of the substitute Harvard players starting the game had played during the season, all in the loss to Princeton, 8–6, the week before. Harvard had a lot of injured players on its varsity, including its quarterback who wrenched his knee in the Princeton game, and Coach Houghton, looking beyond the Carlisle game, wanted to save his regulars for the Dartmouth and Yale games still on the schedule.

On hand for the game at Soldiers' Field in Cambridge were 35,000 fans. Jim Thorpe played with an injured leg bandaged tightly from his toes to above his knees. The first half ended with Harvard in the lead, 9–6. However, when the Crimson fell behind in the third quarter, 15–9, Percy Houghton, sensing defeat, sent in his first-team players to start the fourth quarter. Regardless, Carlisle held on to win the game, 18–15, and take their season record to 9–0. Thorpe ran for 173 of the 334 Indians rushing yards. On one series of downs he ran for 70 yards in nine plays for a TD. He scored all the Indians points, running for a touchdown and kicking four field goals from different angles (two over 40 yards, one for 48 yards) for 12 points. Back in Carlisle, Pennsylvania, students went wild over the Indians victory and snake danced through the downtown streets. Later Thorpe called the Harvard game the second greatest game he ever played in.

The Indians' undefeated season would come to an end the following week when they were defeated by Syracuse, 12–11. The game was played before 11,000 fans in Syracuse's Archbold Stadium in deplorable weather conditions. The temperature was frigid and heavy rains had left the field deep in mud which slowed down the Indians' rushing attack. Jim Thorpe scored both of the Indians touchdowns. However, his conversion kick following his first touchdown missed the mark, providing the margin of victory for the Orangemen.

The Carlisle Indians completed their 1911 season with two more victories. On November 25, the Indians defeated Johns Hopkins, 29–6, and then on November 30, at Providence with a crowd of 12,000 in the stands at Andrews Field, they beat the Brown Bears, 12–6, with Thorpe kicking two field goals.

It had been a remarkable season for the 11–1 Carlisle Indians, and Jim Thorpe gained national notoriety playing halfback, defensive back, place-kicker and punter for the Indians. In honor of his achievements Thorpe was named as captain for the 1912 Carlisle squad. The national accolades and honors followed immediately. Twenty-five Eastern college football coaches said that Thorpe was the best halfback ever developed. Then Thorpe was named by Walter Camp as a First Team All-American halfback. Joining Thorpe as backfield selections were quarterback Art Howe of Yale, halfback Percy Wendell of Harvard and fullback Jack Dalton of Navy.

While Jim Thorpe had played brilliantly, much of the success of the Carlisle Indians in the 1911 football season was due to the play of quarterback Gus Welch, who only two years prior had never touched a football. Pop Warner remarked that Welch was the best quarterback he had at Carlisle since Jimmy Johnson. Also Carlisle captain and end Sam Burd was selected by coaches from the East and West as an outstanding contributor to the Indians' success.

1911 CARLISLE FOOTBALL SCORES

09/23	Carlisle	53	Lebanon Valley	0
09/27	Carlisle	32	Muhlenberg	0
09/30	Carlisle	17	Dickinson	0
10/07	Carlisle	46	Mount St. Mary's	5
10/14	Carlisle	28	Georgetown	5
10/21	Carlisle	17	Pittsburgh	0
10/28	Carlisle	19	Lafayette	0
11/04	Carlisle	16	Pennsylvania	0
11/11	Carlisle	18	Harvard	15
11/18	Carlisle	11	Syracuse	12
11/25	Carlisle	29	John Hopkins	6
11/30	Carlisle	12	Brown	6

6

The 1912 Olympic Games

As spring arrived in 1912 Jim Thorpe was focused on making the 1912 United States Olympic track team, and the thought of playing baseball was not even a passing thought. To accomplish the goal, Pop Warner had a plan for him. To prepare for the Olympic pentathlon and decathlon contests, Pop Warner wanted Thorpe to compete in from five to seven events in every meet that spring.

At a meet at Franklin Field in Philadelphia, Penn defeated Carlisle 85–32. However, Jim Thorpe scored 22 of the Carlisle points, taking first place in the high jump, shot put and 220-yard low hurdles. Carnegie Tech was in the meet, too, but failed to score a point. As the 1912 track season progressed Thorpe excelled, winning gold medals in several major meets such as the Boston Athletic Association (gold medal, 100-yard dash); Pittsburgh Athletic Association (gold medals 12-pound shot put, 60-yard hurdles, 60-yard dash and high jump); and Middle Atlantic Association (AAU) (gold medals, 12-pound shot put, 16-pound shot put, and 75-yard dash).

In May, at the Eastern Olympic trails for the pentathlon at Celtic Park in New York, Jim Thorpe was in a class all by himself. In the meet Thorpe took first place in three of five events (broad jump, 200-meter dash, discus throw) and finished second in the other two (javelin and 1500 meter run). In winning the broad jump, the first event of the day, Thorpe leaped 21 feet, 8³/₈ inches. But it was not a sensational jump for Thorpe, who had previously been on record with a broad jump of 23 feet, 4 inches. In the 200-yard dash Thorpe had the rest of the field eating his dust, winning by more than ten yards, in a time of 23 and ³/₅ seconds. In the discus throw Thorpe won with a toss of 115 feet, 4¹/₂ inches. Also Thorpe came in second in the 1500 meter run, finishing about three yards behind the winner, Tom McLoughlin.

But it was Thorpe's heave of the javelin that caused the bystanders to take notice. Thorpe was inexperienced with the javelin so not much was expected of him. Thorpe grabbed the spear in an awkward manner, walked up to the line and heaved it 136 feet, 7¹/₂ inches, to finish second to Bruno

Jim Thorpe, 1912.

Broad of the American-Irish A. C., a former world record holder, who threw the javelin 157 feet, 6 inches. Thorpe, not knowing the rules of the meet, had been practicing his javelin throwing from within an 8 foot, 2 inch circle; he did not know that in the meet he was allowed an unlimited run towards the line before tossing the spear.

James E. Sullivan, a founder of the AAU and forthcoming American commissioner to the Olympics, was the referee at the meet in Celtic Park.

Following the meet Sullivan remarked, "Thorpe showed his all round ability in so pronounced a fashion, that it is a foregone conclusion he will win the decathlon if it is staged next week. There is no use to make Thorpe come all the way from Carlisle to New York again. I think the committee will decide to call off the decathlon tryouts."[1]

However, the trials were held and Thorpe participated. At the United States Olympic team trials at the Polo Grounds, Thorpe qualified for the 1912 Olympic team in the high and broad jump. He was selected for the pentathlon and decathlon based on his all-around athletic ability. In the high jump trials he jumped 6 feet, 5 inches — within 5/8 inch of the existing world record which at that time was held by Mike Sweeny.

Thorpe remarked that he had done better. He stated that some of his best marks were made at Carlisle and they were not put in the books. This included a broad jump of 24 feet and quarter-mile run of 48 seconds. Another time he maintained that he had run a 220-yard dash in a little over 21 seconds.

The final event for Thorpe prior to his official selection for the Olympic team came on June 8, at the Eastern Olympic tryouts held at Soldiers' Field, Cambridge, the site of some of his recent gridiron glory.

His selection official, Jim Thorpe joined the other 163 members of the 1912 U.S. Olympic team, including his Carlisle track teammate, Louis Tewanima, selected from regional tryouts in Cambridge, Chicago and Stanford University, and left for the V Olympiad in Stockholm, Sweden, from New York on June 14, 1912, aboard the Red Star liner S.S. *Finland.*

Since that departure, for nearly 100 years a debate has ensued over whether or not Thorpe refused to train on the ship. One version of this story has it that en route to the Olympics, Thorpe spent his time at sea lying in a hammock, while his teammates took endless runs around the deck. However, many of Thorpe's teammates came forward over the years to refute this allegation. Avery Brundage, who later became the President of the U.S. Olympic Committee, remarked that Thorpe participated in regular daily workouts while at sea. Still others have stated it was Pop Warner, chosen by Olympic trainer Mike Murphy, the Penn track coach, to come along to the Olympics and work with both Thorpe and Tewanima, who kept Thorpe inactive on the ship. "Mike Murphy was also the father of Hollywood movie star and later U.S. Senator, George Murphy."

Whatever the case may have been, when the ship reached Sweden, at the suggestion of teammate Johnny Hayes the marathon men, including Louis Tewanima, were taken to a private training ground outside of Stockholm. Warner took Thorpe there, too, at his own expense. There Thorpe worked out daily, preparing for his appearance in the games. Thorpe remarked that he benefited much more working out there than he would have on the steamer.

According to Johnny Hayes, Thorpe had peculiar methods of training. Hayes stated that one day he looked out the window of their quarters in Sweden and saw Thorpe get up out of a hammock and walk to the sidewalk. Then he marked off about 23 feet by chalking off both corners of the distance. Hayes was shocked! He thought that Thorpe was about to practice his broad jumping on a cement sidewalk. To his surprise, Thorpe walked back to the hammock, climbed back in and fixed his eyes intensely on the two chalk marks. After a while, apparently satisfied with his perception of the distance and convinced he could accomplish the jump, Thorpe rolled over in the hammock and went to sleep.

Later Thorpe stated, "There is no denying I was lazy in my training. However, I will say this for myself—no meet or game ever came along that did not find me in condition. And at least, I never left my best performances on the practice field."[2]

The first of the modern Olympic Games had taken place in Greece in 1896. Just 13 countries and 285 athletes participated. The United States dominated the games, winning ten gold medals in track and field alone. Tom Burke collected two of them, winning the 100-meter dash in 12 seconds flat and the 400 meters in 54.2 seconds. Robert Garrett also won two gold medals, with an 11.22 meter shot put and a discus throw of 29.15 meters.

The V Olympiad, held at Stockholm, Sweden, took place between May 5 and July 22, 1912, and participation among nations had grown considerably. Twenty-eight nations participated with 2,407 athletes; 48 women and 2,359 men competing in 102 events. In 1912, for the first time the Olympic Games were opened to women divers and swimmers. However, James E. Sullivan, American commissioner to the Olympics, refused to allow American women to compete.

Baseball made an appearance at the 1912 Olympics as a demonstration sport. A game between the United States and Sweden was played on July 15, 1912, with the Americans winning, 13–3, in six innings. Two Americans, Wesley Oler and Ben Adams, played on the Swedish team. The game was umpired by former major league great George Wright, and eight Olympic medalists took part in the game. The attendance was sparse with most spectators being either Americans or Swedish-Americans. A second game before a much larger crowd was played the following day on July 16 between two clubs of Americans representing the East and West. In this game Jim Thorpe played right field and had one hit, a double, in two at-bats.

The first event for Thorpe in the 1912 Olympic Pentathlon was the broad jump. He took first place with a leap of 23 feet, 2$^{7}/_{10}$ inches. According to Thorpe, the day during pre-events training when contemplating his jump while lounging in a hammock, he hadn't placed those two chalk marks quite far enough.

Jim Thorpe's overall performance in the 1912 Olympics was nothing short of overwhelming. Without the benefit of formal training in track, Thorpe won gold medals in both the pentathlon and decathlon. At the time Thorpe's pentathlon and decathlon marks were new world records. Back in America every newspaper in the country carried huge stories about Thorpe, proclaiming him the greatest athlete ever. Jim Thorpe was now a superstar of previously unknown proportions.

Thorpe took first place in the pentathlon with 7 points (winning 4 of 5 events: running broad jump, 200 meters dash, discus and 1500 meter race, losing only in the javelin). Second place was taken by F.R. Bie of Norway with 21 points; James J. Douglas of the United States took third place with 29 points.

JIM THORPE — PENTATHLON EVENTS

Running broad jump	23'2$^{7}/_{10}$"	1st place
200 meter run	22.9 seconds	1st place
1500 meter run	4 minutes, 40.8 seconds	1st place
Discus throw	116'8$^{4}/_{10}$"	1st place
Javelin throw	153'2$^{19}/_{20}$"	3rd place

Thorpe won a gold medal in the decathlon with 8,413 of the available 10,000 points (winning 4 of 10 events, 1500 meters, 110 meter high hurdles, high jump and shot put) setting an Olympic mark (8,413 points) that would stand for two decades. Second place was won by Hugo Wieslander of Sweden and third place was won by Charles Lomberg of Sweden.

JIM THORPE — DECATHLON EVENTS

1500 meter run	4 minutes, 40.1 seconds	1st place
110 meter high hurdles	15.6 seconds	1st place
High jump	6'1$^{6}/_{10}$"	1st place
Shot put	42'5$^{9}/_{20}$"	1st place
Broad jump	22'2$^{3}/_{10}$"	3rd place
Pole Vault	10'7$^{19}/_{20}$"	3rd place
Discus throw	121'3$^{9}/_{10}$"	3rd place
100 meter run	11.2 seconds	3rd place
400 meter run	52.2 seconds	4th place
Javelin throw	149'11$^{2}/_{10}$"	4th place

Thorpe's Carlisle track teammate Louis Tewanama finished second in the 10,000 meters behind Kannes Kolehmainen of Finland, known as the

"Flying Finn." No American would run a better time than Tewanama had in the event until Billy Mills in the 1964 Olympics at Tokyo.

On July 15 Jim Thorpe met with Sweden's King Gustav V to receive his gold medals. In his epic pronouncement the monarch told Thorpe, "You, sir, are the greatest athlete in the world."[3] To this accolade, Thorpe simply replied, "thanks, King." King Gustav V then presented Thorpe with gifts including a bust of himself and a 30-pound silver likeness of a Viking ship, lined with gold and containing precious jewels, from Czar Nicholas of Russia. The gifts had an estimated value of $50,000.

Thorpe stated in an interview for *Sports World* magazine in 1949 that someone had started a rumor that when King Gustav V requested to meet him, he remarked that he couldn't be bothered to meet a mere king. He could use the sleep better. Thorpe stated that story was completely false, as were other rumors that he was too busy to meet with the king because he was busy lifting heavy steins of Swedish beer. Thorpe further stated that meeting King Gustav V was the proudest moment of his life.

Thorpe did not return to the United States with the American Olympic team. He stayed in Europe with several of his teammates, including Louis Tewanima, to compete as individuals in some meets on the continent.

Abel Kiviat was Thorpe's roommate in Stockholm. Kiviat won a silver medal at the 1912 Olympics in the 1500 meters. According to Kiviat, there wasn't anything Thorpe couldn't do. He would see something and he would do it, better — he had brute strength, stamina and endurance. According to Kiviat, Thorpe didn't know how to throw the javelin or the discus, but it didn't matter. He just went in and threw them farther than almost anyone else. Following the games the American team took a trip to Paris. In the dining room of the hotel where they were staying there was a chandelier, and several of the team got to betting on whether someone could jump up and touch it. Kiviat says that Plat Adams, a 6'5" gold medalist Olympic high jumper from Brigham Young, tried it and failed. Then Thorpe took one leap and could have made like Tarzan as he brushed the crystals.

During the voyage overseas for the Olympics, regardless of the historical dispute of his refusing to train, otherwise Thorpe had been all business. However, on the return trip he drank heavily and ran around the decks shouting that he was a horse. It prompted Pop Warner to warn Thorpe that he had to behave himself. Thorpe, like so many before him and after, had simply not comprehended the magnitude and responsibilities of his sudden fame. Already back in the United States a suggestion was made to have Jim Thorpe appear on the five-cent piece featuring a Buffalo on the reverse that was about to replace the V Nickel or Liberty Nickel in 1913.

When Warner, Thorpe and Tewanima arrived back in the United States, they were greeted with a huge celebration. In Boston on August 10, 1912, Mayor John "Honey Fitz" Fitzgerald, grandfather of future President John F. Kennedy, challenged Thorpe to a 100-yard dash. The Mayor said he would take no handicap — he was good enough to give Thorpe a race.

Back in Carlisle some observers, including the school paper, were wondering if Jim Thorpe would return to play football in the fall of 1912 or would sign a major league baseball contract. On August 12, 1912, Jim Thorpe told the *Boston Post* that he liked professional baseball, liked Boston and its people, and could be induced to play for the Red Sox next year. Thorpe said that if he decided to play baseball he wanted to be with a winner. However, at the moment he had another year before finishing school at Carlisle.

The Boston reporters asked Thorpe about the rumor that he might sign a professional baseball contract with the Pittsburgh Pirates. Thorpe replied, "Pittsburgh has never tried to sign me up. I was there at an athletic meet last winter and a Smokey City man was showing me around town. He knew the Pittsburgh owner (Barney Dreyfuss) and we were in the vicinity of his office, took me up and introduced me. Nothing was talked about me becoming a Pirate. I suppose the fact that I visited the office gave rise to the story."[4]

There were also suggestions being made formally and informally that Thorpe, with his multi-sports talent, might be the "white hope" that boxing and white America were seeking to unseat Jack Johnson as heavyweight champion. Johnson, professional boxing's first black heavyweight champion, had won the title in 1908 by knocking out Tommy Burns in a bout held near Sydney, Australia. Following his victory, white America was outraged and the bigotry that ensued called for a white fighter to reclaim the title.

Johnson, however, openly defied the bigotry; he married three white women and spent his money in a free and lavish style. He flashed his gold teeth, drove around in an expensive sports car, held extravagant parties and carried a gold walking stick. When it was suggested to Thorpe that he might be able to reclaim the heavyweight crown from Johnson for white America, he declined, stating that he could run too fast to ever figure as a white hope. However, it was probably good for Jack Johnson that he had not become the wrestling heavyweight champion. Thorpe was a great wrestler and may have entertained such an offer to grapple with Johnson, but more for the sport of it, rather than any racial circumstance or notion of superiority. Thorpe himself was too well acquainted with bigotry to allow himself to be a party to such antics.

Prior to Thorpe's Olympic victories at Stockholm, the view held by many Europeans was that any American winning an event in the Olympics was

merely a naturalized Swede, German or Frenchman. Thorpe's victories left
no doubt that a real American had beaten all the competitors from the Old
World.

On Friday, August 16, 1912, at 12:30 P.M., the trio of heroes, Warner,
Thorpe and Tewanima, arrived in Carlisle aboard the Cumberland Valley
train to one of the grandest of celebrations the little industrial town had seen
since the end of the Civil War. At 2:00 P.M. thousands of people lined the
sidewalks as a huge parade in honor of the Olympic stars passed by. Following
the parade 7,000 people gathered at Biddle Athletic Field for a formal celebration. The presiding officer, Mr. Conrad Hambleton, opened the ceremonies
with a brief speech, then introduced Carlisle Superintendent Moses Friedman.

Superintendent Friedman stated in his address that the celebration in
Carlisle was a national celebration. The heroes they were welcoming concerned
the entire country and it was proud of their success and achievements. Friedman then began to speak about Silver Medal winner Louis Tewanima. He
said that five years earlier; Tewanima had arrived in Carlisle as a prisoner of
war. "His people, the Hopi Tribe of Arizona, had been giving the Government
much trouble and were opposed to progress and education. It was finally
decided to send twelve of the head men and most influential of the tribe to

Lewis Tewanima 1912.

Carlisle to be educated in order to win them over to American ideas. Tewanima was of this party." Friedman said that the Hopis arrived with long hair and earrings. However, after a while in the confines of Carlisle they asked to have their hair cut like the other boys. They took up their studies and worked at various trades, making rapid progress. Soon they could read and write and had become Christians. "Louis Tewanima, here is the twelfth of that party. He is one of the most popular students at the school. You all know of his athletic powers — I wanted you to know of his advancement in civilization and as a man." Then Friedman officially welcomed Louis Tewanima back to Carlisle.

Next Friedman spoke about Jim Thorpe. Friedman said, "The world's greatest athlete is also an Indian. We welcome you, James Thorpe, to this town and back to your school."[5]

On July 29, 1912, President William Howard Taft had sent a letter to Thorpe by way of Moses Friedman congratulating him on his Olympic victories at Stockholm. So Friedman read the letter to the assembled crowd.

"Mr. James Thorpe
Carlisle, Pa.
My Dear Sir:
     I have much pleasure on congratulating you on the account of your noteworthy victory at the Olympic games in Stockholm. Your performance is one of which you may be proud. You have set a high standard of physical development, which is only attained by right living and right thinking, and your victory will serve as an incentive to all to improve those qualities which characterize the best type of American citizen.
     It is my earnest wish that the future will bring you success in your chosen field of endeavor.
     With heartiest congratulations, I am,
     Sincerely yours,
     Wm. H. Taft"[6]

Friedman concluded his remarks by welcoming back coach Glenn "Pop" Warner and calling him the foremost athletic coach in America. He further stated the victories of Thorpe and Tewanima would have been impossible without Warner.

Then there were brief remarks from Warner, Thorpe and Tewanima. All that Thorpe said was, "All I can say is, that you showed me a good time."[7] Then the 7,000 assembled on the field moved off and a baseball game between Carlisle and the Wood team of Chambersburg was played. The game went 14 innings. That evening Warner, Thorpe and Tewanima were the guests at a banquet held by the Carlisle Elks. Later the celebration was concluded with a band concert on the square in Carlisle.

On August 24, there was a huge parade for the American Olympic Team in New York down Fifth Avenue and Broadway to City Hall. According to an article in the *Chicago Daily Tribune*, Thorpe "sat alone in an automobile in embarrassed silence. He was perhaps the chief attraction in the line, but he pulled his Panama hat over his eyes, chewed gum, pinched his knees and

Jim Thorpe is greeted by Mayor Gaynor in the Olympic Games ceremony at New York's City Hall, 1912.

seldom lifted his gaze. Piled in front of him in the car were his trophies, above which fluttered the Carlisle Pennant."[8]

Following all the post–Olympics hoopla, Louis Tewanima spent about a month at Carlisle, then went home to his Hopi tribe in Arizona to tend his sheep and raise his crops. He rarely if ever left the reservation again. In 1954 the Helms Foundation flew Tewanima to New York to be honored as a member of the all-time U.S. track and field team. At the age of 90, on January 18, 1969, Tewanima died after falling off a 70-foot cliff on the reservation in Arizona. He had lived on the reservation all but five years of his life, those spent at Carlisle. Tewanima had attended a religious ceremony at Kiva and was returning to his home at Shonogopovi about a mile away. He apparently mistook a beacon light, took the wrong trail and fell down the cliff.

On Labor Day, 1912, in New York City, Thorpe, with no training since the Olympics and competing on a muddy field, won the A.A.U. all-round championship in a track & field event at Celtic Park by the largest total (7476) ever scored in the annual event. The former mark was set in 1909 by Martin Sheridan (7385).

While it had been a hugely successful spring and summer for Jim Thorpe, it had also been a grueling affair. The A.A.U. meet in Celtic Park would be the last major amateur track meet in which Jim Thorpe would ever compete. His glory days in track and field had been short. Now fall was looming and there was football in the air. As Thorpe and Pop Warner left New York City, they began to focus on the first game of the 1912 Carlisle football season just over the horizon on September 21.

7

The 1912 Carlisle Football Season

The Carlisle Indians began their 14-game 1912 football schedule on September 21 with a victory over Albright, 50–7. Four days later on September 25, the Indians defeated Lebanon Valley, 45–0. Pop Warner withheld his regular players in both games, playing his substitutes to provide them with game experience for the long campaign ahead.

Next on the schedule, September 28, was Dickinson, the Indians' feisty intra-city rival in Carlisle. Dickinson had played hard against the Indians in 1911 and came on the gridiron determined again to defeat them. At the end of the first half the score stood 0–0. Then Jim Thorpe scored two quick touchdowns in the second half and the Indians went on to roll-up a 34–0 victory.

On October 2, Warner once again played his substitutes the entire game as Carlisle took its season record to 4–0 with a 65–0 drubbing of Villanova.

Three days later, on October 5, Carlisle was held to a 0–0 scoreless tie by Washington & Jefferson. The game was played on a bad field. Following the Washington & Jefferson game Jim Thorpe was feeling low. To help cope with his melancholy, Thorpe turned to his usual remedy and got drunk, drinking beer after ducking out on the team at Pittsburgh. Pop Warner went after Thorpe, caught up with him in front of a hotel, and ordered him to apologize to the team or quit the squad.

The following week, on October 12, the Indians, with a chastened Thorpe, ran off a 33–0 victory over Syracuse. The score was 0–0 at the half. The field was muddy and Thorpe was having trouble with sweeping end runs. In the locker room during the half, Warner told Thorpe to run the ball up the middle. But Thorpe was reluctant, telling Warner that it didn't make sense to run over them when you can run around them. But Warner prevailed, got Thorpe to hit the middle, and he scored three touchdowns in the second half.

The Carlisle record now stood at 5–0–1 with Pittsburgh next on the schedule, October 18 at Forbes Field. Prior to the game, Panthers coach Colonel Joe Thompson stated that Pitt had figured Jim Thorpe out and vowed that he would not run through his team again. However, Thorpe scored two touchdowns and kicked one field goal and six conversions, as Carlisle defeated Pittsburgh, 45–8. Thorpe's first touchdown was a 45-yard run in the first quarter, followed by a kick through the uprights. The Indians showed Pitt their offensive depth as both Gus Welch (two touchdowns) and Alex Arcasa (two touchdowns) made sweeping end runs throughout the game with one side of the Carlisle line in front of them providing interference.

Sitting in a box at Forbes Field watching the Carlisle vs. Pitt game was the Pittsburgh Pirates' great shortstop, Honus Wagner. A reporter asked Wagner if he thought that Jim Thorpe might sign with the Pirates for next season. Wagner simply replied, "Dunno." While Wagner was in awe at Thorpe's ability on the gridiron, all he really wanted to talk about was fishing and hunting. "Do you know it is real excitement to break a sweat on a cold day pulling in a fish," said Wagner. "Say no wonder the King of Sweden sent for Thorpe. Look at him now. He could have taken that kick on the fly, but he let it take a hop so that he could figure out his play and his interference...."[1]

On October 26, in Washington, D.C., Carlisle scored all of its points in the first half in defeating Georgetown, 34–20. The Indians' record now stood at 7–0–1. Two days later, on October 28, Carlisle traveled north of the border to play Toronto University. The first half of the game was played under American rules and the second half under Canadian rules. Under the American rules the score was Carlisle 45, Toronto 0. The game ended Carlisle 49, Toronto 1.

At South Bethlehem, Pennsylvania, on November 2, Carlisle defeated Lehigh, 34–14. Lehigh had won six games with its famous forward pass. However, on this day, Jim Thorpe was there to intercept one of Lehigh's All-American quarterback Pat Pazetti's passes about five yards deep in the end zone directly over the line of scrimmage. Instead of touching the ball down for a touchback and bringing the ball out to the 20 yard line, Thorpe, surrounded by players, started weaving around, avoiding opposing players, and by the time he had reached the 10 yard line, he was in the clear and on his way to a 105-yard touchdown with Pazetti, Lehigh's fastest man, in pursuit. Thorpe had made 23 points in the game and the Indians' season record now stood at 9–0–1.

Next up for Carlisle was Army at West Point. During the nearly 100 years since the Carlisle vs. Army game was played on November 9, 1912, there has been much ballyhoo created over the event. The 1912 Army Cadets were a good football team that played a tenacious defense. However, Army was hardly a powerhouse, the stuff of legends that time, myth and some authors have made the team out to be after the fact. The 1912 Cadets were not ranked in the top 10 and had only one Third Team All-American on their squad, tackle Leland Devore.

Going into the Carlisle game on November 9, the Cadets had a record of 3–1, having beaten Stevens, 27–0, beaten Rutgers, 19–0, lost to Yale, 6–0 in a game in which they held the opposition to four first downs, and beat Colgate, 18–7. The Cadets would finish their 1912 campaign with a 5–3 record, losing to Carlisle, 27–6, defeating Tufts, 15–6, and Syracuse, 23–7, and ending the season with a loss to Navy, 6–0.

Part of the reason that the 1912 Carlisle vs. Army game has become so mythicized is the everlasting fame of some of those who were part of the game. On the Carlisle side, there was Jim Thorpe, greatest athlete in the world, and Pop Warner, a gridiron legend in the making. On the Army side, there was right half back Dwight D. Eisenhower, future supreme commander of Allied troops in Europe in World War Two and future 34th president of the United States. Also on the Army squad was Omar Bradley a future five-star general, World War Two hero and chairman of the Joint Chiefs of Staff. Bradley was better known during his days at West Point for playing baseball, in which he lettered three times.

Carlisle had played Army in football once before, in the 1905 season. The 1912 game required authorization by the War Department as there were some concerns about having the two squads oppose each other. Nonetheless, Carlisle had played Navy in 1902 without incident.

Some authors have peddled the idea that the 1912 Army game was a civilized payback opportunity for the Indians against the U.S. Army for the massacre at Wounded Knee in 1890. To reinforce their point, most of those authors usually quote Pop Warner, according to sports writer Bill Stern, delivering a metaphorical pre-game address to his team in the locker room. This story has Warner telling his squad in his pep talk that it had been their fathers who had fought the Cadets' fathers. That his players were Indians and the Cadets soldiers, the soldiers were the long knives, etc., etc., etc. But the reality is that the long knives reference or any other part of Warner's alleged talk has never been substantiated. In fact, it was never substantiated by Pop Warner, much less Jim Thorpe.

Jim Thorpe said, "as we came up to the Army game at West Point we were confident that we were a high rolling team and would give the Cadets a very bad afternoon indeed. And we did."[2] Thorpe never made any reference to the Cadets being characterized by Warner as "long knives."

There have also been insinuations that Army's Dwight Eisenhower was personally out to get Jim Thorpe in the game. Author Lars Anderson in *Carlisle vs. Army* was even so bold to suggest that for Eisenhower the Carlisle game was his chance to create his legacy at West Point. If Ike could stop Thorpe or even knock him out of the game, then Army was ensured of victory.

The game plan for Army was simple — stop Jim Thorpe, the key to the explosive Carlisle offense, and win the game. However, Dwight Eisenhower did not have any personal agenda or ridiculous concerns about building a legacy on disabling Jim Thorpe in the game. The fact was that Eisenhower, just like his teammates, was simply concerned with the normal task of taking care of business in the game and winning.

The game was played late in the afternoon, amidst dark gray November skies at West Point with only 3,000 in attendance. When it was over Carlisle had crushed Army, 27–6, using Pop Warner's new double-wing formation, which frustrated Army. Jim Thorpe played wingback and rooted out Army's captain and All-American right tackle Leland Devore, who got so mad he was ejected from the game for slugging Carlisle left tackle Joe Guyon. At one point, Thorpe threw six straight passes to Arcasa, resulting in a Carlisle touchdown.

Early in the second half, Thorpe re-injured his left shoulder that had been aggravated in earlier games, after being stopped by Dwight Eisenhower and a teammate with a high-low double tackle after a ten-yard gain. As Thorpe lay on the field, Pop Warner rushed out to make sure he had not fractured his collarbone. The referees instructed Warner to take Thorpe off the field as his injury was delaying the game. However, Army captain Devore told the referees to give them all the time they needed. About a minute later, after first-aid was administered, Thorpe leaped to his feet and walked back to his position behind the line to a thunderous cheer from the partisan West Point crowd.

While Thorpe scored only one touchdown despite running for 215 yards, his one touchdown came after he took a kickoff at the 10 yard line and ran the length of the field. However, the touchdown was called back as Carlisle had been off-side. When Army kicked off again, Thorpe took the ball on the 5 yard line and again ran the distance of the field for a touchdown. After the game Thorpe said, "I guess that was the longest run for a touchdown I ever made. Ninety and 95 make 185 yards."[3] Thorpe scored 22 of Carlisle's 27 points vs. Army. The New York Times reported, "Thorpe went through the West Point line as if it were an open door; his defensive play was on par with his attack and his every move was that of a past master."[4]

As for Dwight Eisenhower, he injured his knee when he collided with one of his teammates attempting another high-low double tackle of Thorpe. While Eisenhower was taken out of the game, he later stated that he was not

Opposite: Part of the 1912 Army (West Point) football team. Cadet Dwight D. Eisenhower is second from left. Cadet Omar N. Bradley is second from right.

hurt badly and asked to be sent back in. But the rules of the day prevented a player who was taken out of the game from returning to the game in the same quarter. So Eisenhower remained on the sideline. By the time he was eligible to re-enter the game, Carlisle had put the game out of Army's reach and Eisenhower was instructed by the Army coach Captain Ernest Graves to go to the showers. Jim Thorpe had respect for Dwight Eisenhower as a football player and remarked that Eisenhower was a pretty good player, not great. But he had plenty of guts and determination.

Next up on the schedule for the 10–0–1 Carlisle Indians was Pennsylvania on November 16. The week before, Pennsylvania, with a record of 5–4, had upset Michigan, 27–21, after having lost four straight games to Swarthmore, 6–3, Brown, 30–7, Lafayette, 7–3 and Penn State, 14–0. With Carlisle coming off an impressive win at West Point, 30,000 spectators, including a large contingent of the Carlisle student body, were in the stands at Franklin Field in Philadelphia for the game.

Carlisle played its worst game of the season and Pennsylvania, led by its All-American fullback F. LeRoy Mercer, handed the Indians their only loss of the 1912 season, 34–26. The loss was a sort of déjà vu for Carlisle. It had been almost at the same point in the 1911 season that they had pulled off a great victory over Harvard and were being heralded as the greatest football team in the country; then the following week they were defeated by a struggling Syracuse squad.

Pennsylvania led at the half, 20–13. While Carlisle would take the lead in the third quarter and score four touchdowns in the game, the backfield played a game filled with mistakes, fumbles and missed opportunities to complete forward passes over the goal line. Jim Thorpe was expected to carry the load for Carlisle because his fellow running backs were not going to play. Fullback Powell was not suited up for infringements of team rules and right halfback Arcasa was out of the game due to an injury.

While Jim Thorpe scored a touchdown on a 75-yard run, carelessness on his part played a part in the loss. In fact, the winning touchdown for Pennsylvania came on a long pass from quarterback John Minds to right end Lon Jourdet. Thorpe was playing safety for Carlisle and just stood there as Jourdet grabbed the pass. When questioned on the play by Warner after the game, Thorpe replied that he saw the ball and saw Jourdet. But he never thought he'd get under it.

After Minds kicked the goal after the touchdown, Mercer kicked off, sending the ball over the Carlisle goal line. Carlisle ran the ball out to the 25 yard line where it was fumbled. Pennsylvania quickly scored again as Mercer ran around right end for a touchdown, Minds kicked another goal, and the fate of Carlisle was sealed.

On November 23, Carlisle rebounded with 30–24 victory over the Springfield Y.M.C.A. in Springfield, Massachusetts, in a hard-fought game that saw Indians quarterback Gus Welch tackled hard and taken out of the game in the third quarter. Jim Thorpe scored all of Carlisle's points.

One of the stars of the game for the losing Springfield team was Les Mann, who beginning in 1913 would play major league baseball for 16 years in the National League for Boston, Chicago, St. Louis, Cincinnati and New York, and in the Federal League for Chicago, finishing with .282 lifetime batting average. In the Carlisle game Mann scored two touchdowns.

The game almost didn't come off because Carlisle wanted a $2,000 guarantee plus a percentage of the gate. But the Springfield team wanted to play the Indians, and team captain Dan Kelly talked the athletic board into approving the game. Following the game, the Indians got $2,700, picking-up the extra $700 on the percentage agreement. So they decided not to take the train back to Carlisle, with their final game of the season with Brown only five days away on Thanksgiving. Instead the Indians went to Leicester, only a short distance from Springfield, and practiced on an adjacent field Monday, Tuesday and Wednesday. Then on Thursday morning the Indians took the Worcester to Providence train for the Brown game.

However, the Springfield game would deal Jim Thorpe a strange turn of fate. According to Dan Kelly, it was following this game that Jim Thorpe's professional status first surfaced. Standing on the sideline during one of the Carlisle practices at Leicester was a spectator from Southbridge, Charles Clancy, manager of the Winston-Salem baseball club of the Eastern Carolina League, along with a reporter from the *Worcester Telegram*. When Thorpe ran toward the sideline, skirting an end, Clancy remarked to the reporter that he knew that guy Thorpe. He had pitched for him a couple of years ago. The story didn't get an immediate admission from Thorpe because the reporter got one of the facts wrong. However, for Thorpe, the cat was out of the bag and it was the beginning of the end for his amateur athletic status. Actually Thorpe had pitched for Rocky Mount in 1909 when Clancy, then manager of Fayetteville, saw him. When the story broke, Pop Warner asked Thorpe if he had pitched for Winston-Salem. He replied that he hadn't. It was 1910 when Clancy was managing Fayetteville and traded pitcher Bert Boyle to Rocky Mount for Thorpe.

Joe Libby, a teammate of Thorpe's at Carlisle, was stunned to learn that Pop Warner had asked Thorpe if he had played at Winston-Salem. According to Libby, it was Warner who suggested that Thorpe, Jesse Youngdeer and he play ball in Rocky Mount.

Nonetheless, Thorpe's version of the Clancy recognition story was very different from Dan Kelly's. According to Thorpe, after he was traded in 1910 from Rocky Mount to Fayetteville, where Clancy was the manager, a group of the players went out hunting one day following a game and a photographer took a picture of them. Thorpe said that he was sitting on a mule in the picture. That fall Clancy took a print of the picture home and hung it in his ranch house. Late in 1912, the reporter from the *Worcester Telegram* was visiting Clancy's home and saw the picture. Thorpe said that the reporter immediately connected his likeness in the picture with the Jim Thorpe who had won all the medals in the Olympic Games that past summer. That chance circumstance became the basis for the reporter's scoop that in a few months would resound around the world.

On Thanksgiving Day, November 28, 1912, Jim Thorpe played his last football game for Carlisle. Brown had just beaten Pennsylvania and was very confident that they could give the Indians a very tough game. With 8,000 spectators on hand at Andrews Field in Providence, under a driving snow storm, the Indians overwhelmed Brown, 32–0. Jim Thorpe was unstoppable, had two 50-yard runs and scored three touchdowns in the game.

It had been another remarkable season for the Carlisle Indians as they finished with a record of 12–1–1, outscoring their opponents, 505–120.

1912 CARLISLE FOOTBALL SCORES

09/21	Carlisle	50	Albright	7
09/25	Carlisle	45	Lebanon Valley	0
09/28	Carlisle	35	Dickinson	0
10/02	Carlisle	65	Villanova	0
10/05	Carlisle	0	Washington & Jefferson	0
10/12	Carlisle	33	Syracuse	0
10/19	Carlisle	45	Pittsburgh	8
10/26	Carlisle	34	Georgetown	20
10/28	Carlisle	49	Toronto All-Stars	7
11/02	Carlisle	34	Lehigh	14
11/09	Carlisle	27	Army	6
11/16	Carlisle	26	Pennsylvania	34
11/23	Carlisle	30	Springfield Y.M.C.A.	24
11/28	Carlisle	32	Brown	0

It had been another great season for Jim Thorpe in which he made 25 touchdowns and scored 198 points. The 1912 Carlisle football roster listed his weight as 178 pounds. While Jim Thorpe was a member of the Carlisle football team (1907, 1908, 1911, 1912) its won-lost record was 43–5–2.

In recognition of Thorpe's achievements, Walter Camp named him as a First Team All-American for 1912. Joining Thorpe in the backfield were G. M. Crowther of Brown, Charlie Brickley of Harvard, and F. LeRoy Mercer of Pennsylvania. Thorpe called Harvard fullback Eddie Mahan the greatest all-around backfield man he had ever seen. Mahan was named by Camp to First Team All-American status in 1913, 1914 and 1915.

Prior to the Brown game, speaking from the Leicester Inn about four miles from Worcester, Massachusetts, where the Carlisle team was staying, Jim Thorpe told the press that following the game, he would leave Carlisle and drop out of the sporting world. Thorpe was concerned that his notoriety since the Olympic Games was beginning to be burdensome. Suddenly, with his chance encounter with Charles Clancy, Thorpe was becoming aware of what a small world it was and he was beginning to have concerns that there was a ticking time bomb in his future beyond Carlisle, just waiting to explode.

In late December 1912, Jim Thorpe left Carlisle and returned to central Oklahoma. He arrived in Prague early in the morning while it was still dark. Soon he began to mingle with his tribesmen, hunting wild turkeys, deer and quail through the hills of the Sac and Fox and Creek Indian countries. Despite his international fame, the local townspeople still called him Jimmie. While everyone was glad to have their famous native son home, speculation on his future was on everyone's lips.

8

Thorpe Loses His Olympic Medals

By early January 1913, the question of Jim Thorpe's amateur status was fast becoming a major media event. According to sports columnist Edward Moss, the first article to be published on his professional baseball experience appeared in the *Charlotte Observer* on July 18, 1912, while Thorpe was still in Sweden. The article stated in part, "Jim Thorpe, who in the Olympic games in Stockholm proved himself the greatest all-round athlete in the world, was once traded for Pete Boyle, now a member of the Winston-Salem team in the Carolina League. Thorpe was playing for Jim Connor, an old friend of Clancy's at Rocky Mount, and was not doing much on the slab, but was keeping his stick work, which is a way he has, when a four cornered deal, which startled the tight little circuit, was announced. Clancy had traded Pearltree, a light-hitting outfielder, for Schumann, a veteran, who had led the league in batting the year before, while Connor was to give him Thorpe for Boyle. The big silent Indian proved the very man Clancy needed."[1]

The A.A.U. had a very broad organization in 1912, including sectional offices in the south and southwest, as well as the huge A.A.U. middle–Atlantic office in Philadelphia. Nation-wide there were about 200 men on the A.A.U. payroll. Nonetheless A.A.U. officials were totally oblivious to the article referencing Thorpe's professional baseball experience published in the *Charlotte Observer* in July 1912, while the Olympic Games were being concluded. Furthermore the Southern Association, headquartered in New Orleans, with regional offices in Atlanta and Birmingham, and the South Atlantic Association, with headquarters in Baltimore, made no attempts to alert the A.A.U. or the Olympic Committee to Thorpe's professional status.

But then all hell broke loose when on January 17, 1913, a former pitcher on the Fayetteville team of the Eastern Carolina League, turned sportswriter for a Worcester, Massachusetts, newspaper, who has eternally remained anonymous, broke the story on Jim Thorpe playing professional baseball in 1909-1910. The editor of the *Worcester Gazette* decided to withhold the story of Thorpe playing professional baseball for eight days for further fact-checking. The editor sent a 20-year-old reporter to Winston-Salem, North Carolina, to check on a rumor that Thorpe had played for the Rocky Mount team of the Eastern Carolina League.

What the reporter found out was devastating to Jim Thorpe. It was revealed that he was traded by Rocky Mount to Fayetteville in 1910. A group photo of the team out hunting one afternoon following a game had been taken and then hung by the manager Charles Clancy in his ranch house. Jim Thorpe was in the picture. It was Charles Clancy who moved Thorpe to first base, not being impressed with him as a pitcher when he came over to Fayetteville from Rocky Mount in 1910.

No request for a retraction of the story was requested by anyone. At the moment Jim Thorpe, Pop Warner, and even Charles Clancy were all denying the accusations in the Worcester paper. However on January 26, 1913, the *New York Tribune* reported its study of the Eastern Carolina League records disclosed that Jim Thorpe played professional baseball in 1909-1910. All at once, ballplayers were coming forward to confirm Thorpe's participation in the Eastern Carolina League. One of the first was B. C. Stewart, who was still playing in the Eastern Carolina League. Furthermore it was even revealed that during Thorpe's Eastern Carolina League experience, he had played against some current major league players, including Steve Yerkes, Boston Red Sox second baseman, and Bunny Hearn, St. Louis Cardinals pitcher. However, these players chose to remain silent on the matter.

The rumor mill had suddenly become prodigious. One rumor circulating was that the previous fall while the Carlisle Indians were in Pittsburgh for their football game with Pitt, Thorpe had signed a contract to play ball with the Pirates calling for $7,000 a year. If the Pittsburgh rumor proved to be false, major league baseball owners and managers were sure that Jim Thorpe would soon be seeking a contract and they were beginning to line up to sign him, even before his amateur status had been decided.

Nixey Callahan, manager of the Chicago White Sox, told the *Chicago Tribune* that if it could be arranged, he would like to give Thorpe a tryout. "I never saw Thorpe," said Callahan, "but judging from the great feats he accomplished as a college athlete, I think he ought to be a great baseball man. A fellow with his speed and strength should make a great base runner and batter."[2]

When Charles McDonald, former sporting editor of a Raleigh paper, and Sherwood Upchurch, an umpire, stated in the *New York Tribune* that Thorpe played ball in North Carolina, suddenly Jim Thorpe found himself being pressured on all sides for full disclosure. To face the mounting controversy, Thorpe decided to leave Oklahoma, return to Carlisle, and seek the counsel of Pop Warner.

Almost immediately upon his arrival, Thorpe was faced with new controversy. The assistant storekeeper at the Carlisle school was charged with selling liquor to Thorpe and Gus Welch on Saturday, January 13. Thorpe brushed aside the controversy and kept focused on what he should do about confronting the growing hullabaloo over his amateur status.

Thorpe had become worried about public opinion and he had been receiving many telegrams asking if the accusations that he had played professional baseball were true. Thorpe decided to take the telegrams to Pop Warner and tell him the whole story about playing baseball in North Carolina. According to Thorpe, Warner thought the best route of disclosure for him to take was to offer a written statement, in what amounted to an admission of guilt through ignorance of the rules. Then Warner would personally deliver the statement to James E. Sullivan in New York and plead his case. The statement read as follows:

Department of the Interior, United States Indian Service,
Carlisle, Pa., Jan. 26, 1913
James E. Sullivan,
New York, N.Y.
Dear Sir:

When the interview with Mr. Clancy stating that I had played baseball on the Winston-Salem team was shown to me I told Mr. Warner that it was not true and in fact I did not play on that team. But so much has been said in the papers since then that I went to the school authorities this morning and told them just what there was in the stories.

I played baseball at Rocky Mount and at Fayetteville, N.C. in the summer of 1909 and 1910 under my own name. On the same teams I played with were several college men from the north who were earning money by ball playing during their vacations and who were regarded as amateurs at home. I did not play for the money there was in it because my property brings me in enough money to live on, but because I liked to play ball. I was not wise in the ways of the world and did not realize this was wrong, and that it would make me a professional in track sports, although I learned from the other players that it would be better for me not to let anyone know that I was playing and for that reason I never told anyone at the school about it until today.

In the fall of 1911, I applied for readmission to this school and came back to continue my studies and take part in the school sports and of course I wanted to get on the Olympic team and take the trip to Stockholm. I had Mr. Warner send in my application for registering in the A.A.U., after I had answered the questions and signed it and I received my card allowing me to compete on the winter meets and other track sports. I never realized until now what a big mistake I made by keeping it a secret about my ball playing and I am sorry I did so. I hope I would be partly excused because of the fact that I simply an Indian school boy and did not know all about such things. In fact, I did not know that I was doing wrong because I was doing what I knew several other college men had done, except that they did not use their own names.

I have always liked sports and only played or run races for the fun of the things and never to earn money. I have received offers amounting to thousands of dollars since my victories last summer, but I have turned them all down because I did not care to make money from my athletic skill. I am very sorry, Mr. Sullivan to have it all spoiled in this way and I hope the Amateur Athletic Union and the people will not be too hard in judging me.

Yours truly,
James Thorpe[3]

Meanwhile Carlisle Superintendent Moses Friedman took immediate action in an attempt to clear the school and distance himself and Pop Warner from any wrong-doing in the Thorpe matter. To that end, Friedman wrote a letter to James E. Sullivan disavowing any knowledge of Thorpe's participation in playing professional baseball. His letter stated in part, "I have just learned that Thorpe acknowledges having played with the Southern professional baseball team. It is with profound regret that this information is conveyed to you, and I hasten to assure your committee that the faculty of the school and athletic director, Glenn Warner, were without any knowledge of this fact until to-day. As this invalidates Thorpe's amateur standing at the time of the games in Stockholm, the trophies which are held here are subject to your disposition. Please inform me of your desires in the matter. It is a most unpleasant affair and has brought gloom on the entire institution."[4]

Fred Bruce was an Indian from Montana. In late 1912 and early 1913 Bruce was working at the Carlisle Indian School as a steamfitter installing the Webster vacuum system. Fred Bruce alleged that Jim Thorpe did not write the statement sent to James E. Sullivan, but rather he copied it from a letter furnished to him. According to Bruce, in late January 1913, he was in a conversation with Thorpe in his room when Pop Warner came in and he was asked to leave. When he returned to the room, he saw Thorpe copying a letter. He asked Thorpe what he was doing. Thorpe said that he was writing to Mr. Sullivan at the A.A.U. in New York City. Bruce stated that both Carlisle superintendent Moses Friedman and Pop Warner knew that Thorpe had been paid for playing baseball before he went to Stockholm for the Olympics.

For years afterward Pop Warner would continue to advance a simplistic notion of his innocence in the Thorpe matter. He said that he knew nothing about Thorpe having played semi-professional baseball when he returned to Carlisle. According to Warner in the late 1940s, when Thorpe decided to play baseball in North Carolina, he didn't plan on returning to school. Thorpe was careless and he never thought about the future, so he played under his own name.

On January 27, Pop Warner carried both Thorpe's letter and Friedman's letter to New York and presented them to James E. Sullivan during a meeting in his office. Immediately, Thorpe's statement was reviewed by the American Olympic Team Selection Committee that had chosen him as a member of the 1912 United States Olympic Team. Members of the committee were Gustavus T. Kirby, President of the A.A.U. and Vice President of the American Olympic Committee; James E. Sullivan, Chairman of the Registration Committee and Secretary of the A.A.U. and American Olympic Committee; and Bartow S. Weeks, Chairman of the Legislation Committee of the A.A.U. and Vice President of the American Olympic Committee. Later that day the following statement was issued:

> The Team Selection Committee of the American Olympic Committee selected James Thorpe as one of the members of the American Olympic team, and did so without the least suspicion as to there having been any act of professionalism on Thorpe's part.
>
> For the last several years Thorpe has been a member of the Carlisle Indian School, which is conducted by the Government of the United States at Carlisle, Penn., through the Indian Department of the Department of the Interior. Glenn Warner, formerly of Cornell, is a man whose reputation is of the highest and whose accuracy of statement has never been doubted, has been in charge of the athletic activities of the institution. During the period of Mr. Thorpe's membership at Carlisle he competed on its football, baseball, and track and field teams, and represented it in intercollegiate and other contests, all of which were open only to amateurs, as neither Carlisle nor any of the institutions with which it competed has other than amateur teams. Thorpe's standing as an amateur had never been questioned, nor was any protest ever made against him nor any statement ever made as to his even having practiced with professionals, let alone having played with or as one of them.
>
> The widest possible publicity was given to the team selected by the American Olympic Committee, and it seems strange that men having knowledge of Thorpe's professional conduct did not at such time for the honor of their country come forward and place in the hands of the American committee such information as they had. No such information was given, nor was a suggestion even made as to Thorpe being other than the amateur, which he was supposed to be. This country is of such tremendous, territorial expanse and the athletes taking part therein are so numerous that it is sometimes extremely difficult to ascertain the history of an athlete's past. In the selection of the American team the committee endeavored to use every possible precaution, and where there was the slightest doubt as to a man's amateur standing his entry was not considered.
>
> Thorpe's act of professionalism was in a sport over which the Amateur Athletic Union has no direct control. It was a member of a baseball team in a minor league and in games which were not reported in the important papers of the country. That he played under his own name would give no direct notice to anyone concerned, as there are many of his name. The reason why he himself did not give notice of his acts is explained by him on the ground of ignorance. In some justification of his position, it would be noted that Mr.

Thorpe is an Indian of limited experience and education in the ways of other than his own people.

The American Olympic Committee and the Amateur Athletic Union feel that, while Mr. Thorpe is deserving of the severest condemnation for concealing the fact that he had professionalized himself by receiving money for playing baseball, they also feel that those who knew of his professional acts are deserving of still greater censure for their silence.

The American Olympic Committee and the Amateur Athletic Union tender to the Swedish Olympic Committee and through the International Olympic Committee to the nations of the world their apology for having entered Mr. Thorpe and having permitted him to compete at the Olympic Games of 1912.

The Amateur Athletic Union regrets that it permitted Mr. Thorpe to compete in amateur contests during the last several years, and will do everything in its power to secure the return of prizes and readjustment of points won by him, and will immediately eliminate his records from the books.[5]

The decision of the A.A.U. had racist connotations, indicating that Thorpe was an Indian of limited experience and education and ignorant in the ways other than those of his people. This has been largely ignored by most writers on the subject. Nonetheless, the fact was that at the time Jim Thorpe was winning Olympic medals, in the United States track and field techniques and events were just barely starting to emerge from the domain of blue-blooded athletic clubs. Compared to the disciplinary standards of today, it is hard to accept the trite justification offered by the A.A.U. for Thorpe's actions.

The following day the headline in the *New York Times* read, "OLYMPIC PRIZES LOST; THORPE NO AMATEUR." Realizing that he had lost his Olympic medals, Thorpe said he had nothing to say. His case was unparalleled. By today's standards the A.A.U. banning of Thorpe seems ludicrous. In today's Olympic Games, professionals from many sports such as basketball, hockey, etc. compete legally as part of the United States team. Jim Thorpe was banned for playing professionally in a sport that the A.A.U. was well aware employed many other college athletes. However, those players became anonymous because they chose to play under false names.

George A. Huff had been the manager of the Boston Red Sox for eight games in 1907. By 1913 Huff was serving as the athletic director at the University of Illinois and during the summer months was a scout for the Cleveland Naps. He was also one of the leading advocates for permitting college baseball players to play for money during the summer. According to Huff, "Amateur rules don't make amateur athletes; they make amateur liars."[6]

It was also well known that while Thorpe was playing football and participating in track for Carlisle, he and other players had received several cash payments from Pop Warner. Furthermore, on any given day Thorpe could stop in a downtown clothing store run by Mose Blumenthal, a Carlisle Indians booster, and be outfitted in new clothes for free. Mose was also known to supply Thorpe with whiskey and money. In today's world of intercollegiate athletics, such under-the-table generosity by boosters is common. In fact most universities have some sort of off-campus slush fund for needy athletes. It's only when a more serious offense against a student-athlete is brought to the fore that booster gratuities, after the fact, come into play in any disciplinary action.

In 1956 the Ohio State University football program was put on probation for one year by Kenneth L. Wilson, commissioner of the Western Conference, and made ineligible for participation in the Rose Bowl because its legendary coach, Woody Hayes, had made personal loans to his players. Furthermore, all of the players who had been the beneficiaries of Hayes' generosity were subject to review for eligibility by the commissioner. The loans that Hayes had made to his players amounted to about $400 total. Hayes, throughout his career, had maintained that college athletes were being cheated by the schools where they played. The same year that Ohio State was feeling the wrath of Western Conference justice, many other schools such as Texas A&M, Alabama, Auburn and Washington were already on probation or being investigated for recruiting violations involving money, or for over-eager boosters making cash payments to players. One former UCLA player had testified that he and his teammates had drawn illegal salaries.

According to Woody Hayes, during the four years that a student-athlete participated in football or basketball, the university made millions of dollars off his name, but in return, the student athlete made nothing. In fact, most did not even earn a college degree. What was true about the hypocrisy in college athletics with Jim Thorpe in 1912 and Woody Hayes in 1956 still exists in the twenty-first century on nearly every college campus in America. One way or another, student-athletes are subsidized to play sports and often cheated out of an education.

With Thorpe disqualified by the Amateur Athletic Union for playing professional baseball in 1909-1910, Hugo (H.K.) Wieslander of Sweden, runner-up, was declared the decathlon winner and F. R. Bie of Norway was declared the pentathlon winner. It has been stated over the years that when Hugo Wieslander received Thorpe's medals, he returned them with a note supposedly stating, "These medals belong to Jim Thorpe, the greatest athlete in the world. I don't know how they do things in America, but I can't accept the medals." At least until now, this note alleged to be penned by Wieslander has not been found and continues to be an Olympic myth.

Believing that he had done no wrong, reluctantly Jim Thorpe packed up his gifts from heads of state, including the silver chalice in the shape of a Viking ship, lined with gold and encrusted with jewels, sent to him by Czar Nicholas II of Russia, and sent them back to the Olympic Committee. While these were personal gifts with a high monetary value of $50,000 and not official Olympic prizes, Thorpe nonetheless returned them. For many years the gifts that Thorpe returned were on display at the International Olympic Committee Museum in Lausanne, Switzerland. Then they would fall into obscurity and be forgotten, until rediscovered in 1972 after an exhaustive three-year search conducted by E. Donald Sterner, who had played tackle with Thorpe on the early professional football team, the Canton Bulldogs, in 1917.

In regard to Jim Thorpe's circumstance, *The Sporting News* wrote, "The 'crime' for which Thorpe has been compelled to surrender the trophies he won at the Olympic games was one of which practically every 'amateur' of note in this country has been guilty. The difference was that Thorpe didn't need the money, while some of the others did, and that the Indian was too simple to play under an assumed name, so used his own. It is refreshing to find such un-sophistication in a country which sophisticates even its children at the earliest possible age."[7]

9

Thorpe Signs with the
New York Giants

Banned from amateur athletics, Jim Thorpe was now ready to officially become a professional athlete. In 1913 semi-professional football was a small regional game played primarily in upper New York state, western Pennsylvania and northeastern Ohio. The players who played in these hard-hitting, sometimes dangerous contests, did so for the love of the game and were paid a pittance.

So baseball was where the money was and Jim Thorpe was ready to sign a big league baseball contract. Later Thorpe remarked, "Football is fine, but all you get out of it is press clippings. In track you get press notices, too, but they won't pay your bills. Baseball lasts longer and pays better."[1] On January 28, 1913, Thorpe sent a telegram to August "Garry" Herrmann, Chairman of the National Commission and President of the Cincinnati Reds, stating he would consider a proposition and sign with the club making the best offer.

By the early teens professional baseball was booming. However, there was suddenly a challenge to the established American and National Leagues by a group of entrepreneurs who wanted a piece of the action and were about to launch major competition with a third league, the Federal League. So major league baseball was eagerly awaiting the arrival of Jim Thorpe in a big league uniform as a drawing card. Several clubs were ready to tender an offer to him, although there were rumors circulating that Thorpe had already been signed to a contract the previous summer by the Pittsburgh Pirates. Another rumor held that Thorpe had a reserve contract with the Beaumont club of the Texas League.

Garry Herrmann wanted the National Commission to take action as a body on Thorpe. However, Ban Johnson, president of the American League and member of the National Commission, disagreed. Ban Johnson was in sympathy with Thorpe. He was advocating his free agency as a chance for him to regain the prestige, both monetarily and personally, he had suffered by the decision of the A.A.U. Johnson said, "If I had one, I have had a dozen requests by managers in the American League to withhold the promulgation of contracts signed by men who did not want the fact they had signed such contracts to be known until they were through with college."[2]

With rumors abounding that he was either the property of the Pittsburgh Pirates or Beaumont, the Jim Thorpe contract signing frenzy began. By January 29, there were five scouts in Carlisle despite the fact that Thorpe was sick in bed. Among the clubs attempting to sign Thorpe were the Chicago White Sox, St. Louis Browns, Chicago Cubs, Cincinnati Reds and Pittsburgh Pirates.

The Pirates sent scout Bill Murray to Carlisle to offer Thorpe a contract to play first base. While Thorpe was in Pittsburgh for the Carlisle vs. Pitt football game in 1911, he was introduced to Barney Dreyfuss, but denied that any contract talk took place. According to Dreyfuss, he was contacted by H. P. Kennedy, an attorney from Uniontown, Pennsylvania, and personal friend of Thorpe's, who stated that he was interested in playing for the Pirates. Then when Thorpe met Dreyfuss he told him that he would not sign any major league contract without first giving the Pirates a chance to sign him. However, Dreyfuss stated that at the time he would have only offered Thorpe a probationary contract calling for $300 a month. But attorney Kennedy got the amount raised to $400.

One of the first clubs to jump on the Thorpe bandwagon and attempt to sign him was the Cincinnati Reds. At the insistence of Reds manager Joe Tinker, Garry Herrmann dispatched business manager Frank Bancroft to Carlisle to sign Thorpe for $4,500. For the past few weeks in late January, Herrmann had been communicating with P.T. Powers, former president of the Eastern League, in his New York office asking him for assistance in signing Thorpe. Surprisingly, Powers suggested to Herrmann that the best person in New York to assist him in signing Thorpe was none other than James E. Sullivan, one of the A.A.U. officials who had just stripped him of his Olympic medals. Powers told Herrmann, "Had I known you wanted him I could have had him signed up before the others got to him. According to the papers here today, McGraw only called him on the phone yesterday."[3]

While other clubs were sending representatives to Carlisle, John McGraw, manager of the Giants, remained in New York. On Thursday, January 30, McGraw made a long-distance telephone call to Thorpe informing him of his interest in signing him. It was the call that Jim Thorpe had been waiting for. The New York Giants, led by pitcher Christy Mathewson, were one of the premier franchises in major league baseball. The Giants had won the 1912 National League pennant race over the Pittsburgh Pirates by 10 games. However, they lost the 1912 World Series to the Boston Red Sox.

At the time, John McGraw did not even know if Jim Thorpe batted right-handed or left-handed, and he always had doubts about the ability of college athletes. McGraw asked Thorpe what the other clubs were offering him. Thorpe stated in the range of $4,000 to $4,500 a year. McGraw quickly responded that he would give him $5,000 a year for three years. Thorpe covered the phone with his hand and asked Pop Warner, who was with him, what he should do. Warner said to tell McGraw he wanted to think it over and would call him back on Friday.

Bill Murray said that the Pirates would match McGraw's offer. Furthermore Thorpe was reminded that he had promised Barney Dreyfuss that he would sign with the Pirates. So Thorpe called Dreyfuss and told him that he was prepared to keep his word, even though he really wanted to play for the Giants and overall their three-year contract was a better offer.

However, Dreyfuss told Thorpe he was released from his promise. Dreyfuss really liked Thorpe and he told the press, "I want to say for Thorpe that he kept his word with me, and acted the part of a gentleman throughout. When he found that Cincinnati and New York were both willing to pay him a large salary, he called me up and told me of it. He said he would sign with me, however, if I wished to hold him to his tentative promise of 18 months previous. I did not want Thorpe to lose anything that he had a chance to gain, so I released him from his promise, and told him to sign where he wished, but that I could not better my offer, as I was not signing him because of the publicity."[4]

The next day Thorpe called McGraw back and told him he was ready to sign with the Giants. Thus Jim Thorpe became the highest paid untried major league baseball player in the history of the game. Furthermore, Thorpe had not even played minor league ball since 1910.

There was a rumor circulating that before Frank Bancroft of the Reds had arrived in Carlisle, a relative of John McGraw's had approached Pop Warner on behalf of the Giants about signing Thorpe. Now the story being circulated was that with the deal about to be done, Warner had been acting as Thorpe's agent and would receive $2,500 for helping to influence Thorpe to sign with the Giants.

On Saturday, February 1, dressed in a natty, navy blue Norfolk suit and slouch hat, probably supplied by Mose Blumenthal, Jim Thorpe arrived in New York with Pop Warner to sign his contract with the Giants. His appearance in New York caused a major media event as he arrived at 2:00 P.M. at the Giants offices at the Fifth Avenue Building among throngs of newsmen, photographers and fans eager to get their first glimpse of Thorpe.

Most of the sportswriters in the room believed that the Giants' signing of Thorpe was just a publicity gimmick. *The Sporting News* stated that Thorpe had little chance to fit into major league baseball based upon his two years of low-level minor league experience and less than sensational performance, and now suddenly jumping to a team that was expected to compete for the pennant.

It was the first time that John McGraw had ever seen Thorpe. McGraw told the assembled media, "I am not going to count anything on Thorpe's record in that little Carolina league. The Indian was only a youngster then and practically all his athletic development has come since those days. Thorpe surely must have had some natural ability as a ball player, judging from what he did with his team down there. He won eleven out of twenty-one games in which he pitched, and that was with a tail ender, which was so bad that it won only a total of twenty-eight games. That record speaks for itself."[5] However at the time, McGraw was not sure what position Thorpe would play. He said he would see what he could do in spring training.

If John McGraw's real intention in signing Thorpe was a publicity gimmick, then he would have made him a pitcher. With Thorpe on the mound and Chief Meyers behind the plate, the Giants would have had an enormous gate attraction in having the only all–Indian battery in professional baseball. But McGraw was well aware of Thorpe's speed, and he perpetually seemed to need outfielders. McGraw just couldn't sign outfielders quickly enough.

After Thorpe signed his three-year contract, McGraw had a private conference with Pop Warner. McGraw wanted to know about Thorpe's personality and capabilities. Warner told McGraw that one thing he could count on was that Thorpe had never failed to make good at anything to which he set his mind on. Warner told McGraw that Thorpe was dogged and persevering and a good listener. Furthermore, Warner told McGraw that he felt that Thorpe might be developed into a real good hitter. He never backed away from the plate and never showed any fear of an opposing pitcher. To summarize, Warner advised McGraw that Thorpe's primary qualities were his speed, arm, eyes, judgment and gameness.

Meanwhile, Thorpe had been talking with reporters, smiling all the while at Giants secretary John B. Foster. Thorpe sat for two hours while photographers snapped his picture and conversed with him. A reporter reminded Thorpe that as he was signing his contract with the Giants, his medals were en route to Europe on the liner *New York*. Thorpe replied that he didn't want to talk about it anymore and the sooner the matter was dropped the better. He had just signed a major league contract and was attempting to focus on spring training. When a reporter asked Thorpe what his Indian name was, he replied, Drags-His-Root.

Having heard rumors about some of Thorpe's classic drinking bouts, some of the reporters had devised a plot to get him drunk because they believed it would be a good story. However, that evening Jim Thorpe returned with Pop Warner, to Carlisle where he intended to remain under his watchful eye until leaving for spring training in Marlin, Texas, on February 18.

While Jim Thorpe had just signed a major league contract, the matter of his free agency had not been completely established. The same day that Thorpe signed his contract with the New York Giants, the Beaumont, Texas, ball club claimed that it had a reserve clause contract on Thorpe because it had purchased the Oklahoma City franchise which had a reserve clause claim on him. To add credibility to the Beaumont assertion an article published in the *Beaumont Journal* dated February 26, 1912, stated that contracts from the Oklahoma players that went with the franchise had been received and players were instructed to report as soon as possible. One of those players named in the article was James T. Thorpe. However, the Thorpe who had played in Oklahoma didn't show up at spring training in 1912.

The Beaumont club was not interested in keeping Thorpe if it indeed did have a claim to him. They felt that the matter was open to compensation. Ed Stedman, president of the club, just wanted to get as much money as he could for Thorpe's contract. On February 5, Stedman sent a letter to Garry Herrmann, telling him that he wanted $6,000 for Thorpe. Stedman told Herrmann that he didn't really know what Thorpe's worth was, but he knew that he would be a big drawing card in the big leagues. So he wanted to get the best possible price.

But with the concern that the Thorpe who had signed to play with Oklahoma City might not have been James F. Thorpe, but rather a player by the name of James T. Thorp, to establish a contractual relationship with Beaumont, the club would have to prove that the Thorpe signed in Oklahoma was the Jim Thorpe who had just signed with the New York Giants.

Suddenly a whole lot of baseball men had opinions on Jim Thorpe's free agency status. John H. Farrell, secretary of the National Association of Professional Baseball Leagues, stated that Thorpe was not bound by the reserve clause in the contract under which he played with the Fayetteville, North Carolina, team. National League president Thomas J. Lynch was telling everyone, including John McGraw, that Thorpe was a free agent based on every precedent in organized baseball. American League president Ban Johnson was saying Thorpe was still property of the Fayetteville club. But when the Eastern Carolina League folded after the 1910 season it automatically made all the players under contracts free agents.

In the end the entire Beaumont claim to Jim Thorpe amounted to little more than a cash-grab by Ed Stedman, president of the Beaumont club, and its manager, Edward Wheeler. Beaumont never received any payment for Jim Thorpe and the matter soon became moot. In fact the National Commission led by Garry Herrmann never did officially declare Thorpe a free agent.

On February 6, 1913, *The Beaumont Journal* published an article stating, "Abner Davis before he shipped his franchise in the Texas League to Beaumont, signed up a player named Thorpe, who lived in Oklahoma. He sent him a contract in 1912, but he did not report to Beaumont in the spring. Thorpe so far as Beaumont was concerned was a dead issue. Probably they would have forgotten about unknown and let him go by default by not sending him a contract by February 1. But they heeded the finger tap of Opportunity, and they have stirred up some small doings.

"The Thorpe they own may not be Jim Thorpe after all. The man Davis signed lived in Oklahoma. Jim Thorpe may not have been there. The great athlete may be able to put up an alibi. What if he does? Beaumont has lost nothing but the price of a few telegrams. But what if James Thorpe is the same Thorpe that signed with Oklahoma City? By all baseball law he belongs to Beaumont, unless that forgotten burg in the Carolina swamps still holds title. And they may be able to get some simoleons for him.

"Opportunity knocked but once, but Stedman and Wheeler had a mutual ear to the keyhole."[6]

After receiving an award in Boston, then stopping in Carlisle to get his uniform and clothes, Thorpe missed the Giants train connection in Harrisburg. He finally caught up with the team in St. Louis, and then at almost every stop along the way to Texas a crowd was at the station asking for Jim Thorpe. In one small Texas town, John McGraw hid Thorpe from a sheriff who boarded the train and requested to see him, fearing a warrant of some sort. It turned out that the sheriff was just one of the legions of Thorpe's admirers and wanted to shake his hand.

The Giants finally reached Marlin on February 19. John McGraw had just signed a new five-year contract as manager calling for $30,000 a year and was confident his ball club would repeat as National League champions. Christy Mathewson had come to spring training, although McGraw really didn't want him or Larry Doyle to start training until a few weeks before the team headed north. Despite the fact that Mathewson had won 23 games in 1912 and Doyle had hit .330, McGraw felt that too much work for both made them stale.

In Jim Thorpe's first at-bat against Christy Mathewson in a spring training intra-squad game he hit a home run. McGraw leaped out of the dugout and yelled, "That's the hardest ball that was ever hit!"[7] This prompted Chicago sportswriter Hugh Fullerton to remark, "It keeps one guessing to decide whether Jim Thorpe's home run off Matty is a boost for Jim or a knock for Matty."[8] However, there would not be many more gargantuan home runs for Thorpe that spring in Marlin; soon after he started having trouble hitting curve balls and striking out a lot. The problem was that he didn't have the patience at bat to wait for a good pitch and swung at everything. This weakness would dog Thorpe throughout his big league career.

Immediately, John McGraw attempted to take Jim Thorpe under his wing and counsel him on becoming a big leaguer. McGraw advised Thorpe to object to everything big league umpires said. McGraw believed that if you objected to everything an umpire said — eventually they would give you the benefit of the doubt. He also told Thorpe to sit in the dugout before a game and when opposing players began parading by to file his spikes to intimidate them. When McGraw quickly became concerned that Thorpe was keeping late hours during spring training, he advised him on the dangers of drinking and playing cards.

The New York Giants beat the Dallas, Texas, club 9–1 in their first exhibition game. Jim Thorpe was in the lineup and had three hits in five at-bats, two singles and a double. He also stole two bases. But John McGraw wasn't happy. Thorpe had appeared at the ball park just five minutes before the start of the game. McGraw sternly advised Thorpe that he should get down to the park with the rest of the club, or he could go back to Carlisle. Instead of just taking it like any of the other players would, Thorpe challenged McGraw. It was apparent almost from the first day of spring training that Thorpe and McGraw would never get along very well.

Although McGraw had signed Thorpe, as spring training progressed he really didn't have much interest in playing him. He didn't like Thorpe's training habits, didn't like him talking back to him and, most of all, didn't believe that Thorpe was seasoned enough for the major leagues.

Using him as a pitcher was out of the question. How could a low minor league pitcher with barely a .500 record expect to find a place on a big league pitching staff that included Christy Mathewson, Rube Marquard, Jeff Tesreau and Red Ames, among others? Fred Merkle, who had hit .309 the previous season, would be playing first base. In the outfield, there was Red Murray in right field and Fred Snodgrass in centerfield.

As for left field, McGraw planned to play George Burns, a young outfielder whom he had been gradually developing for the past two years. In 1912, McGraw decided to keep Burns on the roster, but only played him in 29 games. McGraw told Burns in spring training that year that he would not play much during the season, but he wanted him to be near him on the bench so he could learn. Now in 1913, McGraw believed that Burns was ready and he was right. For the next nine seasons between 1913 and 1921, George Burns would be the New York Giants' starting left fielder, leading the National League in runs scored five times and stolen bases twice. In 1925, George Burns would complete a 15-year major career with 2,077 hits and 383 stolen bases.

Therefore, with the Giants outfield set, there was no room for Jim Thorpe. The fact was that John McGraw was about to exploit Jim Thorpe's popularity. Many in the press criticized McGraw for keeping Jim Thorpe on the roster simply as a drawing card. But McGraw was quick to remind everyone that a lot of big league clubs thought enough of Thorpe's abilities in January to send an army of scouts to Carlisle.

In its edition of March 16, 1913, *The Sporting News* stated that "The idea that a good many people may have had that the Indian Jim Thorpe would be only a sort of circus card with the Giants has been already dispelled by ten days of work at Marlin. McGraw is said to really believe he has a find. The Indian is all that a ball player should be, has the speed, the arm, the eye, the judgment and the gameness — all the physical, mental and moral qualifications. McGraw hasn't determined where he will use him, but he will use him."[9]

Jim Thorpe — New York Giants.

Chief Meyers, a Native American, a member of the Cahuilla Tribe from Riverside, California, was the catcher on the Giants. Before entering into professional baseball, Meyers had attended Dartmouth for a couple of years. However, after school administrators discovered that his high school diploma was false, he dropped out, refusing to take another entrance exam. Not only did Meyers become Christy Mathewson's primary catcher, but he was one of the best hitters in the Giants lineup, having led the team in batting in 1912 with a .358 average.

Chief Meyers became Jim Thorpe's roommate. According to Meyers, because of Thorpe's celebrity, he could not get as much batting practice as the other players. The press would surround him and Thorpe acquiesced to them because he was afraid of being misunderstood by the public.

Meyers maintained that when Thorpe was forced to return his Olympic medals it broke his heart and he never recovered. Meyers stated that one evening Thorpe came into their room and woke Meyers up. He was crying and tears were rolling down his cheeks. "You know Chief," said Thorpe, "the King of Sweden gave me those trophies, he gave them to me. But they took them away from me, even though the guy who finished second refused to take them. They're mine Chief, I won them fair and square."[10]

As spring training camp broke and the Giants began heading north to begin the season, John McGraw left Jim Thorpe with minor leaguers waiting for assignments when the Giants played at Beaumont, Texas. *The Sporting News* stated that McGraw was worried that in Beaumont, Thorpe might be kidnapped and held for ransom.

Meanwhile, as Jim Thorpe was heading for New York and the Polo Grounds, the inevitable question was raised of where he stood historically in regard to other Native Americans or college football players who played major league baseball.

As previously stated, the first American Indian to play in the major leagues was James Madison Toy, who played in the American Association in 1887 and 1890. Later Louis Sockalexis, a Penobscot Indian who had played baseball at both Holy Cross and Notre Dame, played in the major leagues for the Cleveland Spiders of the National League, 1897–1899. Sockalexis had a career batting average of .313.

Likewise Jim Thorpe was not the first college football player to play major league baseball. Both George Barclay, who played for the St. Louis Cardinals and Boston Braves, 1902–1905, and Christy Mathewson of the Giants had played football at Bucknell University. Also David Fultz (Brown), John Gammons (Brown) and Fred Crolius (Dartmouth) had preceded Thorpe as college football players transitioning into the big leagues. Furthermore Jim

Thorpe would not even be the first major leaguer to play non-league professional football; he was preceded by Ed Abbaticchio and Rube Waddell.

The New York Giants opened their 1913 season on April 10. But Jim Thorpe wasn't in the lineup. By the end of spring training his status on the Giants had been reduced to that of a "fine prospect." John McGraw told the press, "He has a lot to learn about baseball, and so has any player who has been operating in the minors or at college. I never expected that Thorpe could jump in and make good the first season. He has the natural ability and the brains to make a good player, but on a club, he is up against trained competition — men who have gone through the school of experience. You must remember that Jim never was taught much about baseball. However, I notice that he is a keen observer and he is improving right along."[11]

McGraw was also irritated at the insinuation in the press that both he and the Giants front office were exploiting Thorpe and intended to toss him out after the first western road trip. "The Giants are good enough to be the best drawing team in the country, regardless of any side shows. We spend more money in putting up a championship front than any club in the country, any expense is not spared in rounding out a formidable team,"[12] said McGraw.

Jim Thorpe would make his first major league appearance in the second game of the season, pinch-hitting for pitcher Jeff Tesreau. While it was the first of 698 at bats in Thorpe's controversial big league career, suddenly he was 0-for-1.

As the season progressed, Thorpe continued to sit on the bench near McGraw and be educated in the game. During a game in Pittsburgh, Fred Snodgrass played two long fly balls very awkwardly. Immediately, McGraw counseled Thorpe on how to play such balls. He told Thorpe not to back out, but turn and sprint until he was ahead of the ball. The following day McGraw inserted Thorpe in the lineup and he made a fine catch in the outfield, doing just what he had been told to do. Thorpe's play prompted McGraw to remark to the press, "In another month or so the Indian will be a really good outfielder. He starts well now, knows how to play a ball when he reaches it, and, with his speed, can go a thundering long way for 'em. He has one of the best throwing arms on the club. After a while he'll be a good hitter."[13] Still, to a lot of observers the infrequent playing time hurt Thorpe. When he played regularly he hit well. But when he was once again relegated to the bench by McGraw his average dropped.

Although Jim Thorpe was now a professional baseball player, he still liked to participate in horseplay and pranks. Such behavior didn't sit well with John McGraw. Thorpe had always been a fantastic wrestler. Aboard a train on a Giants road trip, Thorpe got into a wrestling match with pitcher

Jeff Tesreau, who stood 6' 2½" and weighed 218 pounds. When Thorpe tossed Tesreau over a couple of seats, he was ordered by John McGraw never to touch another player or face dismissal from the team.

As the season progressed McGraw became increasingly concerned about Thorpe's drinking. After hearing a rumor that Thorpe had been drinking in a New York bar, McGraw confronted Thorpe in the dugout, telling him that he shouldn't drink. Then McGraw got personal by telling Thorpe, "Besides no Indian knows how to drink." The way that McGraw emphasized "Indian" annoyed Thorpe. So he shot back, "What about the Irish."[14] McGraw, a well-known figure in barrooms around the National League, took offense and reprimanded Thorpe, telling him not to get smart with him. Thorpe quickly told McGraw that he was not getting personal with him, it just so happened that he was part Irish too. The exchange really highlighted the tension that existed between the two, and from that point on Jim Thorpe was eternally in John McGraw's doghouse.

After a slow start the Giants coasted to the 1913 National League pennant. Led by a pitching staff that featured three 20-game winners, Christy Mathewson (25–11), Rube Marquard (23–10) and Jeff Tesreau (22–13), the Giants finished 12½ games ahead of the second-place Philadelphia Phillies. Jim Thorpe played in just 19 games, mostly as a pinch-hitter, finishing with a batting average of .143.

In the 1913 World Series, the New York Giants were beaten handily by the Philadelphia Athletics, four games to one. The Giants hit only .201 in the series with four players in the starting lineup hitting below .200 (Larry Doyle, 2B, .150; George Burns, OF, .158; Buck Herzog, 3B, .053; Tillie Shafer, 3B & OF, .158). Another outfielder, Red Murray, hit just .250.

Just prior to the World Series, Fred Snodgrass, who had played in 133 games for the Giants during the 1913 season, strained a tendon in his leg. In the Series the injured Snodgrass had only three at-bats and attempted to play one game at first base. Outfielder Claude Cooper, who played in just 15 games for the Giants in 1913, hitting .300, was used in two World Series games and had no official at-bats. Still, with his outfielders not hitting and Snodgrass ailing, John McGraw elected not to play Jim Thorpe in the Series, not even giving him one at-bat. Christy Mathewson pitched great ball for the Giants, winning one game and losing another. Mathewson finished with a 0.95 ERA and pitched a shutout in the second game for the Giants' only win. It was the third year in a row that John McGraw had lost to the American League in the World Series.

For Philadelphia, Eddie Plank was 1–1 in the Series, pitching a two-hitter in the fifth and final game to beat the Giants and Mathewson, 3–1. Chief

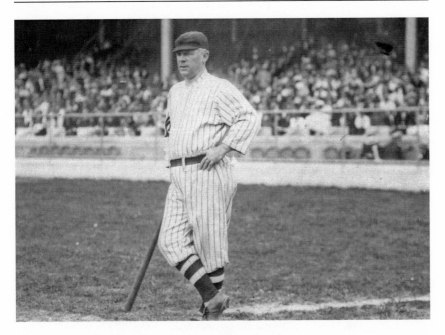

John McGraw at the Polo Grounds, 1912.

Bender won two games for the Athletics. The heavy damage done to Giants pitchers other than Mathewson was by two Athletics, Frank Baker and Eddie Collins. The two accounted for 17 of the Athletics' 46 hits in the series, a combined batting average of .436. Furthermore Baker and Collins scored seven of the Athletics' 23 runs. Baker and Collins also drove home ten runs. In game one, Baker, living up to his legend as "Home Run" Baker, hit a two-run shot off Rube Marquard, who finished the series with a 7.00 ERA for nine innings.

Later Pop Warner maintained that John McGraw never handled Jim Thorpe properly. "Jim was a horse for work and McGraw didn't give him that work. Otherwise he'd have been one of the finest baseball players of all time."[15]

The World Series ended on October 11. Three days later, on October 14, Jim Thorpe married Margaret Iva Miller. The two had met in 1911 at Carlisle. While Thorpe had been tight-lipped about his relationship with Iva while at Carlisle, he had spent considerable time courting her by spending a great portion of his allowance on double portions of ice cream and soda. Iva was two years ahead of Thorpe in school at Carlisle.

Their wedding took place at St. Patrick's Roman Catholic Church in Carlisle. The ceremony was performed by Father Mark Stock, a friend of Thorpe's, and the best man was Gus Welch, captain of the Carlisle football team in 1913. The bridesmaid was Miss Margaret Chisholm of Oklahoma. Ushers were Carlisle students.

Margaret Iva Miller was the daughter of a hotel proprietor from Muskogee, Oklahoma. She claimed to be a Cherokee and transferred to Carlisle in 1909 from the Chilocco Indian School where her sister was a teacher. But before marrying Thorpe she confessed to him that she had no Indian ancestry.

The union of the two would bring about the birth of four children. Their only son, Jim Jr., died at the age of 4½ from polio during the influenza epidemic of 1918. The three girls born to the couple were named Gail, Charlotte and Grace. Jim and Iva Thorpe would be married for ten years before divorcing.

For their honeymoon the Thorpes joined the New York Giants and Chicago White Sox on a World Tour.

John McGraw was a strong advocate for players being married. According to McGraw, "I am convinced that nothing helps a young man so much in baseball or in any other profession as a good wife. It is the real wholesome woman of good, hard, common sense who helps the ball player to success. Often she has been my very helpful ally in getting a player to improve his work or to take care of himself."[16] McGraw further stated that a player should get married right after the World Series. Then when the next season began, he was capable of understanding things.

10

The 1913 Giants and White Sox World Tour

Following the 1912 World Series, John McGraw, manager of the New York Giants, went on a 15-week vaudeville tour delivering a monologue about baseball written by Bozeman Bulger. After a performance at the Palace in Chicago, McGraw got together for drinks at "Smiley" Corbett's bar with National Commission chairman and president of the Cincinnati Reds, August "Garry" Herrmann, John Bruce, secretary of the National Commission, and Charles Comiskey, president of the Chicago White Sox. After conversing for a few minutes, Comiskey called McGraw over to a private table and asked him, "Say John, what do you think of taking our teams on a trip around the world?" McGraw asked when. Comiskey replied, right after the 1913 season. McGraw enthusiastically agreed to go.

McGraw said later, "That's all there was to it. Mr. Comiskey and I began making arrangements shortly afterward. Between us we financed the entire proposition. And we never had one scrap of paper between us in the way of an agreement."[1]

The idea of a major league world tour was not novel — it had been done before. In fact, the first major league teams to play abroad were the Boston Red Stockings and the Philadelphia Athletics of the National Association, who played in England July 16 — August 16, 1874. The tour had been organized by Boston pitcher Albert Goodwill Spalding. However, once in England, the English wanted to play cricket rather than baseball. The Americans, led by Athletics pitcher Dick McBride and Boston's Harry Wright, both skilled and tested bowlers, proceeded to defeat the English decisively at their own game, even whipping the famed Marylebone Cricket Club. The secret to the Americans' success in cricket was two-fold. First, McBride bowled (pitched) fireballs at the English. Second, the English had a habit of swinging at every wicket (ball) bowled, whereas the Americans were disciplined at bat and waited for a bowl that they could drive past the fielders. Consequently, the English charged the Americans with "dirty cricket."

By 1888, Albert Spalding was in the sporting goods business and hoping to open up worldwide markets. So he put together major league baseball's first world tour. An All-American squad led by John Montgomery Ward and a Chicago squad featuring Cap Anson made the junket, which included games on its itinerary in Australia, Ceylon, Cairo, Rome, Florence, Paris and England. The two teams played 30 games, two of them in the shadow of the Great Pyramids. In all, more than 60,000 people viewed the games on the tour. While baseball never caught on in England, its popularity was starting to spread in Cuba, Nicaragua and Japan. While Albert Spalding lost money on his tour, later he remarked that every country where baseball games had been scheduled on his World Tour fought on the Allied side in World War One.

A lot of the Giants and White Sox players were not eager to go on the World Tour and opted out, preferring to stay home because they needed the income from their winter jobs. Others could not afford to take their families with them. So the roster was filled with players from other major league teams who were eager to make the tour. However, John McGraw was able to convince several of his players to go, including Fred Merkle, Larry Doyle, Bunny Hearn, George "Hooks" Wiltse and Jim Thorpe. The Giants tour roster would be supplemented by Hans Lobert and Mickey Doolan (Philadelphia Phillies), and Lee Magee and Ivy Wingo (St. Louis Cardinals).

Likewise Comiskey was only able to get a few of his players to make the trip, such as Buck Weaver, Joe Benz, Tom Daly, Red Faber, Jim Scott and manager Nixey Callahan. Players joining the White Sox from other clubs for the tour included Sam Crawford and Lefty Lorenzen, (Detroit Tigers), Tris Speaker (Boston Red Sox), Dick Egan (Cincinnati Reds), John Bliss and Steve Evans (St. Louis Cardinals), and Germany Schaefer (Washington Nationals).

To make expenses for the trip, the Giants and White Sox agreed to play a schedule of 35 exhibition games on the way to the west coast, where they would depart for the Orient. Four games were rained out. Several other players, including some stars, agreed to join the tour as far as the west coast. They included Christy Mathewson, Chief Meyers, Fred Snodgrass, Jeff Tesreau, and Art Fromme of the New York Giants; Ray Schalk, Hal Chase, Reb Russell, Doc White, Frank Isbell, Wally Mattick and Joe Berger of the Chicago White Sox; and Walter Johnson of the Washington Nationals.

Umpires Bill Klem and Jack Sheridan also agreed to join the tour.

In some towns scheduled on the US portion of the tour, it would be the first time major league baseball exhibition games had ever been played there. The players were to be paid a share of the gate in every city. Cincinnati was chosen as the starting point for the tour in deference to its being the birthplace of professional baseball in 1869. There were no VIP seats issued and the only persons not paying admission were the members of the press. In fact, for the first game in Cincinnati, Garry Herrmann, Charles Comiskey and Ban Johnson all paid for their boxes for the game.

Jim Thorpe would play right field regularly and be a major drawing card on the tour, not just in the remote towns of the USA where fans had never seen him play baseball or football before, but all around the world. It was an opportunity for John McGraw and Jim Thorpe to form a friendship, but the rigid personalities of both would prevent that from happening.

John McGraw was telling the press that he hoped to give Thorpe a lot of experience on the trip, thereby enabling him to become a starter for the Giants in the 1914 season. The press also was hopeful for Thorpe, pointing out that Claude Cooper, another outfielder who shared the Giants bench with Thorpe during the 1913 season, playing in just 27 games, had jumped to the Federal League.

Nonetheless, the press wasn't letting McGraw off the hook for losing the 1913 World Series to the Athletics. They were stating that during the tour McGraw would be able to use other players such as Mickey Doolan and Hans Lobert of the Phillies, and Lee Magee of the Cardinals, to shore up the weaknesses in his line up at shortstop, third base and left field that had allowed the Philadelphia Athletics to win the 1913 World Series, despite the brilliant pitching of Christy Mathewson.

In Cincinnati on October 18, 1913, the World Tour began in grand style. However, with a cold day and swampy field, only a small crowd of about 5,000 turned out for the game, which had been hyped for several days by the Cincinnati newspapers. The New York Giants and Chicago White Sox appeared at Redland Field wearing their new uniforms trimmed with the national colors, with the American flag worked on their sleeves and a U.S. shield on the neckband. For the tour the players would be provided with two sets of uniforms, one that had a blue background and a second with a white background.

The Giants won the game in Cincinnati, 11–2. Jim Thorpe had three singles and scored two runs in the game. There had been a lot of local requests for Christy Mathewson to pitch for the Giants. He did and gave up one run and four hits in four innings.

A 100-yard dash had been planned between Hans Lobert, one of the fastest runners in major league baseball, and Jim Thorpe prior to the game. However, Lobert backed out, stating that if he started running here, he would have to do it everywhere the tour played. The two had actually met the day before the World Series began in New York, and the speedy Lobert had defeated Thorpe.

For the record, there were a lot of disgruntled gamblers in Cincinnati who collectively had lost $300,000 on the Giants in the World Series. The smart money had all gone on the Athletics, and one Cincinnatian, E. E. Smathers, won $40,000 on Philadelphia.

It was customary for Garry Herrmann to entertain visitors, royally and the Giants and White Sox contingency were not disappointed during their brief stay in the Queen City. In the morning before the game, the tour entourage, numbering nearly 80 people including the players, were put on a special streetcar, given a tour of the city and taken to the zoo. Eventually they wound up at a local saloon, Smearcase John's, for an elaborate luncheon that included standard Garry Herrmann Teutonic fare of sausages, limburger cheese, and pig's knuckles. The affair lasted so long that the party was late in arriving at the ballpark, causing waiting fans to wonder if something had happened to them. Following the game, Herrmann entertained Charles Comiskey, Ban Johnson, John McGraw and a few other notables at a dinner at the Havlin Hotel.

Garry Herrmann and a band of about 25 people went to Chicago for game two of the tour. The Cincinnati, Hamilton & Dayton Rail Road furnished the train for the American leg of the World Tour from Cincinnati to Vancouver. The train carried 65 persons representing the Giants and White Sox. This included the players, Jim Thorpe's bride Iva, managers and umpires, Harry Sparrow, who acted as the business agent for the tour, two newspapermen, Joseph Farrell of the *Chicago Tribune* and Gus Axelson of the *Chicago Record-Herald*, Ted Sullivan, a baseball personality turned author and lecturer, and John McGraw's doctor, Frank Finley. In addition, Charles Comiskey took his wife Nancy and son J. Louis and his recent bride Grace. White Sox manager Nixey Callahan also took his wife. Rounding out the entourage were several well-connected persons close to McGraw and Comiskey. The all-steel train was made up of three sleepers, an observation car and combination baggage and buffet car. The entourage would spend 26 nights on the train.

The second game on the American leg of the tour was played in Chicago on October 19, with 8,000 fans in attendance on a day when the weather was more suited for football than baseball. The Giants defeated the White Sox again, 3–1.

The following day at Springfield, Illinois, with snow falling while the game was played, Jim Thorpe hit a home run off White Sox pitcher Jim Scott, giving the Giants their third straight win, 6–4.

The tour entered Iowa where at Ottumwa, with 2,000 fans in attendance, the White Sox finally beat the Giants, 7–3. Jim Thorpe continued to hit well, going 1-for-2 with a double. While the game was riddled with errors, six for the Giants and two for the White Sox, the fans were pleased with the home runs of Fred Merkle of the Giants and Tom Daly of the White Sox.

On October 26, at Kansas City, as each player came to bat for the first time, umpire Bill Klem introduced him to the crowd. The greatest noise occurred when Jim Thorpe was introduced. Later in the game Thorpe made a fine play in the outfield, depriving Sam Crawford of a sure triple as the Giants beat the White Sox, 6–2.

Then the tour proceeded through Jim Thorpe's backyard into Oklahoma. On October 28, at Tulsa, prior to the game the over-crowed right field bleachers collapsed. Company I of the Ninth Infantry out of Fort Root, Arkansas, was passing under the bleachers when it collapsed, sending 500 men, women and children, and the frail wooden boards and strained metal of the stands down upon them. Fifty people were injured and one soldier, Pvt. Chester Taylor, died from a fractured skull. Oklahoma Governor Lee Cruse and his staff were seated only a few feet away from the collapse. In fact, if the collapse had happened only minutes before it would have trapped three wives of Giants players, Rea Lobert, Anna Meyers and Edith Doyle, who had passed under the stands to avoid the huge crowd at the main gate. Nonetheless, following a 30-minute delay, while the area around the collapse was cleared and the injured removed, the game was played with the White Sox victorious over the Giants, 6–0, behind a nine-hit complete game by Walter Johnson. Christy Mathewson had started for the Giants but left tired after four innings and behind, 2–0. Following the game, the players and their wives partied most of the night before boarding the train for Muskogee, where a game was played the next night.

On October 30, the teams played in Bonham, Texas. On Halloween the teams arrived in Dallas. The Texas State Fair was in progress and the game between the Giants and White Sox was an added attraction.

After playing in Arizona the tour moved into California. Hans Lobert stated that on November 11, when the tour arrived at 7:00 A.M. in Oxnard, California, the hometown of Fred Snodgrass, their train was met by ten stage coaches that took the players to a big ranch for a huge barbecue. The players had a breakfast that day consisting of roasted ox, lima beans with onions, and beer.

Then the mayor of Oxnard put speedy Lobert on the spot. He asked him if he would race a horse around the bases. The locals were curious to see whether a specially trained cattle horse could beat a man around the bases. Lobert held the record at the time for circling the bases in 13^4/$_5$ seconds. Lobert was reluctant, stating that he was there to play baseball. However, he eventually agreed to the race.

There were 5,000 people in the rickety wooden stands and several hundred cowboys on horseback watching the game in the outfield. With the Giants leading 2–0 in the seventh inning, Christy Mathewson had tired and was resorting to throwing a spitball. The Lobert vs. horse race had been hyped prior to the game and the cowboys were getting restless and demanding that the race get started. As the cowboys became more vocal, John McGraw suddenly feared a riot. He told Lobert that he would have to run now or they couldn't finish the game.

So during the seventh-inning stretch, reluctantly, Lobert approached home plate and lined up with a beautiful black horse to be ridden by a Mexican vaquero dressed in chaps and spangles that glittered like jewels in the sunlight. Pathé News was there to film the race. Umpire Bill Klem discussed the line of progress with the participants and then shouted out the command to Go! Off down the first base line went Lobert and the horse. Lobert and the horse reached third base neck and neck with the cowboys whooping and hollering. Coming down the third base line to the plate, Lobert was abreast with the horse. Then all at once the horse jetted into a sudden burst of speed and finished two yards ahead of Lobert. Lobert had circled the bases in 14 seconds. Not even the speedy Jim Thorpe could have done any better.

The cowboys were satisfied that they had gotten what they paid for, so the game was resumed. Mathewson got out of a couple of jams in the eighth and ninth as the Giants won the game, 3–2, over the White Sox. Following the game Hans Lobert would learn that a considerable amount of money had been wagered on the race.

The past few games Jim Thorpe had been having problems fielding the ball in the outfield. The White Sox took notice of Thorpe's dilemma and began deliberately attempting to drive the ball to him in right field. On November 13, at Oakland, California, the White Sox beat the Giants, 5–2, when Thorpe dropped a long fly ball to right field off the bat of Sam Crawford allowing two runs to score. Then on November 18 at Portland, Oregon, with 6,000 fans in attendance, in the fifth inning Thorpe fell on a muddy field going for a fly ball by Sam Crawford, allowing two runs to score that provided the 2–0 margin of victory for the White Sox over the Giants.

Germany Schaefer, who was playing second base for the White Sox, tried to ease Thorpe's pain by injecting a little humor into his circumstances. Schaefer said actually Thorpe played good ball during the journey from Chicago to the west coast because it was "Indian Summer."

The final game scheduled for the American leg of the tour was to be played at Tacoma, Washington, on November 19, but was rained out. The Giants and White Sox had played 35 games in 31 different cities across America.

Following the California games, Christy Mathewson left for home. While Jim Thorpe and Chief Meyers had been very popular with the Indians on the cross-country trip, most of the white fans wanted to shake hands with Christy Mathewson. While the white fans respected Jim Thorpe for his athletic ability, he was simply more of a curiosity. But Christy Mathewson, "Big Six," was a baseball superstar. Furthermore in 1912 Mathewson's autobiography, titled *Pitching in a Pinch*, had been published and it had been read by tens of thousands of school boys across the Great Plains and Far West. As a

Christy Mathewson (Sports Story Reprints).

result youngsters were chafing at the bit to meet their hero.

However, according to *Los Angeles Times* reporter Harry A. Williams (White Sox Had Grudge Against Matthewson" Nov. 12, 1913), some of the White Sox, mostly American Leaguers, considered Christy Mathewson snobbish and aloof. In fact, one of the White Sox players said that Mathewson went out of his way to avoid recognizing the White Sox players on the street. As a result, during the American leg of the tour, the White Sox often attempted and sometimes succeeded in unloading on Matty.

One American League player on the tour told news reporter Ring Lardner he didn't see how Mathewson got by. Either the batters in the National League knew nothing about hitting or he was such an old man they felt sorry for him.

On November 19, the tour left from Vancouver, B. C., aboard the R.M.S. *Empress* of Japan bound for Yokohama, Japan. However, due to rough seas caused by one of the worst typhoons to hit the Northern Pacific in two decades, nearly every member of the party got seasick, with the exception of Germany Schaefer, Mickey Doolan and Jim Thorpe. Joe Benz was sick 12 days; Sam Crawford was sick for ten days and both managers, John McGraw and Nixey

Callahan, were disabled for two days. Red Faber was so sick that he was under the care of the ship's surgeon.

The tour and its recovering party finally landed in Japan on December 5. On December 6 and 7, the Giants and White Sox played two games in Tokyo with the White Sox winning both, 9–4 and 12–9. The first game was the second game of a doubleheader, with the Giants and White Sox initially playing as a combined team against one of the better Japanese college teams, Keio University. The combined Giants and White Sox won the game 16–3. A third game, in Tokyo was rained out.

Japan had been playing baseball since the 1870s. John McGraw said, "Of the non-speaking countries we found the Japanese better informed on baseball than any other people. All the big universities there have teams and they have advanced rapidly in the finer points of baseball. In a few years I expect to see Japan as much of a baseball country as Cuba."[2]

On December 11, the tour arrived in Shanghai but rain prevented the game from being played. As the tour arrived at the wharf at 9:00 A.M. a thousand well-wishers and players from teams in the local Shanghai Amateur Baseball League had gathered and they all wanted to see Jim Thorpe. While cricket was more popular than baseball in British-dominated Shanghai, the game had been heavily promoted and a crowd of 25,000 was expected to turn out for it at the city's elegant race track. A tarp had been laid over the infield at the track and the local Chinese worked hard to keep the field in possible playing condition. However, as a steady torrent of rain continued to fall, Comiskey and McGraw had no choice but to cancel the game.

Next games were played in Hong Kong, Manila and Australia. Baseball had been introduced into Australia by American gold miners in the 1870s and kept alive by Australian cricket clubs. It was in Melbourne on January 7, 1914, that Jim Thorpe played his best game on the tour, hitting two home runs and making several spectacular catches in the outfield. The next day, Thorpe hit a home run in a game played at Adelaide, Australia.

The next games were scheduled to be played in Ceylon and Egypt. The tour boarded the R.M.S. *Orontes* for the voyage. It was the dog days of summer in Australia, and the stifling heat prompted Sam Crawford to wish for snow. According to Crawford, taking a breath of air at Perth was like breathing in air from a furnace. Iva Thorpe had much the same opinion.

During the long voyage from Adelaide, Australia, to Ceylon, the players and their wives amused themselves by playing childish games. It was decided on January 12 to play a game of follow the leader. Jim Thorpe, always agreeable to horseplay, was selected as the leader and proceeded to lead the men and women all over the decks of the ship indulging in stupid actions. When

Thorpe spotted Charles Comiskey lounging in a deck chair, the prankster leaned over and gave "The Old Roman" a big wet kiss. Everyone following Thorpe's lead proceeded to smooch Comiskey accordingly. Comiskey, a man with a need for considerable distance in personal space, who rarely shook hands with his own players, found no amusement in the affection showered upon him.

There was also a lot of shuffleboard played on the way to Ceylon. Surprisingly, John McGraw and Jim Thorpe teamed up and were the second-best team aboard ship, only exceeded by the skill of Dick Evans and Steve Evans.

The tour finally arrived in Ceylon and on January 23 played a brief five-inning game won by the White Sox, 4–1, before a sparse crowd at the Colombo racetrack. Then the tour quickly departed for Egypt.

Arriving in Cairo on February 1, the players and their entourage were taken by trolley to the Heliopolis Hotel where in the lobby the entire party stood upon most expensive rug in the world, a Smyrna measuring 75 × 40 feet with a value of 75,000 francs. A tour of the Sphinx and pyramids was organized. In deference to the exact spot near the pyramids where the Spalding World Tour had played in Cairo 25 years before, many of the players stood in tribute.

That afternoon, under a blazing desert sun and with the last Khedive of Egypt in attendance, the Giants and White Sox played on the worst field of the tour. The infield was like cement and a wire fence surrounded the outfield. Despite the playing conditions, competition between the two teams was fierce. McGraw was now two games down to the White Sox and wanted to win badly.

The White Sox team was proud in representing the American League and began to ride the Giants, especially Fred Merkle and Fred Snodgrass, goats of Giants teams past. This caused a stormy response from John McGraw. While the game ended in a 3–3 tie, called because of darkness after ten innings, Jim Thorpe had a great day. He accounted for all the Giants runs, leading off the game with a home run and adding two run-scoring hits. A second game was played the following day with Thorpe going 4-for-4 in a 6–3 Giants win. For the single players on the tour such as Buck Weaver, Fred Merkle and Steve Evans, the bawdy nightlife of Cairo was a delight.

From Egypt the tour sailed across the Mediterranean Sea to Europe, its fifth continent in three months. Arriving in crowded Naples, John McGraw and Charles Comiskey were disappointed to learn that no suitable field could be found to play a game. Some of the tourists decided to sightsee around Naples and were shocked as they discovered the unsanitary conditions in which pasta was manufactured.

In Rome, all three games were rained out. Other than the tour's private visit with the Pontiff in Vatican City, about the only significant event of the Rome visit occurred on the floor of the ancient Coliseum, where Jim Thorpe and Fred Merkle were talked into participating in a wrestling match. Thorpe quickly won the contest, pinning the six foot one, 190-pound Giants first baseman with ease, then placing his foot in the small of the vanquished back.

A more artistic side of Jim Thorpe surfaced when he visited an art museum in Rome and purchased three reproductions of paintings for his and Iva's apartment back home.

The tour's visit to Italy was also marked by a harrowing near-miss of a fatal accident when the engineer of the train carrying the party missed a signal notifying him that a 20-foot section of track over the Volturno River was out. Fortunately workers along the route shouting at the top of their lungs got the engineer's attention before he plunged the train into the river gorge.

In addition to the other misfortunes of the Italian leg of the tour, Charles Comiskey became ill on the train and began to exhibit all the symptoms of a heart attack. An American doctor from Virginia happened to be on the same train and diagnosed Comiskey's condition as severe indigestion.

The tour arrived in Nice, France, on February 14 and the White Sox defeated the Giants 10–9 on a rocky soccer field with a large contingent of wealthy vacationing Americans in the stands. Prior to the game, Jim Thorpe acquiesced to the wishes of the crowd and put on a display of his Olympic Games feats, throwing a shot put and a discus. The following four games scheduled for Paris on February 18–21, were rained out.

With the rain postponing games, Jim and Iva Thorpe used the time to take advantage of seeing the wonders of Paris. They went to the Louvre, the theatre, the opera and the Moulin Rouge. Thorpe had been to Paris during the 1912 Olympic Games when the track team took advantage of some open days at the end of the games. However, Thorpe had no money then, not even a nickel for a beer, and saw very little of the tourist attractions in the French capital. But this time around it was a different matter and the couple hardly slept for the four days the tour was in Paris.

On February 22, the tour departed France for England. On February 26, the last game on the tour's schedule was played in London. It was an 11-inning game played at the Chelsea football ground before 35,000 fans including King George V. Tommy Daley hit a home run as the White Sox triumphed over the Giants, 5–4.

John McGraw and Nixey Callahan were notified that following the game they would be received by King George V in his box. So McGraw and Callahan had to scurry about locating top hats and frock coats. Just as they were about to start for the box, word was received that the King had stated that an ordinary bowler or derby would do.

The main American attraction in London was once again Jim Thorpe. Wherever he and Iva went, to the theatre, the museums, they were mobbed. The sight of Thorpe was cultural shock for the British. They were used to seeing the stereotyped American Indians in Wild West shows that came to London. They were surprised to see that Thorpe had no war paint on his face and was not decked out in feathers. It confused the British that Thorpe resembled a white man.

On February 28, the Giants and White Sox sailed for home aboard the ill-fated *Lusitania*, arriving in New York on March 7. Two celebratory banquets were held, one in New York on March 7, the other in Chicago on March 10. However, with spring training about to begin in Marlin, Texas, neither John McGraw nor any of the Giants players attended the Chicago banquet.

The same day that the tour arrived in New York, March 7, 1914, Babe Ruth hit his first professional home run in the same ball park in Fayetteville, North Carolina, where Jim Thorpe had hit his first home run playing in the Eastern Carolina League. However, the fans remembering Thorpe's long blast stated that the Babe's home run had traveled 60 feet further.

During the World Tour, Jim Thorpe had thrived on playing every day. He hit good major league pitching and was wildly cheered at every stop. He even challenged Tris Speaker for top hitting honors on the tour. Unfortunately, following the tour, Jim Thorpe and John McGraw were no closer than they had been went they set out on their odyssey. In fact, they had become more distant. Conflict between McGraw and Thorpe developed over the usual issues, drinking, horsing around and wrestling. Often during the tour, McGraw lectured Thorpe on what he called inappropriate behavior for a married man.

Nonetheless, Iva Thorpe was a big surprise to onlookers all around the world. They were impressed with her plain but vivacious beauty and the fact that she always had a smile upon her face. And it was very clear that she was deeply in love with Jim.

Thorpe's feats in the Olympic Games had made him a world-wide celebrity and unlike the other ball players on the tour, he was well known in the Philippines, Japan, China, Egypt, Italy, and every country in which the Giants and White Sox played. He didn't disappoint the fans that came to see him play. He was blazing fast in the field and on the bases. Furthermore in every country, fans felt compelled to remark on his loss of the medals he had won at Stockholm, what an outrage and injustice it was.

Most believe that the World Tour was profitable; some say that McGraw and Comiskey made over $75,000 on the junket, although the exact figures have never been revealed. Nonetheless, the tour had been successful in showcasing the American game around the globe. Nearly 100 years following the Giants and White Sox World Tour there are now players representing 30 countries and territories playing in major and minor league baseball. More than 30 percent of the players on current major league rosters were born outside of the USA.

11

Congress Investigates Carlisle

During the fall of 1913 and winter of 1914, while Jim Thorpe was on the New York Giants and Chicago White Sox World Tour, a Congressional investigation of the Carlisle Indian School began. Not only had accusations of embezzlement and the scandal surrounding Thorpe's Olympic medals led to the investigation, but questions of financial improprieties had been charged in the athletic department run by Glenn S. "Pop" Warner.

Fred Bruce, an Indian from Montana who in late 1912 and early 1913 had been working at the Carlisle Indian School as a steam fitter installing the Webster vacuum system, had alleged that Jim Thorpe did not write the confession statement he sent to James E. Sullivan, but rather he copied it from a letter furnished to him. Bruce stated that in late January 1913, he was in a conversation with Thorpe in his room when Pop Warner came in and he was asked to leave. When he returned he found Thorpe copying a letter.

When Fred Bruce completed his work at Carlisle he went to Chilocco, Oklahoma. However, he still harbored unresolved issues resulting from his experience at the Carlisle Indian School. On November 18, 1913, Bruce wrote to Mark Griffen, Secretary of the Indian Rights Association, stating that he had been present when a meeting took place in late 1912 or early 1913, among a group of the Carlisle athletes. According to Bruce, William Garlow, the center on the Indians football team, told the group that he tried to find out what was happening with all the money the athletic department was taking in. Garlow said that when he asked, they gave him $50 and told him to sign a paper — that's as close to money as he could get.

Furthermore, Bruce stated that he attempted to find out what the athletic money was used for. He asked a few employees and they told him they didn't know. A few buildings were constructed on the campus. Bruce alleged that they were valued twice as high as they actually cost. Bruce concluded his letter to Griffen by stating, "I am pretty sure that Mr. Friedman and possibly Mr. G. Warner will have a good many dollars of the athletic money in the banks in their names."[1]

Mark Griffen did not ignore Fred Bruce's letter. Griffen had been hearing rumors of questionable administrative behavior at the Carlisle Indian School for some time and immediately sent a letter to Cato Sells, the Commissioner of Indian Affairs in Washington, D.C. In his ten-page letter, Griffen described what he called "an unwholesome and unsatisfactory condition of affairs at the school — a situation calling for a prompt and thorough investigation, in the interest of all concerned."[2]

Griffen stated that in his opinion, academics received secondary consideration at the school in favor of athletics and the band. In particular, Griffen cited several areas of concern that he felt the Bureau of Indian Affairs should investigate.

According to Griffen, a severe state of discontent and disrespect existed at Carlisle that was highlighted during the commencement ceremonies of March 1913. The ex–Assistant Commissioner of Indian Affairs was addressing the class and began to heap praise upon Superintendent Moses Friedman. This brought about a loud chorus of boos from the assembled pupils. Griffen also cited, as another example of discontent at the school, the marked increase in runaways. In October 1913, eight boys at one time had run away from the school.

In addition, Griffen stated that he had been informed that there were a large number of complaints from students regarding the status of their individual accounts with the school bank, in that they had nothing to show what the balance was to their credit.

There were also a large number of cases of alleged immorality cited by Griffen in which 32 girls and 15 boys were dismissed from the school. Griffen felt that circumstance alone indicated there was something radically wrong with the school's management. Griffen mentioned that he had been informed through a reliable source that, several years earlier, one of the female students participating in the "outing system" was put into service in a home in Washington, D.C., where she was wronged by a visitor who was said to be a surgeon in the U.S. Army. The situation had been reported to Superintendent Friedman, who in turn reported it to the Bureau of Indian Affairs. However, due to the prominence of the offender, the affair was quashed. Soon after, the young lady died.

Griffen also cited rampant use of and access to alcohol by the students. In one instance on June 13, 1913, according to Griffen, 52 male students returned to the campus clearly under the influence of alcohol. Griffen had received a letter from a student named Louis Schweigman, corroborated by another student, alleging that, following the Harvard game in 1912, William Garlow said that when he encountered Superintendent Friedman drinking in an establishment, Friedman gave him 15 dollars and told him to go and have a good time. Then Friedman told Garlow if he wanted to he could sleep with the girls.

It was also alleged that another football player, quarterback Gus Welch, had been drunk on the school grounds, accompanied by a school employee. Welch's condition was reported to Friedman, but he chose to do nothing about it. The school employee was a white man who should have been prosecuted for giving liquor to an Indian, but instead was allowed to quietly leave the school.

Griffen also cited several instances of corporal punishment being administered on students who were stripped and whipped with a heavy leather strap. In one instance Griffen alleged that Coach Warner was present as a witness. Another time a large girl was whipped.

As for the Athletic Department, Griffen stated that was solely supervised by Superintendent Friedman and the student body had no say in athletics. Griffen stated, "The Athletic fund appears to be managed as a 'close corporation' by Supt. Friedman, Coach Glenn Warner and a Mr. Miller. It is understood that these gentleman are the absolute custodians of this fund and are not even answerable for its use to the Indian Bureau."[3]

As for the matter involving Jim Thorpe, Griffen offered the letter he had received from Fred Bruce as proof that records in the Carlisle office demonstrated clearly that Thorpe had played professional baseball before he participated in the 1912 Olympic Games.

According to informants to Griffen's office, student-athletes were paid directly or indirectly for their services in the form of credit orders to a local store in the amount of $50. It was also alleged that on some occasions, direct payments to student-athletes were made using these credits to cover up cash payments.

Griffen concluded his letter by asking Cato Sells for a thorough and searching investigation of Superintendent Friedman's complete administration by Inspector E. B. Linnen, whose report he felt should carry great weight due to his record of exceptional honesty and efficiency.

While a four-member Congressional joint sub-committee was being formed to investigate the school, the Bureau of Indian Affairs did send E. B. Linnen to Carlisle to investigate the allegations in Mark Griffen's letter. Linnen's report was soon completed and it not only corroborated the allegations in Griffen's letter, but went beyond in describing not only questionable administrative practices of Moses Friedman, but also unhealthy and unsanitary conditions that were hardly in the best interest of expediting the educational process.

Linnen described a campus in disrepair and one in a state of near rebellion against Friedman. The dining hall was poorly equipped with less than adequate cups, plates and linen, and the crockery was chipped. Less than a balanced diet was served to the students, usually consisting of oatmeal, one slice of bread, gravy, rice and beans. Butter was served once a week and there was consistently a shortage of other staples such as milk, syrup and bread, although Carlisle maintained its own bakery. Furthermore, there had been instances of corporal punishment and questionable practices originating out of the athletic department.

Outrage by the student body toward the Carlisle administration had been fueled in part by the way Superintendent Friedman and Coach Warner had handled the Olympic medals affair involving their hero Jim Thorpe. However, their major discontent had risen over the action of Friedman in allegedly urging a Pennsylvania judge in Cumberland County to mete out 60-day jail sentences to a female and male student for an infraction that under the existing law was punishable only by a fine. While the exact charge is not known, it has long been held that it was debauchery.

In a signed petition to Cato Sells, Commissioner of Indian Affairs, 55 Carlisle students, including football star Joe Guyon, sought the removal of Glenn "Pop" Warner as athletic director. The students alleged that Warner possessed weak character, used profane and abusive language in the presence of students, and used the football team for the purpose of gambling. It was charged that Warner was incapable of coaching either baseball or basketball and had abolished the baseball team out of selfish motives.

Now broader controversy began to surround Pop Warner. Both on the school campus and outside, it was alleged that every superintendent of Carlisle, including Pratt, had turned his head from Warner's profiting from selling tickets and road trips while making money off his student-athletes.

On January 24, Superintendent Friedman arrived in Washington in an attempt to launch a pre-emptive strike in defense of his administration of the Carlisle Indian School. He told Commissioner Cato Sells that the charges against him were instigated by former superintendent General R. H. Pratt. Sells refused to hear Friedman and immediately ordered him to return to his post at Carlisle.

The four-member joint sub-committee of the Indian Affairs Committee of the Senate and House formed to formally investigate the Carlisle Indian School consisted of Senators Joseph Taylor Robinson of Arkansas and Harry Lane of Oregon, and Representatives David Carter of Oklahoma and John H. Stephens of Texas. During January and February, 1914, the sub-committee would hear what would eventually amount to 632 pages of typewritten testimony.

In late January the sub-committee made an unannounced visit to the school and met with E. B. Linnen, who was proceeding with his investigation for the Bureau of Indian Affairs, several students, employees and residents of the town. One of those to give testimony was Gus Welch, captain of the highly successful 1913 Indians football team that finished with a record of 10–1–1. Welch testified that Coach Warner was a man of no principles. Other players testified that they had seen Warner selling football game tickets in hotel lobbies and pocketing the money. It was also alleged that in the 1913 Dartmouth game, Warner had bet heavily.

Following the visit, Senator Robinson, head of the sub-committee, stated that they had found conditions at the school unsatisfactory. While the press was barred from the meetings, it was learned that the sub-committee found Superintendent Friedman's action in having the female and male student arrested and given a 60-day jail sentence reprehensible and the incident demonstrated his incompetence.

In regard to corporal punishment being administered at Carlisle, the sub-committee found that the Bandmaster, Claude M. Stauffer, had allegedly used a club, inflicting severe injuries in disciplining a female student, and also punched her in the face. The facts were that Stauffer had spanked the Indian girl at the order of the superintendent and the matron of the girl's department. The instrument used to administer the punishment was not a club as reported, but rather a piece of wood broken from a soap box. Nonetheless, when the incident became public Stauffer was upheld by Friedman.

It was also charged that Stauffer on many occasions had failed to provide proper nutrition to the girls by withholding bread from them, so that the boys who had worked at manual labor on the farms would have an ample supply.

Following the sub-committee's visit to Carlisle, Commissioner Cato Sells immediately suspended Moses Friedman and Claude Stauffer. To fill the post of superintendent, Sells appointed Oscar H. Lipps, a supervisor in the U.S. Bureau of Indian Affairs in Washington, D.C.

In early February, the sub-committee began to focus its investigation on the Carlisle athletic department. Senator Robinson stated, "There are some other matters relating to the accounts of the superintendent connected with the athletic fund, and his accounts as superintendent that are under investigation."[4] On Friday, February 6, 1914, the joint commission met in the Y.M.C.A hall on the Carlisle Indian School campus and heard testimony from William H. Miller, who was employed at Carlisle as a financial clerk.

Senator Robinson, chairman of the sub-committee, asked Miller, "Have any loans or advances been made to boys on the football teams at various times?"

"Yes," said Miller, admitting that $200 had been advanced to Albert Exendine and $300 to Louis Tewanima, and on another occasion $50. When Robinson pushed the matter of the money advanced being as loans, Miller stated that the money was not repaid. Furthermore, Miller stated that the loans or advances were authorized by the superintendent.

Next Senator Robinson asked Miller, "Have you checked up to see how much was paid to football boys in 1908?" Miller said that he had. Robinson went on, "It appears from the memorandum furnished to me that, on December 10, 1908, the total amount paid on this account was $4,283." Miller replied, "That was the amount of the check."

Robinson continued, "I find also by check No. 508, December 4, there is an item of $3,667.63. What account was that paid from, and what was it for?" Miller replied, "From the athletic account, and for the boys." "For the football boys?" asked Robinson. "Yes, sir," replied Miller.

So it appear that the players on the Carlisle football team had been paid a total of $7,950.30 for the 1908 season. If each varsity player got an equal share it amounted to $567 each. It paid to play for Carlisle.

Robinson then asked Miller, "What other advances in the nature of bonuses are usually made to the football boys? What other allowances?" Miller replied, "Since the practice of paying the money was abolished, they have been allowed an overcoat and a suit of clothing each year." The money was paid out of the athletic fund and orders were given to local merchants in the town.

With veiled threats of misuse of athletic funds and possible prosecution swirling about him, Glenn S. "Pop" Warner testified that profits from football had enhanced the campus facilities and infrastructure. He said the football money paid for a new printing office, business department, remodeling of the dining hall and a new heating system and lights for the dorm. Another charge leveled at Warner was that he had paid two sports writers, Hugh R. Miller and E. L. Martin, to boost the school's athletics.

While the sub-committee chose not to find any direct evidence of misappropriations of the athletic funds at Carlisle, or any direct evidence of wrongdoing by Coach Warner, it was revealed that at one time the Carlisle athletic fund had grown to a whopping $25,000! Some of those funds had even been invested in Northern Pacific and Reading Railroad bonds.

Regardless of the controversy surrounding Warner, the record showed that he had taken Indians from the plains and mountains, green talent who knew nothing about football, and developed them into All-American football players and Olympic track champions at Carlisle. Notwithstanding great athletes such as Jim Thorpe, Chief Bender and Louis Tewanima, the list of players Warner developed at Carlisle was long and impressive: Albert Exendine, William Gardner, Jimmy Johnson, Frank Mount Pleasant, Bemus Pierce, Jim Phillips, Edward Rogers, Gus Welch and Jonas Metoxen, among others.

Superintendent Friedman, on the other hand, was suspected of destroying papers showing he had misappropriated funds belonging to the school. An affidavit had been obtained by Cato Sells from an Indian student, Siceni Nori, who worked at the school as chief clerk. Nori alleged that Friedman had directed him to burn the evidence. But by mid–1915 all charges of embezzlement and conspiracy against Friedman would be dropped. In early May, 1914, Friedman had voluntarily stepped down as superintendent at Carlisle. He charged that he had been harassed out of his position by Cato Sells and a Democratic administration in Washington that wanted Republicans out so they could make appointments of their own. A year after Friedman's resignation, acting superintendent Oscar H. Lipps was appointed permanently.

Glenn S. "Pop" Warner returned to Carlisle to coach the Indians in the 1914 football season. However, the Congressional hearings had left the once proud and powerful Indians football program in shambles. Joe Guyon, a second team Walter Camp All-American halfback in 1913, who had leveled charges against Warner, left school. Later Pop Warner would say that Joe Guyon was every bit as responsible for the success of the Carlisle football program as Jim Thorpe.

Quarterback Gus Welch quit the team. However, midway through the schedule with the Indians' record at 3–6, having lost six straight games, Warner convinced Welch that they could mend their differences, and he returned to the squad. However, Carlisle was immediately walloped by Notre Dame, 48–6, at Comiskey Park in Chicago. Gus Welch, out of condition, was injured in the game so badly that he was hospitalized.

With a demoralized squad, Warner's 1914 Carlisle Indians finished with a 5–10–1 record. The only significant Indians victory was over Alabama, 20–3, in the second-last game of the season. The Pop Warner era at Carlisle had come to an end. Warner resigned and took the head coaching job at the University of Pittsburgh. His career coaching record at Carlisle was 114–42–8. Warner would coach at Pitt from 1915 to 1923, establishing a record of 60–12–4, while winning national titles in 1915, 1916 and 1918. Introducing a double wing formation, Warner won his first 29 games at Pitt.

12

Thorpe Struggles with the Curve Ball

A few weeks after completing the World Tour Jim Thorpe reported for spring training at Marlin, Texas. For the moment the animosities that existed between Jim Thorpe and John McGraw seemed to be on hold. Thorpe was attempting to improve as a player and even tried switch-hitting in a game at San Antonio, getting three hits, two from the right side and one from the left.

It was during spring training in 1914 that the greatest myth of Jim Thorpe's baseball career was born. During a spring training game in Texarkana, Texas, a town on the Texas–Arkansas border, Thorpe hit three home runs — a considerable accomplishment that could stand alone. However, for some reason, Thorpe felt a need to embellish the feat. So he began spinning the yarn that not only had he hit three home runs in the game, but the clouts had landed in three different states. According to Thorpe his first round tripper was an inside-the-park job. So that home run was hit in Texas. His second home run cleared the right field fence and landed in Arkansas. His third home run of the day was hit over the left field fence and landed in Oklahoma. There is no dispute on the final destinations of his first two home runs, but the third — well, the fact was that the Oklahoma border was some 40 miles beyond the left field fence.

Two Giants outfielders had signed with the Brooklyn Federal League team for 1914, Claude Cooper and Danny Murphy. So a lot of observers felt Jim Thorpe just might be a starter for New York in the coming season, or at least he would play a lot more than the previous season.

As opening day neared, on April 12, 1914, 10,000 showed up at a New York theatre to see films of the Giants and White Sox World Tour.

Regardless of the creditable spring that Thorpe had and the fine job he did on the World Tour, he was once again destined to ride the bench for the New York Giants in 1914 . When he did play, he usually performed well. Such was the case on May 26 at West Side Park in Chicago. In a wild Giants 10–

7 come-from-behind victory over the Cubs, Thorpe started the winning rally with a pinch-hit double in the sixth inning, driving in two runs off Chicago starter Hippo Vaughn. His hit also sent another runner to third, who was then driven in with a sacrifice fly. However, those two RBI would be the only ones that Thorpe would have in the 1914 season. Thorpe would play in only 30 games with 31 at-bats for the Giants, hitting a paltry .194.

The New York Giants, after leading the National League for most of the season, slumped in late August and early September. Consequently the Giants finished the 1914 season in second place, 10¹/₂ games behind the Boston Braves. The fact that McGraw did not play Jim Thorpe made absolutely no sense. The reserve outfielders that McGraw played instead of Thorpe hardly did much better. Dave Robertson hit .266 in 256 at-bats and Red Murray hit .223 in 139 at-bats.

In spring training at Marlin, Texas, in 1915 John McGraw was telling reporters that he believed Jim Thorpe might win a regular job in his outfield this coming season. Then in a game at Waco, reporters watched in amusement as Thorpe chased curve balls and missed by a mile, fooled by 19-year-old pitcher Jimmy Zinn.

Following the game John McGraw addressed reporters. "This is the year Jim gets his real chance to show what he can do. You say he looked bad on that curve this afternoon. Well, that is very apt to always be his way. He may look bad on one ball, as he did to-day, but you have not mentioned that he pickled the next one. He may go through the big league in just that manner, showing up bad now and then, but coming back and leathering the ball," said McGraw. "He is as good an outfielder as Heinie Zimmerman is a third baseman and I guess anybody will concede that Heinie is a great man to have in a baseball game,"[1] added McGraw.

However, the reality was that McGraw's outfield was already set with three experienced outfielders, Murray, Burns and Snodgrass. Still carrying 30 players on this roster, McGraw needed to cut his roster to 21 by opening day on April 14. So the day before the season started he sent eight players to Rochester and one to Jersey City. As McGraw had two outfielders under long-term contracts, Thorpe and Robertson, he was forced to send standout prospect Sandy Piez to Rochester. Piez, who played college baseball at Rutgers, had played in 35 games for the Giants in 1914, hitting .375 in eight at bats. Piez would never return to the major leagues.

On opening day 1915 the Giants were greeted by 20,000 fans at the Polo Grounds. However, they were overshadowed by the Federal League opening game in Harrison, New Jersey, where the Newark Peppers lost to the Baltimore Terrapins, 6–2, before 26,000 fans. In the second game of the season Rube

Marquard pitched a no-hitter for the Giants against the Brooklyn Robins at the Polo Grounds.

Although Thorpe didn't have a very good spring, McGraw started him in the outfield as the season began, believing that if he played more it would benefit him. However, Thorpe was soon benched and wound up playing in just 17 games for the Giants, hitting .231.

With the third year of a three-year contract beginning, calling for $5000 a year, on April 27 McGraw put Thorpe on waivers and had club secretary John B. Foster send telegrams to all other clubs. As soon as he passed waivers, McGraw sent Thorpe to the Jersey City club of the International League. Joining the Jersey City Skeeters, Thorpe became the highest paid player in the International League.

At the same time the Giants put Jim Thorpe on waivers, they also put John Murray and pitcher Arthur Fromme on waivers. But the other clubs passed on picking up the two and because they had contracts which required their consent to be sold or traded, they would remain with the Giants. Fromme was winding up a ten-year major league career. He came to the Giants in 1913 in one of the worst trades ever made by the Giants in John McGraw's tenure as manager. In return for Fromme, the Giants sent Red Ames, Heinie Groh, Josh Devore and $20,000 to the Cincinnati Reds. For years following the trade, McGraw would attempt to persuade Reds president Garry Herrmann to make a deal sending Groh back to New York.

While on the Jersey City club and away from the discipline of John McGraw, Thorpe let his free spirit take over his personality. He got angry at teammate and roommate Al Schacht at a party after being joshed by him. According to Schacht, when Thorpe got mad, he grinned. The wider the grin, the madder he was. As Schacht kept kidding Thorpe, his grin kept getting broader. Suddenly he grabbed Schacht by the scruff of the neck and with one hand dangled him outside a window three stories above the street.

On June 3, 1916, Thorpe would file a $10,000 libel suit with the New Jersey Supreme Court against a Jersey City newspaper that printed a story alleging that on June 15, 1915, he and Catcher Reynolds of the Jersey City club had attacked 24-year-old Edward La Forge in a Jersey City saloon, knocking him out cold for an hour. The paper stated that Thorpe had been taken into custody but was later released. So Thorpe was suing on the grounds the story was false and malicious and had harmed his personal reputation as a ball player, caused him loss of employment and depreciated the value of his services.

The Jersey City club had had enough of Thorpe's antics and sent him to Harrisburg of the International League. Then in early July Thorpe was released back to the Giants. The Harrisburg club told John McGraw that

Thorpe had a disturbing influence on the team. In Jersey City and Harrisburg that summer, Jim Thorpe continued to be plagued by his inability to hit a curve ball. Still, Thorpe played in 96 games in the minors in 1915 and had a combined batting average of .303 (112 hits in 370 at-bats). When he went four-for-four (two triples, a double and a single) in a game against Buffalo, it started a rumor around baseball that Thorpe could hit in the minors, but couldn't hit in the majors.

On August 20, Thorpe rejoined John McGraw and then sat on the bench for the rest of the season as the New York Giants imploded. With Christy Mathewson (8–14) having the worst year of his brilliant career, the Giants finished in last place in the National League, a humiliating 21 games behind the pennant-winning Philadelphia Phillies.

Center fielder Fred Snodgrass was having such a miserable season, hitting just .194, that in August McGraw sold him to the Boston Braves. Also Rube Marquard, who had pitched a no-hitter in the second game of the season, was in constant conflict with McGraw all summer long. So on August 31, Marquard arranged his own trade to Brooklyn for the waiver price.

Although Jim Thorpe was not playing for the Giants, a humbling experience for an athlete recognized just a few short years ago as the greatest athlete in the world, he allowed himself to enjoy the perks of being on a major league roster. Larry McLean, the Giants' trainer, said that Thorpe ate gargantuan breakfasts. According to McLean, on the road Thorpe would come into the hotel dining room at 10:00 A.M. and order a breakfast of grapefruit, cereal, a half-dozen fried eggs with ham, a sirloin steak with onions, two orders of fried potatoes, country sausage, wheat cakes, rolls and a pot of coffee.

In an article published in the *Pittsburgh Leader*, November 27, 1915, International League umpire Frank Brown stated that he believed that Thorpe had no interest in the game. He cited incidents where Thorpe struck out and then threw his bat down with indifference. When an opposing catcher would mention to him that he had just struck out again, supposedly Thorpe remarked that it did not cut out any of his $5,000 contract. Brown also said he saw Thorpe let fly balls drop in front of him in the outfield.

While baseball was paying his bills and he still had a contract with the New York Giants, Jim Thorpe missed the glory of football and was beginning to have second thoughts about competing exclusively on the diamond. Suddenly he started to refocus on football. In September 1915, Indiana University hired Thorpe as the first assistant football coach to head Coach Clarence C. Childs, formerly of Yale. It was agreed that Thorpe would report as soon as the baseball season came to an end and take over in charge of the team's backfield and kickers.

Indiana finished the 1915 football season with a record of 3–3–1. With Thorpe coaching the backfield, Indiana walloped Miami (Ohio), 41–0, before losing to the University of Chicago the following week, 13–7. In practice, Thorpe would kick off for the freshman team vs. the varsity.

But just booting the ball in practice was simply not enough contact for the former All-American. So Jim Thorpe returned to football as an active player, joining the Pine Village team in Indiana. The Pine Village team had been organized by a small western Indiana livestock and poultry dealer, Chris Rhode.

On November 25, 1915, at Lafayette, Thorpe helped Pine Village defeat the University All-Stars, 20–0. In the game Thorpe broke free for a 55-yard run and punted the ball 80 yards. He was paid $250 for the game, and being on the gridiron felt like an enormous homecoming.

13

Thorpe Plays for the Canton Bulldogs

While Jim Thorpe was coaching and playing football in Indiana during the fall of 1915, in Canton, Ohio, a businessman and sports promoter named Jack Cusack was advancing the fledgling sport of professional football.

The first professional football player is thought to be "Pudge" Heffelfinger of Yale, who was paid $500 to play a game for the Allegheny Athletic Association in 1892. Three years later Heffelfinger, along with three other players, were paid twice their railroad fare by the Allegheny club to play a game against another Pittsburgh team. Heffelfinger scored all the points in that game as Allegheny won, 6–0.

So it was that between 1892 and 1906, professional football had its roots in Pennsylvania cities such as Pittsburgh, Latrobe and Greensburg. Also to a lesser degree football was being played in New York cities such as Syracuse, Watertown and Ogdensburg. However, by 1904 most of the clubs had folded.

But the game found a new home in Ohio in cities such as Canton, Massillon and Akron. In the early 1900s all Canton closed when the Canton Athletic Club played. In 1906 the Canton AC became the Canton Bulldogs. Betting on the games was very popular. According to Max Ozner, a tackle on the 1905 Canton AC, "one fellow lost his barber shop betting on the team."[1]

Professional football would have a rocky start in the Buckeye State. A fierce rivalry had developed between teams from Canton and Massillon, two little eastern Ohio cities about 12 miles apart. The Massillon Tigers got their name when Ed Steward, who worked for the Massillon *Independent* newspaper, went to Princeton College, purchased all of the football team's used black and orange stripped jerseys, brought them back to Massillon and outfitted the local team in them.

Canton and Massillon had played a series of exciting, but brutal contests in the early 1900s with the Tigers usually prevailing. Then a scandal occurred in one of two 1906 games that would jeopardize the growth of professional football for nearly a decade.

The second game between Canton and Massillon in 1906 was won by the Massillon Tigers, 12–6. Immediately following the game, charges of crooked play were alleged by the Massillon *Independent*. The paper charged that Canton coach and captain Blondy Wallace had attempted to fix the game with some of the Massillon players and its coach, S. H. Wrightman, offering him $4,000 to permit Canton to win. Wallace filed a $25,000 libel suit against the paper that was later dropped. But it was a fact that prior to the game several players had been induced by higher pay to quit the Massillon Tigers and join the Canton Bulldogs. Later it was alleged that a Massillon player, Walter East, had lined up John T. Windsor, an Akron businessman, to bankroll the fix. In Canton the amount of money bet on the game was huge and the Bulldogs' loss caused considerable unrest among their fans. Even today a cloud hangs low over the outcome of that game in Canton.

As a result, football in Canton and Massillon reverted back to club or sandlot status for several years with intra-city games and occasional road contests to cities like Akron and Salem. Players were paid by passing the hat and dividing the take at the end of the season.

In 1912 another professional team was organized in Canton and games were played at League Park in that city, located at the top of the hill at the east end of Meyers Lake. That same year, although there was no official league, teams were organized in Cleveland, Toledo, Columbus, Cincinnati, Shelby and Elyria in Ohio and Pittsburgh in Pennsylvania. Soon other teams would be organized in Salem, Youngstown and Dayton in Ohio, and in Detroit, Michigan. Most of the teams were made up of local players without college experience. It soon became apparent that the teams with the most former college players won the most games. But former college players demanded more money than the locals, so a salary system was introduced, replacing the profit split from the games.

By 1914, the game was beginning to become moderately profitable with games between Canton and Akron drawing about 2,500 fans at 50 cents per admission. The game now showed enough interest that in Canton a local brewer, J. J. Foley, arranged for a bank to set up a $10,000 line of credit for Jack Cusack, the Canton Bulldogs' part-time secretary-treasurer.

Cusack knew that the most important factor in promoting professional football was the creation of rivalries. So it followed that the Canton team needed Massillon back in the game. There was some hope of resurrecting the Massillon team in the summer of 1914 when Cusack met with the Massillon Chamber of Commerce. However, he was disappointed to learn that the plans for introducing a new Massillon team included raiding the Akron Indians team for players. Cusack was appalled, reminding the Chamber that that was exactly how the troubles had begun in 1906. Furthermore he told the Chamber that Canton would refuse to play any team from Massillon under those conditions, despite the fact that he knew how profitable a game between the two teams would be. However the whole matter would become moot when Massillon decided not to organize a team for 1914.

It was during the 1914 season that the reality of how rough a game football was became apparent when a local young man from Canton, Harry Turner, who played center for the Bulldogs, died of injuries he suffered in a game with Akron. In making a tackle, Turner fractured his back and completely severed his spinal cord.

The following year, Jack Cusack was given a choice by his full-time employer, the East Ohio Gas Company, a subsidiary of the Standard Oil Company of New Jersey; either work for the gas company or pursue a career in professional football. Cusack chose the latter. It would follow that in the 1915 season, professional football would become a permanent fixture on the American sports scene.

In 1915 Massillon fielded a team and agreed to recruiting principles. Consequently, Jack Cusack knew that Canton would have to field the most powerful team possible. To that end, Cusack attempted to recruit almost every former college All-American he could locate by mail or in person. At the time, college football had a monopoly on the sport of football and boldly opposed the introduction of professional football. So a lot of former college players were reluctant to join professional teams, both out of allegiance to their alma maters and a belief that playing professional football would taint their college gridiron legacies. Nonetheless Jack Cusack was able to recruit several former college players who demanded that they play under assumed names. This included some college coaches who feared losing their jobs. Some of the former college players did use their own names such as Bill Gardner, a tackle from Carlisle, and Hube Wagner, an All-American end from Pitt.

Cusack was also able to sign Earle "Greasy" Neale (using an assumed name) who had been an outstanding college defensive end and was currently coaching at West Virginia Wesleyan. In 1916 Neale began an eight-year career in the major leagues, playing for the Cincinnati Reds and Philadelphia Phillies. Neale would also continue playing professional football in the off-season during his major league career and later would become the head coach of the Philadelphia Eagles in the NFL. In 1973 Greasy Neale was elected to the Professional Football Hall of Fame.

The 1915 Canton Bulldogs began their season with a 75–0 win over a team from Wheeling, West Virginia. Then they beat the Columbus Panhandles, 7–0. However, in their next game they were beaten by the Detroit Heralds, 9–3, on the road. The following week Canton defeated the Cincinnati Celts, 41–12, a team made up primarily of former college stars. Then on November 8, the Canton Bulldogs defeated the Altoona Indians, 38–0. Altoona was comprised of many former Carlisle Indians players.

Now waiting for the Canton Bulldogs were the newly organized Massillon Tigers. Jack Cusack knew how popular the reprised rivalry would be between Canton and Massillon, so he arranged for two games with the Tigers on the 1915 schedule.

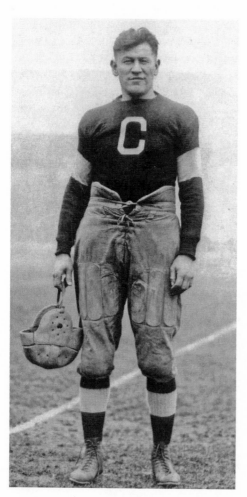

Jim Thorpe — Canton Bulldogs.

Then Jack Cusack showed his brilliance as a promoter. He contacted Jim Thorpe in Indiana and signed him just in time for the first game with Massillon. Cusack sent Thorpe's old Carlisle teammate Bill Gardner to Indiana to talk with him. Cusack offered to pay Thorpe $250 a game to play in the two upcoming games with Massillon, the same amount he had been paid earlier in the fall by the Pine Village team in Indiana. While Thorpe agreed, some of Cusack's business advisers were anxious, feeling that $250 a game was an outrageous sum and could lead the Bulldogs into bankruptcy. However, Cusack was convinced that Jim Thorpe was considered a living legend in football and his appearance on the field would increase attendance dramatically, thereby offsetting his pay.

Cusack's business instincts were correct. The Bulldogs had been averaging about 1,200 fans during the 1915 season. With

Thorpe as an attraction, attendance at Massillon and Canton for the next two games increased to about 6,500 and 8,000, respectively.

The 1915 Canton vs. Massillon games were the stuff of legends. Most of the star-studded Massillon team of former collegians played under assumed names. However one who did not was the Tigers' left end, Knute Rockne of Notre Dame.

The first game played at Massillon was won by the Tigers, 16–0. The game was played on a slippery field that prevented Jim Thorpe from scoring a touchdown. After breaking through the Massillon line in the second period, Thorpe was on his way to the goal line, with only Massillon quarterback Gus Dorias (Rockne's Notre Dame teammate) in close pursuit, when he slipped and went out of bounds on the 8-yard line. Later after running around Rockne at left end, Thorpe slipped again with a clear field in front of him. Led by the drop-kicking of Gus Dorias and a touchdown plunge by fullback Edward Hanley (Western Reserve), Massillon continued their domination over Canton on the gridiron.

To beef up the Bulldogs line for the second game at Canton, Jack Cusack signed a trio of former college linemen, Robert Burke, an All-American tackle from Wisconsin, E. C. Able, an All-American tackle from Cornell, and Charlie Smith, a tackle from the Michigan Aggies. Charlie Smith is believed to be the first African American to play professional football. Then Jim Thorpe was appointed team captain.

On game day, November 29, 1915, League Park in Canton was packed with 8,000 fans. Cusack, not wanting to lose any potential gate receipts, sold standing room tickets in the end zones. So ground rules were established that Massillon agreed to, stating that "any player crossing the goal line into the crowd must be in possession of the ball when he emerged from the crowd."[2] At the game's end fate would shine favorably on the Bulldogs as they would benefit from the ground rules.

The game was won by Canton, 6–0, as Jim Thorpe kicked two field goals for the winning margin. His first was a drop-kick from the 18-yard line and the second was kicked from placement on the 45-yard line. Canton entered the fourth quarter with a 6–0 lead, but then the Massillon passing attack led by Tigers quarterback Gus Dorias began to click. Bulldogs tackle E. H. Abel seemed to be slowing down considerably. He was suffering from a heavy cold and tired. When Thorpe, as the Bulldogs captain, did call for a replacement, Abel was replaced by Charlie Smith. Apparently, Thorpe had reservations about replacing Abel because he had been an All-American tackle.

With only a few minutes left in the game, Gus Dorias hit his right end Briggs with a pass on the Canton 15-yard line and he raced across the goal line into the "Standing Room Only" crowd in the end zone. Apparently Briggs fumbled, or at least that is what everyone thought, as the ball popped out of his hands in the end zone into the hands of Charlie Smith. The referee, mindful of the ground rules that had been established before the game, ruled the play a touchback. Briggs argued that the ball had been kicked out of his hands by a uniformed policeman. Briggs insisted he saw the brass buttons on the officer's coat. There was just one problem; Canton did not have a uniformed police force in 1915.

The Canton vs. Massillon game had been billed as the championship game for the so-called Ohio League, so emotions ran high among the fans. Had the referee allowed Briggs' touchdown to stand, the score would have been 6–6, putting the Tigers in a position to capture the championship. With about three minutes left in the game, the fans decided to take matters into their own hands. Thousands of Massillon and Canton fans stormed through the fences surrounding the players' area and raced onto the field. The Massillon fans were vehemently protesting the referee's decision and the Canton fans were adamantly defending it. The officials were unable to clear the field and called the game.

Following the game, Jack Cusack was offered a side bet of $10,000 to play a third game against Massillon. But Cusack turned down the bet. "Sunday night a side bet of $10,000 was shoved in my face for another game, with the same men as we used Sunday," said Cusack. "But I'm through for this year."[3]

About ten years after the 1915 Canton vs. Massillon game Cusack, who had left Ohio to work in the oil industry in Oklahoma, returned to Canton for a visit. He was riding on a streetcar in Canton when a conductor wearing a brass-buttoned coat that he had known sat down beside him and began to reminisce about the glory days of Canton Bulldogs football. The conductor told Cusack that when Briggs had plunged across the goal line in the second 1915 Canton vs. Massillon game, he had fallen in the end zone right in front of him. So he kicked the ball out of Briggs' hands and into the arms of Charlie Smith. When Cusack asked him why he had done it, the conductor replied, "I had 30 dollars bet on that game and, at my salary, I couldn't afford to lose that much money."[4]

For years after, Knute Rockne, the Massillon Tigers left end, would talk about the second Canton vs. Massillon game in 1915 at many banquets and in particular his epic encounter with Jim Thorpe in the game.

Rockne would tell how he had thrown Thorpe for a loss. Thorpe then rose to his feet and said, "You shouldn't do that, Sonny. All these people came to watch old Jim run." On the next play, Rockne, confident that he could stop Thorpe again, crashed into him, only to be leveled by his shoulder and momentarily knocked out. As a dazed Rockne rose to his feet, Thorpe had traveled 40 yards downfield for a touchdown. As Thorpe came back up field towards Rockne, he shouted, "That's good, Sonny, you let old Jim run."[5]

Of course there is a bit of the Rockne Notre Dame blarney in his story; Jim Thorpe did not score a touchdown in either of the Canton vs. Massillon games. Furthermore, the fact that Thorpe had knocked out Rockne by hitting him with his shoulder just added grist to the mill for a rumor that his shoulder pads were made of sheet metal or cast iron. Of course the insinuation was completely false. The only metal in Thorpe's shoulder pads was just a small bit in the interior ribbing to hold the layers of felt padding in place. The pads were constructed of hard sole leather that was riveted together. In fact, Jack Cusack and Thorpe had plans to market the pads, but a manufacturer they approached was wary of them, concerned that they might be classed as illegal. So they abandoned the project.

Knute Rockne (Sports Story Reprints).

By 1916 Jim Thorpe was receiving paychecks from playing both professional baseball and football. The U.S. Government took notice, declared Thorpe self-supporting and began to tax him. Up until this time Thorpe had been rated a "ward of the government."

At spring training at Marlin, Texas, in March of 1916, John McGraw became convinced more than ever that Jim Thorpe could not hit a curve ball. So McGraw thought it might help if he had Thorpe experiment with batting left-handed. The experiment quickly faded. On April 1, before the 1916 season started, McGraw sent Thorpe back to the minor leagues, under an option agreement with the Milwaukee Brewers.

Regardless of Thorpe's difficulty during spring training in convincing John McGraw that he could hit the curve ball, an incident coming north on train from Marlin sealed his fate for the season. Thorpe got drunk on the train and as he came ricocheting down the corridor of the Pullman car he found his favorite wrestling partner, pitcher Jeff Tesreau, about to climb into his overhead bunk. All at once, Thorpe picked up Tesreau and heaved him into his bunk, bruising his pitching arm. It was the second time that Thorpe had injured the pitcher. Although McGraw fined Thorpe $500 for the incident, he came to a decision that he would have a more disciplined ball club without him and shipped him to AAA ball in Milwaukee.

Going to Milwaukee was perhaps the best thing that had happened to Jim Thorpe in his professional baseball career. Playing almost every day in 143 games for the Brewers in the summer of 1916, Thorpe had a fine season, hitting .274 with 157 hits including 10 home runs. He also stole 48 bases to lead the American Association. However, Thorpe still had the habit of swinging at almost every pitch, so he also led the league in strikeouts.

It was still the deadball era in baseball in 1916, and Thorpe's 10 home runs in the season were a noticeable accomplishment. In fact, only four players hit more home runs that season in the major leagues. Dave Robertson of the Giants led the National League with 12 home runs and Wally Pipp of the Yankees led the American League with 12. The Giants had retained an option on Thorpe. John McGraw was pleased with the season Thorpe had in Milwaukee, so he told him to report to Marlin for spring training in 1917.

As for John McGraw's Giants in the 1916 pennant race, they got off to an inconsistent start, losing eight straight at home, followed by winning 17 straight on the road. McGraw believed that to compete for the pennant he would have to rebuild the Giants infield. By May he was once again attempting to get the Reds to trade third baseman Heinie Groh back to the Giants and looking to get rid of Bill McKechnie, who was playing the hot corner.

On July 20, McGraw arranged a deal with the Reds, but it did not include Groh. The Giants traded Christy Mathewson, Bill McKecknie and Edd Roush for all-around infielder Buck Herzog and outfielder Red Killefer. Also on August 20, the Giants traded first baseman Fred Merkle to Brooklyn for catcher Lew McCarty.

Finally, on August 28, the Giants traded second baseman Larry Doyle to the Chicago Cubs for third baseman Heinie Zimmerman and shortstop Mickey Doolan. So as McGraw could not pry the Heinie he wanted (Groh), away from Garry Herrrmann in Cincinnati, he had to settle for the Heinie (Zimmerman) that he could get at third base.

With McGraw's rebuilt infield in place, in September the Giants would win a record 26 games in a row at home, before losing to Boston on September 30. However the Giants still finished the season in fourth place, seven games behind pennant-winning Brooklyn.

For McGraw, trading Mathewson to the Reds was difficult. McGraw told the press that Mathewson was not only the greatest pitcher he had ever seen, but he was also his friend. But by 1916 Mathewson was showing strong signs of slowing down. In fact Mathewson knew that his days as a dominant pitcher were over. The Cincinnati Reds were less interested in having Mathewson pitch then in having him manage the team, and McGraw thought it would be a great opportunity for him.

However, almost immediately the trade of Edd Roush would turn out to be another blunder by McGraw. Roush would blossom into one of the best outfielders in the major leagues and win two National League batting championships, beginning the next year in 1917 with a .341 average. Roush led the Reds to the 1919 NL pennant while winning his second NL batting crown with an average of .321. Roush played 18 years in the major leagues, finished with a .323 lifetime batting average and was elected to the National Baseball Hall of Fame in 1962. Nonetheless, McGraw with his rebuilt infield would win the 1917 National League pennant.

For Jim Thorpe, the trade of Mathewson, McKecknie and Roush to the Reds would eventually lead to an opportunity for him to play in the major leagues again during the 1917 season.

In the fall of 1916, Jim Thorpe began playing professional football fulltime for the Canton Bulldogs. As soon as the American Association schedule was completed, Thorpe reported to Canton and suited up for the Bulldogs.

Jack Cusack had built a powerhouse team in Canton for the 1916 season. Among those recruited by Cusack was former Georgetown All-American halfback Harry Costello, who besides being great at running the ball was also a skilled passer and drop kicker. Also Cusack had four former college All-Americans sitting on his bench as reserves. The Canton line averaged 213 pounds and overall team weight averaged around 200.

In the first ten games of the 1916 season, Canton allowed only seven points to the opposition. The first Canton victory came on October 2, 23–0 over the Altoona Indians. Then the Bulldogs beat Pitcairn, 7–0, a very good team from Pennsylvania. Just prior to the game with the Buffalo All-Stars, Dr. Hube Wagner left the Bulldogs to devote more time to his medical practice. Wagner was replaced by end Ernie Soucy of Harvard, another All-American, and the Bulldogs swamped the Buffalo All-Stars, 77–0. The Buffalo game was the first game that Jim Thorpe played in for Canton following the baseball season. With 254-pound former Wisconsin All-American tackle Howard Buck playing left tackle, Canton clobbered the New York All-Stars, 76–0. On November 5, 1916, Canton defeated the Cleveland Indians football team, 27–0, as Thorpe tore off on a thrilling 71-yard run after catching a punt.

By late November, with the Bulldogs undefeated, another classic confrontation arrived with a two-game series between Canton and Massillon for the 1916 championship of professional football.

The first game was played at Massillon on November 27 with the Canton Bulldogs the favorites of the odds makers by 3–5. On a day when the weather was cool and a wind whipped across a muddy field, 10,000 fans witnessed a hard-fought 0–0 tie between the Bulldogs and Tigers. So the second game scheduled for December 3 at Canton's League Park took on new meaning.

Once again 10,000 fans packed the stands for the second clash between the Bulldogs and Tigers, and the weather and playing field were hardly any better than in the first game at Massillon. But a pugnacious Canton defense prevented Massillon from ever getting past the 30-yard line as the Bulldogs defeated the Tigers 24–0.

The Bulldogs' first score came in the first quarter when center Ralph "Fat" Waldsmith of the University of Akron scooped up a fumbled punt return and ran 15 yards unchallenged into the end zone.

One of Jim Thorpe's former teammates at Carlisle, fullback Pete Calac, played a determined game and bulled his way through the husky Massillon defensive line for a touchdown in the second quarter to give Canton a 12–0 halftime lead. Early in the fourth quarter, left end Ernie Soucy caught a 15-yard pass from quarterback Milton Ghee to make the score Canton 18, Massillon 0. Then, late in the fourth quarter, Thorpe scored Canton's final touchdown with a plunge from the 3-yard line.

The 24–0 final score only showed half the reality of how badly Canton had dominated Massillon. The game statistics were remarkable in their clarity.

	Canton	Massillon
Forward passes attempted	14	16
Forward passes completed	3	5
Yards gained on forward passes	63	38
Attempts to advance by rushing	39	26
Yards gained by rushing	175	54
Number of punts	5	6
Distance covered by punts — yards	159	217

	Canton	*Massillon*
Penalties inflicted on, yards	96	30
First downs	10	5

Robert Nash, the big Massillon tackle from Rutgers, said in regard to the Bulldogs line following the game, "It was the most powerful line I ever played against. We couldn't stand against it, for the charge of the Canton line simply carried us out of the way. If we resisted, we were lifted bodily out of the path of the man with the ball, shoved aside like a bag of flour."[6]

While all of Canton celebrated the following day, the *Evening Repository* reported, "After a decade and a half and oft-time costly effort, Canton at last can boast the professional football championship of the country; which also means the world and Massillon. The Bulldogs of 1916, assembled and whipped into shape by the great Jim Thorpe, battled their way to the crown Sunday afternoon at League park, crushing the Massillon Tigers 24–0 in a struggle that bubbled over with Canton superiority. It was the first real triumph of the red and white over the orange and black in all the years of striving. And it was worth waiting for, this complete annihilation of the Tiger hopes."[7]

Betting on the 1916 game had been sparse because most of the Canton fans were leery of the jinx that had seemed to plague the Bulldogs in past Massillon games. However, Jim Thorpe had no fear of placing a wager on his team. Prior to the game Jim Thorpe had encountered a Massillon fan in the lobby of the Courtland Hotel telling all that the Canton Bulldogs had no chance against the Massillon Tigers. Thorpe approached the man and asked him if he wanted to back up his words with a bet on the game. Thorpe suggested a bet of $2,500 and the boastful Massillon fan covered it.

14

McGraw Loans Thorpe to the Cincinnati Reds

The 1917 major league baseball season was scheduled to start in less than a week when President Woodrow Wilson signed a joint resolution adopted by Congress declaring war on Germany. The Selective Service Act required that all males from 21 to 30 years of age report to their election precinct polling places to register for the draft during June. Jim Thorpe, although not a voter, registered for the draft, but he listed his age as four years older, making him appear 33 years old, rather than 29.

After playing professional football for the past two seasons, Jim Thorpe had reached a crossroad in his athletic career. He was now firmly established as a star in the young and growing sport of professional football. Also he was in demand as a coach. Furthermore, he had wisely used a portion of the money from his multi-year contract with the New York Giants to purchase a good-sized farm in Oklahoma. Jim Thorpe did not need baseball. But baseball wasn't sure that it didn't need him. So as the 1917 baseball season began, the New York Giants exercised their option on Thorpe and invited him to spring training camp in Marlin, Texas.

On April 24, 1917, one of the most unusual deals ever in major league baseball took place. Unofficially Jim Thorpe was sold by the New York Giants to the Cincinnati Reds for the regular waiver price of $1,500. But the fact of the matter was that Thorpe was only being loaned to the Reds.

Centerfielder Edd Roush, the Reds' best hitter, was injured. Leftfielder Tom Griffith had a sore arm. That left the Reds with two other outfielders, Greasy Neale and Manuel Cueto, a Cuban who was hitting below .200. Reds manager Christy Mathewson desperately needed an extra outfielder. So Matty placed a distress call to John McGraw. As a courtesy to his good friend, McGraw agreed to send Jim Thorpe to the Reds for cash with the stipulation that the Giants would retain the privilege of recalling him should Cincinnati decide to release him. While the deal was unprecedented in baseball history, the other National League owners signed off on it.

Harry N. Hempstead, the president of the Giants, sent the following letter to Garry Herrmann, president of the Reds, detailing the terms of the Thorpe deal.

> Apr. 24, 1917
> Mr. August Herrmann,
> Cincinnati, O.
> My dear Mr. Herrmann:
>   This will advise you that the services of Player Jim Thorpe have been released to the Cincinnati Base Ball Club in accordance with the telegram from you to Mgr. McGraw. The New York Base Ball Club is to have first call on the services of Thorpe at any time the Cincinnati Club may desire to release him. We have paid the Player up to and including Apr. 23, 1917 at the full rate of his contract which I am enclosing to you. There will be due us a sum for railroad transportation from here to Cincinnati, the amount of which we will apprise you later.
>   Sincerely yours,
>   H.N. Hempstead
>   P.S. The purchase price as we understand it is $1500.00 the regular major league waiver price. Please remit to this office.[1]

In New York, John McGraw was publicly stating to the press that he was sorry to see Jim Thorpe go and believed that he would eventually turn into a good ball player. Privately McGraw was continuing to say that Thorpe couldn't hit a curve ball. Also, despite his speed on the base paths and in the field, McGraw had concerns that Thorpe had trouble judging long-hit fly balls. Still, for some reason, John McGraw could not completely cut ties with the former Olympic champion and move on. The Reds were not the only club that still had an interest in Thorpe. Barney Dreyfuss would have gladly taken him off McGraw's hands, but unlike the loan to the Reds, the Pirates would have wanted Thorpe outright.

In Cincinnati, Thorpe was joining Earle "Greasy" Neale, who had played professional football in the off-season with Thorpe as an end on the Canton Bulldogs in 1915. Both Thorpe and Neale, marginal major league baseball players, would eventually be enshrined in the Pro Football Hall of Fame. With Roush out of the lineup, Mathewson moved Greasy Neale to center field and Tommy Griffith to right. Although Griffith had been doing very good job with the bat, he had recently been bothered with a sore arm and couldn't throw.

The deal appeared to be a good one for Jim Thorpe. People in Ohio were familiar with Thorpe's heroics as a member of the Canton Bulldogs in the 1916 football season and they welcomed him with open arms in Cincinnati. However, the Cincinnati *Commercial Tribune* couldn't resist insulting Thorpe and wrote about his acquisition, "The aborigine comes for a purely cash consideration."[2]

With Jim Thorpe on his way to Cincinnati, Manuel Cueto came to the conclusion that he was about to become the odd man out in Christy Mathewson's outfield. Starting in the outfield against the Chicago Cubs the day before Thorpe arrived in Cincinnati, Cueto suddenly found his stroke and went 2-for-4 with a single and home run.

On April 24, 1917, Jim Thorpe played his first game for the Cincinnati Reds, starting in right field. It was not exactly a brilliant debut. Thorpe was still experimenting with switch-hitting and went 1-for-4, an infield single, as the Reds lost to the Cubs, 8–4. Batting left-handed in his first at-bat against Al Demaree, Thorpe hit a scorching line drive into the hands of Cubs first baseman Les Mann that had triple written all over it. Thorpe also attempted to steal second and was thrown out.

Going into the top of the fourth inning, the Reds were leading, 4–2. However, two infield errors led to the Cubs scoring four runs. In the top of the sixth inning, Jim Thorpe fielded a long drive hit by his ex–Giants teammate Larry Doyle. As he drew back to make a throw to keep Rollie Zeider from taking third, the ball slipped from his grip, allowing Zeider to score. Umpire Bill Klem ruled that Thorpe did not have the ball in his possession long enough and let Doyle take second. In the end Thorpe's faux pas was inconsequential to the Reds' loss, and most observers at Redland Field were impressed with how much ground Thorpe could cover in the outfield.

On May 2, 1917, on a cold and windy day at Weeghman Park in Chicago, the Cincinnati Reds and

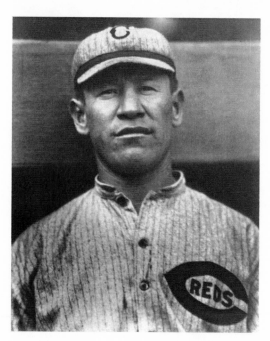

Jim Thorpe — Cincinnati Reds.

Chicago Cubs squared off in what is arguably the greatest baseball game ever played. Jim Thorpe would play a pivotal role in bringing home the winning run during a double no-hitter pitched by the Reds' 6' 6", 245-pound right-hander Fred Toney and the Cubs' 6' 4", 215-pound left-hander James "Hippo" Vaughn.

As Vaughn was a hard-throwing left-hander who threw a wicked curve, Christy Mathewson decided to start an all right-handed hitting lineup. But it had no effect as Vaughn shut down the Reds inning after inning. As the Cubs entered the bottom of the eighth, the best they had done against Toney in seven innings was for Cy Williams to draw two walks, one in the second and one in the fifth. Then banter began with the players in the Cubs dugout attempting to get the team hyped-up to score a run off Toney. When one of the Cubs yelled, "Hell, we ain't even got a hit off him,"[3] Vaughn realized that he and Toney were locked in a double no-hit game.

After nine innings Hippo Vaughn, backed up by some slick fielding by his infielders, had held the Reds hitless, allowing but one baserunner to reach second. Likewise, Fred Toney had held the Cubs hitless for nine innings, allowing only Williams to reach second. Vaughn had ten strikeouts, including fanning Jim Thorpe and Dave Shean twice. When Heinie Groh struck out with his bottle bat on his shoulder, he protested the call and was thrown out of the game. Fred Toney had only three strikeouts.

In the top of the tenth inning, with the steel stands rocking with thunder, Hippo Vaughn took the mound. Vaughn set down the first two Reds batters. Then Larry Kopf hit a clean single and advanced to third when Cy Williams dropped a fly ball hit by Hal Chase.

This brought Jim Thorpe to the plate with two outs and two men on. Hal Chase stole second unchallenged. With the count two balls and one strike, Vaughn threw a curveball to Thorpe. He hit a slow roller to the left of the mound and sped down the baseline like a deer. Vaughn seemed to become frozen. Then he scooped up the ball and threw it to catcher Art Wilson, bouncing it off his chest protector, allowing Kopf to score the only run of the game. Whether or not Vaughn would have been able to throw Thorpe out at first base is subjective. The third out came as Wilson recovered the ball in time to tag Hal Chase at home plate attempting to score behind Kopf.

In the bottom of the tenth inning Fred Toney set down the Cubs in order, striking out the last two batters he faced.

W. A. Phelon wrote in the *Cincinnati Times-Star*, "When Thorpe sent his little grounder to Vaughn, there were two outs, and it looked as if Vaughn could have wheeled and sent the ball to first ahead of the agile Injun. But, as Vaughn afterwards admitted, the play on Kopf as he ran home tempted the big pitcher and drew him astray. 'It seemed to be right in front of me,' said Hippo, 'and I thought all I had to do was to toss it in and end it all.'"[4]

Hippo Vaughn had pitched a brilliant game but lost. In the first nine innings he had faced the minimum 27 batters. Two Reds had reached first on walks and one on an error by shortstop Rollie Zeider. But two of those baserunners became outs in double plays and another was thrown out attempting to steal. In the fifth inning Jim Thorpe had come within inches of ending Vaughn's no-hitter when he hit a hard drive to left field that landed about six inches foul.

Fred Toney had previously pitched a 17-inning no-hitter in the minors on May 10, 1909, pitching for Winchester, Kentucky, against Lexington. Reds president Garry Herrmann had accompanied the team to Chicago and witnessed the game from a box behind the Cincinnati bench. Following the game Herrmann personally congratulated Toney.

Following the double no-hitter in Chicago, Jim Thorpe's little Baltimore chop deserved to become as much of the baseball folklore in the greatest game ever played as the incredible pitching of Vaughn and Toney.

On May 11, Jim Thorpe made his return to the Polo Grounds. While Thorpe got two of the Reds' four hits, Giants pitcher Ferdie Schupp spoiled his homecoming by pitching a complete game as New York won, 9–2. In the seventh inning Thorpe singled and scored on two errors and a walk. In the ninth inning Thorpe hit a line drive home run to right. Following the game, John McGraw had no comment.

In two short years, John McGraw had rebuilt the New York Giants, and on June 27, 1917, they took over first place in the National League and held it for the rest of the season. Although the Giants outfield — former Federal League star Benny Kauff in center field, Dave Robertson in right field and George Burns in left field — were all playing well, McGraw felt he needed bench strength for the stretch run. So on August 1, McGraw recalled Jim Thorpe from the Reds.

At the time, Thorpe was hitting .247 in 77 games for the Reds. Back in New York, Thorpe would once again sit on the bench, playing in only 26 games and hitting .193. In one of the few games that McGraw played Thorpe, he dropped a fly ball in the outfield.

Sitting on the Giants bench was Jimmy Smith, a veteran outfielder who would become the father-in-law of light heavyweight boxing champion Billy Conn. Smith was a pretty tough fellow too and very sure of himself. When Thorpe dropped the ball, McGraw told Smith to get in the outfield and tell Thorpe he was through for the day. However, the two-fisted Smith was reticent. He told McGraw, "No sir, Mr. McGraw, you go on out there and tell the Indian yourself."[5]

The New York Giants won the 1917 National League pennant by ten games over the second-place Philadelphia Phillies. Thorpe, by being in a Giants uniform, became eligible for a cut of the players' World Series money.

The New York Giants lost the 1917 World Series to the Chicago White Sox, four games to two. Jim Thorpe would become a tragic figure in the 1917 World Series, suffering a deep humiliation in game five. The series was tied at two games each. For game five John McGraw inserted Thorpe in right field, batting sixth. But in the top of the first inning, McGraw removed him. After the Giants quickly scored two runs, the White Sox replaced starting pitcher Reb Russell, a left-hander, with right-hander Eddie Cicotte. With Thorpe coming up to bat, McGraw sent left-handed hitting Dave Robertson up to pinch-hit for him. Consequently, Jim Thorpe would never get one at-bat in the Series and never have another chance to play in the World Series. In fairness to Dave Robertson, he played in all six games of the series and hit .500 (11–22).

Hall of Fame outfielder Edd Roush, who played with Jim Thorpe on the Reds in 1917, said Thorpe was a good ball player, but just couldn't hit right-handed pitching and couldn't hit curve balls. Roush was quick to add that Thorpe was fast in the outfield. He said Thorpe could outrun a deer. In fact, Roush was a pretty fast runner himself and stole 268 bases in his 18-year major league career. According to Roush, Thorpe had a long stride in the outfield. If you don't have a long stride, your head bobs up and down too much and it makes it hard to follow the flight of the ball. Thorpe would take only two strides to Roush's three. Roush would run just as fast as he could, but Thorpe would keep up with him by just trotting along. Roush asked Thorpe if anyone in the Olympic Games ever made him run his best. Thorpe replied that he never saw a man that he couldn't look back at.

Following the 1917 World Series, Jim Thorpe once again joined the Canton Bulldogs. Although professional football was growing in popularity, as a result of the United States' involvement in World War One, it would struggle in the 1917 season. A lot of players were serving in the armed services and attendance was down. Despite the burden of the country being at war, Canton still fielded a very formidable squad. Leading up to the first game with arch-rival Massillon, the Bulldogs won seven straight games, outscoring their opponents, 217–7.

Attendance was down at the Bulldogs games, but many historians believe that the war was not the only reason for the sag in attendance at Canton. There is also the notion that Jack Cusack may have been responsible in part because his 1916 Bulldogs team was so overpowering that Canton fans were so confident about winning every game, except those against very strong teams such as Massillon, that they stayed home and read the games' results in the newspaper.

Following the Canton Bulldogs' 49–0 shellacking of the Rochester Jeffersons, Leo Lyons, the Rochester coach, was walking off the field with Jim Thorpe. He told Thorpe, "You know Jim, some day this game will draw like professional baseball. We should form a league."[6]

There had recently been some talk among major league baseball magnates about starting a professional football league. However, when Connie Mack of the Philadelphia Athletics and Barney Dreyfuss of the Pittsburgh Pirates informed the owners of the huge losses they had suffered when they attempted to form a pro football league in 1902, the idea was quickly scrapped.

For the 1917 season, the Massillon Tigers signed Harvard All-American Charlie Brickley, a great drop-kicker, and named him team captain. The Canton Bulldogs had re-signed former Dartmouth All-American quarterback Milt Ghee, possibly the best pro quarterback of his era. During the 1917 season Ghee would throw 17 touchdown passes, an incredible number for the era.

The first of the two Canton vs. Massillon games was played on November 26, before 6,000 fans at Massillon. Brickley decided to start a Tigers line of smaller Ivy League players, believing that the added speed would help the Tigers. This would be a huge mistake for Massillon. At a time when professional teams had very little time to practice together, the Massillon Tigers were always changing their lineup. So they never had the cohesiveness that existed on the Canton Bulldogs. Jack Cusack, on the other hand, believed in teamwork and developed a core starting lineup that included Jim Thorpe, Greasy Neale, Eugene "Horse" Edwards, Pete Calac, Milt Ghee, Ralph "Fat" Waldsmith, Fred Sefton, Pat Dunn, John Kellison and others. While some of Cusack's players would not arrive at the field until the morning of the game, just in time to do a run-through of the plays, they still had the advantage of game experience with the same players.

As a result, on the first Canton possession of the game, the Bulldogs drove the ball straight downfield 77 yards, culminating with Jim Thorpe going over the goal line for a touchdown. While the Tigers began substituting their bigger lineman, it was too late. Canton was victorious in the first contest, 14–3. The victory was cause for Canton to declare itself the Ohio Champion.

However, in order for Canton to claim the U.S. Championship, they next had to play the Detroit Heralds at Navin Field on Thanksgiving Day. The Heralds were the Michigan Champions and had already beaten three Ohio teams: the Cincinnati Celts, Toledo Maroons and Columbus Panhandles. In addition they had annihilated the All-Buffalos from New York and easily whipped two Indian teams. The Heralds' only loss of the season was to the Camp Custer service team.

The key for Canton in defeating Detroit was to stop their fast and powerful halfback Norb Stacksteder, formerly of the Dayton Triangles, who had made more than a half-dozen breakaway end runs for touchdowns during the season.

With 8,000 fans in the stands on Thanksgiving Day, the Canton Bulldogs held Stacksteder in the first quarter and the period ended with the score 0–0. Jim Thorpe entered the game in the second quarter. After being stopped for a one-yard loss in his first attempt to run the ball, from that point on, Thorpe and Pete Calac began hitting the Detroit line and drove the ball downfield 70 yards. Then Milt Ghee hit Greasy Neale with a short pass for the touchdown. The Bulldogs drive delivered the only points of the game as the second half turned into a defensive battle, with Canton winning the game, 7–0.

The second Massillon game was played at Canton on December 3. Perhaps the Canton Bulldogs were still exhausted from the difficult game they had with the Detroit Heralds, or they were over-confident, or perhaps the old Massillon hex had returned. Nonetheless it was the Bulldogs' third game in eight days and the game turned out to be a defensive battle with the Massillon Tigers prevailing, 6–0. Massillon won the game on two field goals by former Notre Dame standout Stan Cofall. Although Jim Thorpe was injured in the second quarter as a result of some unsportsmanlike conduct by Cofall, he continued to play the entire game despite limping.

According to Pete Calac, Jim Thorpe's teammate on the both the Carlisle Indians and the Canton Bulldogs, "Pro football in the days of Jim Thorpe wasn't as clean as it is now — and it was a lot dirtier than the college games of that time. Jim was equally as good in college and the pros. But the dirtier the football got, the meaner Jim got. The pros would gouge your eyes, knee you on every play and just outright slug you time and again. With Jim they would just pile on. But he wore longer cleats and when they got him on his back, he would double up and start kicking his way out of the pile."[7]

15

Thorpe's Major League Career Ends

As the 1918 major league baseball season began Jim Thorpe found himself once again in his familiar place on the New York Giants bench. The World War would force an early end to the season on September 2. The war had taken a toll on the Giants roster. Star center fielder Benny Kauff played only 67 games before being drafted. Pitchers Rube Benton and George Kelly had enlisted, while Jeff Tesreau and Walter Holke left baseball to work in the war industries. Still McGraw refused to play Thorpe on a daily basis, preferring to use rookie Ross Youngs in right field.

By June 3, the Chicago Cubs moved into first place and remained there. On July 10, McGraw inserted Jim Thorpe into the lineup in Chicago and he had a fine day. In the sixth inning Thorpe hit a triple off Chicago starter Hippo Vaughn, driving home a run. In the eighth inning he hit a hard drive that was knocked down by Vaughn, who threw wildly to first. Then in the tenth inning, Thorpe hit a home run off Phil Douglas to give the Giants a 7–6 victory. Thorpe scored three runs in the game.

The next day, July 11, Thorpe singled in a run for the Giants in a 9–4 win at Pittsburgh. Thorpe came into the game in the fourth inning when Ross Youngs injured his foot. However, the following day Thorpe was back on the bench as Ross Youngs returned to the lineup. Thorpe was showing that he could play if had the opportunity. On July 24, in a 10–2 Giants loss to St. Louis Cardinals, Thorpe got two of the Giants' four hits. In the game played at the Polo Grounds future Hall of Fame pitcher Waite Hoyt made his debut in relief, striking out two of the three batters he faced.

Jim Thorpe finished the abbreviated 1918 season hitting .248 with 28 hits in 113 at bats. His slugging average was .381 which compared favorably with the Giants' starting outfielders, Ross Youngs (SA .376, BA .302), Benny Kauff (SA .437, BA .315) and George Burns (SA .389, BA .290).

On September 18, two weeks after the major league season ended, the

Carlisle Indian School was closed by the United States Army. The buildings were turned into a hospital for disabled veterans of the World War. From 1879 to 1918, 8,858 Indian students from 140 tribes had gone through Carlisle. The glory days of Carlisle Indian football had long passed and the team had not had a winning season since 1913. The last of the Carlisle football teams, the 1917 squad, finished with a record of 3–6–0 and was unable to score on any of the major college teams on its schedule, losing to West Virginia, 21–0, Navy, 62–0, Bucknell, 10–0, Army, 28–0, Georgia Tech, 98–0 and Pennsylvania, 26–0.

Between January 1918 and January 1919, the great influenza pandemic struck. World-wide the flu was responsible for 21.5 million deaths, including 675,000 Americans. It was also during 1918 that Jim Thorpe's four-year-old son, James Francis, Jr., died of complications associated with infantile paralysis. Al Schacht said that in spring training in 1917, Thorpe had brought his wife and son to Texas. After practice the three of them would sit out on the lawn in front of the hotel and Jim would play with his son. Schacht said he had never seen Thorpe happier. However, after the death of his first-born son, he never seemed the same.

Jim Thorpe would also have three daughters by his marriage to his first wife Iva — Gale, Charlotte and Frances.

In the fall of 1918 the World War continued to take so many players into the armed services that most of the well-known professional football teams such as Canton, Massillon and others decided to forgo the season. Still there was professional football in 1918. Although teams such as the Dayton Triangles, Detroit Heralds and Wabash Indians had also lost many of their players to the service, they were able to keep a lot of the others working in industries deemed essential, and played a full schedule. The Dayton Triangles, under former Canton star Earle "Greasy" Neale, who was the team's coach and star running back, finished with a 9–0 record and were acknowledged as the 1918 champions of professional football.

On January 14, 1919, the heirs of the John T. Brush estate sold the New York Giants to Charles A. Stoneham, John McGraw and Judge Francis X. McQuade. Judge McQuade was a well-known magistrate in New York who won favor in the baseball community in 1917 when he dropped charges against John McGraw and Christy Mathewson after they attempted to play a game at the Polo Grounds on Sunday in violation of the existing law. However, the man who was about to become the new president of the Giants, Charles A. Stoneham, was a bit of a mystery man. Stoneham had lived most of his life in Jersey City, but had powerful connections with New York Tammany Hall politicians such as Al Smith and Tom Foley. Stoneham also had a small stable of good racehorses. When the press asked Stoneham why he had purchased the Giants, he simplistically stated that he had been a Giants fan his whole life and an admirer of John McGraw. For McGraw the part ownership meant that he would no longer have to yield to the power of club secretary John Foster, in whom the Brush family had vested such authority.

McGraw decided to have the Giants set up their 1919 spring training camp in Gainesville, Florida. He was still smarting over the previous season, feeling that the Giants should have won the pennant in 1918 but were prevented by the team being dismantled by the war.

As the 1919 season began, McGraw found the Giants in a tough three-way race with the Cincinnati Reds and Chicago Cubs. The Reds had six very good starting pitchers, Hod Eller, Jimmy Ring, Ray Fisher, Dutch Ruether, Dolf Luque and Slim Sallee, whom Garry Herrmann had plucked off the Giants roster on waivers before the start of the season. The defending National League Champion Chicago Cubs still had Hippo Vaughn, and their pitching staff was bolstered by the return of Grover Alexander from the service.

As the 1919 season got under way, Jim Thorpe began arguing with John McGraw about playing time. Within six weeks of the season starting, Thorpe would be packing his bags for Boston.

According to Al Schacht, who had played with Thorpe in the minors in 1915, the incident that would seal Thorpe's fate with McGraw occurred when he missed a signal while running the bases and it cost the Giants a run. When Thorpe returned to the bench he found McGraw furious. Then McGraw called Thorpe a dumb Indian. The remark so infuriated Thorpe that he began chasing McGraw all over the Polo Grounds. It took half the Giants team to stop Thorpe from assaulting McGraw. It was the end.

According to John McGraw, the reason he decided to send Jim Thorpe packing was because he was a disturbing influence on the team. Thorpe's head-strong attitude and lack of self-discipline in training began to be adopted by other players. When Thorpe was in the lineup for several days in a row, he was the center of attention with the fans and sports writers. The rest of the club was reduced to the role of hero-worshippers. Even though McGraw constantly benched Thorpe, it did little to bring about behavior modification. In fact, such actions only seemed to reinforce Thorpe's desire to flaunt his celebrity and defy McGraw. It was a bad marriage, and the time for a divorce was long overdue.

Regardless of the credibility of either of the two stories, on May 21, 1919, Jim Thorpe was traded from the New York Giants to the Boston Braves for Pat Ragan.

Replying to questions from the press about dealing away Thorpe,

McGraw said, "He has heard so often that he can't hit a right-hander's curve ball that he believes it."[1]

If indeed that was the truth and Thorpe's inability to hit a curveball was the bottom line for McGraw in giving up on him, it would follow that the Giants manager needed to shoulder some of the blame for that deficiency. In all the times that John McGraw sent Jim Thorpe down to the minor leagues while he was under his three-year contract, not once did McGraw do so with a mandate for the minor league manager to provide Thorpe with hitting instructions. Thorpe continued to rely on his own athletic instincts instead of formally learning from minor league hitting instructors how to actually hit a curve ball. Consequently each time Thorpe returned to the Giants from the minor leagues, he was the same player, with the same skills, that McGraw had sent down.

Author Frank Graham maintained that John McGraw got a lot out of his Indian ball players, Jim Thorpe and Chief Meyers. "They hadn't been easy to handle, especially Thorpe. But, within their limitations, they had given him everything."[2]

The fact that Jim Thorpe had never liked John McGraw was nothing unusual. Lots of McGraw's players detested him — Waite Hoyt, Edd Roush, Rube Marquard, Buck Herzog and many others. In fact, Buck Herzog disliked McGraw so much that he told him when he was traded back to the Giants in 1916 in the Mathewson, Roush, McKechnie trade with the Reds that he would play as hard as he could for the Giants, but there was no need for the two of them to be friends in the deal.

If you played for McGraw, known as "Little Napoleon," you liked him, simply respected him, or hated him. Fred Snodgrass played seven and a half years for McGraw and both liked and respected him. Snodgrass said that for some reason people thought that McGraw directed every move his players made on the field, that he was an absolute dictator. "Most of time we ran on our own. We used our own judgment,"[3] said Snodgrass. "McGraw allowed initiative to his men. We stole when we thought we had the jump. We played hit-and-run when we felt that was what was called for. We bunted when we thought it appropriate."[4] Snodgrass said that the formula for getting along with McGraw was very simple; he expected every player on the team to know how to play baseball. When a player didn't know how to play, that's when the trouble began.

Even with pitcher Jesse Barnes returning to the Giants from the Army and leading the National League with 25 wins, New York lost the 1919 pennant to Cincinnati. After losing two crucial doubleheaders to the Reds in August, the Giants never recovered and finished nine games behind.

Going from the Giants to the Boston Braves, Jim Thorpe would leave a club in first place for one in last place. The Braves were confident that Thorpe could deliver runs with his ability to hit sacrifice flies if nothing else. However, Thorpe's arrival in Boston did not preclude John McGraw from giving Braves manager George Stallings an unsolicited reference report on Thorpe. As a result, at first Stallings was afraid to play Thorpe even though the Braves needed outfield help.

By joining the Boston Braves Jim Thorpe became friends with another quintessential free-spirit — shortstop Rabbit Maranville. It wouldn't be long before Thorpe and Maranville would join forces in numerous episodes of mischievous merriment to the displeasure of the Braves management. Among other oddball hi-jinks Thorpe and Maranville would engage in, they would spend a night in adjoining trees pretending they were bobcats. They also found delight in tossing water bags out of hotel windows and even jumped in a pool fully dressed, attempting to catch goldfish.

Since winning the National League pennant in 1914, the Boston Braves had finished second, third, sixth and seventh in the standings. Now, in 1919, manager George Stallings was attempting to rebuild the club. Jim Thorpe was supposed to be part of that effort. However, his camaraderie with Rabbit Maranville did not endear the Braves management to him.

While playing more regularly in Boston seemed to agree with Thorpe and he started hitting, his play in the outfield was spotty. In fact, his poor play in Chicago cost the Braves a win over Hippo Vaughn. During the entire 1919 season Thorpe's future in the majors seemed to be on shaky ground. Furthermore, he was no longer the draw at the gate that he once was. On August 28, 1919, the Boston Braves informed the Seattle club of the Pacific Coast League that they were willing to trade Thorpe for pitcher Lyle Bigbee and outfielder Bill Cunningham. But Seattle turned the deal down.

On September 25, 1919, Jim Thorpe played in his last game in the major leagues, with the Boston Braves against the New York Giants. He started the first game of a doubleheader in left field, had one hit in five at-bats and also scored a run as the Giants pounded out 24 hits in 14–2 victory. Thorpe sat out the second game, won by Boston, 8–4.

One winter in the early 1950s, Jim Thorpe was making an appearance at a Sportsman Show in New York. Ted Williams, the Boston Red Sox slugger, a dedicated fisherman in the off-season, was also at the show demonstrating fly casting. Williams, who always seemed to have trouble with the press during his career, was introduced to Thorpe. Thorpe took Williams aside and told him that, since the press could either make a ballplayer miserable or help him, it was in his best interest to attempt to get along with them.

Then Thorpe digressed to his days in the big leagues, telling Williams that the writers were always insinuating that he couldn't hit a curve ball. Thorpe quickly pointed out to Williams that he had hit .327 one year. Thorpe said while that bothered him, what really bothered him more was that one writer stated in a column that he was bad for the team; he was not a team player. One day the writer who had written that came into the clubhouse. Thorpe, still upset by the article, approached the writer and told him he didn't believe accusing him of not being a team player was a very fair statement. According to Williams, Thorpe asked the writer, "What do you think you would do if somebody wrote something like that about you?" The writer replied, "Well, I guess I'd punch him in the nose." Thorpe smiled that big Indian smile and said, "So I punched him in the nose, and down he went."[5]

Although 1919 was Jim Thorpe's last season in the major leagues, it was his best year, hitting for an average of .327 (52 hits in 159 at bats — New York two games, batting average 333; Boston 60 games, batting average 327). Thorpe finished his six-year major league career with a .252 lifetime batting average.

Toward the end of the season, happiness had returned to Thorpe's life when his wife gave birth to an eight-pound daughter in Boston.

Pop Warner believed that John McGraw mishandled Thorpe. Thorpe was a workhorse and McGraw didn't work him. Other observers believed Thorpe never excelled as a major league ball player because he was a free spirit, didn't care a lot for baseball and refused to take the game or the big league cities seriously. But Thorpe played his major league career in the dead-ball era.

In fact Jim Thorpe played his entire major league career and most of his minor league career in the deadball era. It is possible that if Thorpe had begun playing after the new ball was introduced in 1920 and with more at bats, he may have become more of a power hitter.

With the introduction of a livelier ball in 1920, the number of home runs increased in both the major and minor leagues. With the livelier ball in play and more at bats, Jim Thorpe's home run production also began to increase. He hit 16 home runs playing with the AA Akron, and between 1920 and 1922 with 1528 at bats, Thorpe hit 45 home runs in the minor leagues (1 home run per 34 times at bats). In contrast, prior to 1920, Thorpe hit a total of 7 home runs in the major leagues (1913–1915, 1917–1919) with 696 career at bats (1 home run per 99 times at bats) and 3 home runs in the minor leagues (1909-1910, 1915-1916) with 1209 at bats (1 home run per 403 times at bat).

JIM THORPE'S MAJOR LEAGUE STATISTICS

Year	Team	Games	BA	SA	AB	H	HR	RBI	SB	E	FA
1913	NY N	19	.143	.229	35	5	1	2	2	1	.944
1914		30	.194	.226	31	6	0	2	1	1	.750
1915		17	.231	.327	52	12	0	1	4	2	.933
1917	2 teams CIN N (77G - .247)				NY N (26G - .193)						
Totals		103	.237	.357	308	73	4	40	12	8	.958
1918	NY N	58	.248	.381	113	28	1	11	3	1	.983
1919	2 teams NY N (2G - .333) BOS N (60G - .327)										
Totals		62	.327	.428	159	52	1	26	7	8	.918
6 years		289	.252	.362	698	176	7	82	29	21	.947

16

Post-War Professional Football

With the Great War in Europe over, as the fall of 1919 approached, entrepreneurs and sportsman alike in the United States looked forward to a rejuvenation of professional football. In Canton, Ohio, locals hoped for a reprisal of the so-called Ohio League and the Canton Bulldogs following a year's hiatus. Jim Thorpe was still in Boston playing for the Braves, but he sent a letter to Canton announcing that he intended to return for the 1919 season and would be the player-coach for the Bulldogs. Some of Thorpe's enthusiasm had been fueled by an offer of part ownership in the team.

Actually Thorpe had a previous offer. The New York Giants were interested in having a professional football team formed that would play games on Sundays in the Polo Grounds in the fall. In fact, John McGraw had the audacity to ask Jim Thorpe if he was interested in coaching the team. Thorpe diplomatically told McGraw that he had already committed himself to Canton.

By now Jack Cusack had left Canton and was working in Oklahoma. But a new manager of the Bulldogs rose to the occasion in the person of local automobile dealer Ralph Hay. Jack Donahue was going to be the new manager for Massillon. In Akron, former Canton Bulldog Fat Waldsmith and Vernon Maginnis were ready to put a team on the field. Also there was a possibility of teams being formed in Youngstown and Cleveland.

Jim Thorpe, while struggling to remain in the major leagues, suddenly had an enormous influence in professional football. Ralph Hay would not discuss scheduling the Canton Bulldogs for the 1919 season without Thorpe's approval. Hay arranged a meeting in late July of the managers of the Ohio League in Pittsburgh when the Boston Braves came in on a road trip. In fact, John McGraw sent a representative to Pittsburgh to entice Ohio teams to play in New York in the fall, where they could expect huge gate receipts. Both Canton and Massillon agreed to play games in New York. When Jim Thorpe turned down the New York coaching job, John McGraw hired former Harvard star and Massillon captain Charley Brickley to head the squad.

However, it would turn out that there would be no New York pro football team in 1919.

As the 1919 major league baseball season wound down, Ralph Hay went back to Canton and began building the Bulldogs team. He signed Thorpe's former teammates at Carlisle, Joe Guyon, who had since played at Georgia Tech, and Pete Calac, who had been wounded in the war but was ready to play. Hay also signed Guy Chamberlain, a 6' 2", 190-pound end from the University of Nebraska, and Al Feeney, a 210-pound center who had played at Notre Dame. Feeney would later be elected mayor of Indianapolis. Hay even got the Canton Marine Band to furnish music at Bulldogs home games at League Park.

Then Hay accepted a challenge from C. J. (Paul) Parduhn, the manager of the Hammond Bobcats. Parduhn had signed former Canton quarterback Milt Ghee and assembled of a squad of stars known as "the $20,000 team" that included Doc Hauser, an All-American end from Minnesota, Hugh Blaylock, a tackle from Michigan State, and a bruising 235-pound fullback named Gil Falcon. In addition, Parduhn signed a former University of Illinois end, George Halas, for $100 a game. Halas had also played 12 games for the New York Yankees during the 1919 season.

Parduhn had arranged for his team to play several games at the Chicago Cubs park on the North side to test the popularity of professional football in Chicago. Teams from Minneapolis, Cleveland, Detroit and Massillon had agreed to play in Chicago. Then Parduhn gave Ralph Hay an ultimatum; he would have to play his team in Chicago or he would lay claim to the national title for 1919.

Subsequently, Hay agreed to have Canton play Hammond, and the game was scheduled for early November. To make room on the Canton schedule, the game at the Polo Grounds in New York was cancelled.

Canton opened its 1919 season on October 5 with an unimpressive 13–7 win over the Pitcairn Quakers from Pennsylvania. Jim Thorpe had not yet quite made the transition from baseball to football and fumbled twice in the game.

On October 12, the Bulldogs walloped the Toledo Navy team, 64–0. Jim Thorpe ran for three touchdowns in the game.

The following week, Thorpe, 31 years old and the player-coach of the Bulldogs, preferred to remain on the bench and let Joe Guyon and Pete Calac run the ball as the Bulldogs beat the Columbus Panhandles, 22–3. Next Canton defeated the Detroit Heralds, 27–0. The Bulldogs were now 4–0 and were headed to Chicago for their showdown game with the Hammond Bobcats.

Even though the Bobcats had atracted a lot of hype in the press with their $20,000 payroll, the team was not so glitzy on the field. A week before, the Hammond squad had faced a determined team in Cleveland and narrowly pulled out a 6–0 win on two field goals.

On November 3, 1919, what was billed at that time as the greatest pro football game ever played took place in Chicago between Hammond and Canton before 10,000 enthusiastic fans. The Bulldogs had a tough time just getting to the Cubs park for the game. The bus they were riding in broke down and the team had to hike to the elevated train, arriving late at the park.

The first half ended with Hammond leading, 3–0. However, in the second half Jim Thorpe kicked a 25-yard field goal to tie the score. Then Canton tried to score using long forward passes. Time and time again, the Bulldogs' passes were batted down by the Bobcats, and the game ended in a 3–3 tie. One of the Hammond players batting down Bulldogs passes was quarterback Milt Ghee, whom Ralph Hay had been unsuccessful in attempting to re-sign for Canton.

While both teams were still undefeated, the outcome of the game did not settle the issue that the game was intended to resolve, the so-called national professional title. Immediately after the game, Paul Parduhn offered the Bulldogs a big guarantee to play another game in Chicago. However, with two games scheduled with Massillon on the horizon, Ralph Hay was not sure about the additional game with Hammond. He suggested that if they played it, Thanksgiving would the ideal day. Parduhn accepted immediately.

As the season progressed it was apparent that professional football was becoming popular. The 1919 season was the first year that professional football was played with wide success outside of the college ranks. There was an increase in the amount of chatter from various insiders about forming a professional football league using major league baseball as a model. However, Ralph Hay let it be known that he had no interest in such talks until the season was over.

Such talk about a formal professional football league was sending shock waves through college administration buildings across the nation. They believed that college football had become a national tradition. College administrators and coaches were concerned that their football programs could become feeding systems for the professional teams and that a lot of players would leave college for the chance to play professional football. There was even concern that a lot of talented high school players would defer college for the pros. The colleges felt that many of their student-athletes came from poor families and were working their way through school. Therefore, after they paid their tuition, there was not much money left. Now professional football teams' representatives were showing up on the campuses and tempting the student-athletes with financial inducements to play for their teams, telling them to play under assumed names.

One of those college players playing professional football in the fall of 1919 was left halfback George Gipp, the Notre Dame star who had played as a ringer for the Rockford Grands in a game against the Rockford A.C. under the assumed name of "Baker." Other Notre Dame players in the Grands lineup included Edward "Slip" Madigan at center and Dutch Bergman at right halfback. The Notre Dame players were promised $250 each for the game by Grands coach and quarterback George Kitteringham.

However the $250 per game paid to George Gipp was not the standard pay rate. Most of the collegiate players that put on a pro football uniform on Sunday were paid much less, and the pro teams' managers liked it that way.

At the University of Pittsburgh, Coach Pop Warner was expressing his displeasure with professional football in no uncertain terms, telling all that everything possible should be done to dissolve pro football. Warner was even making the accusation that some of his former players, who were making good money playing pro football, were not giving their best effort unless there were bets made on the games. According to Warner, unless there were wagers on the results, there was little incentive to win. In the pro game the spirit of the college game was lacking and the main incentive was the pay envelope.

The *Chicago Daily Tribune* alleged, "In the east it is a common occurrence for members of certain teams to play collegiate games on Saturday then take a rattler (train) to play with one of the professional teams in Ohio on Sunday. Whether the athletic authorities at these institutions know their players are making money on pro football is not known, but if they intend to take the pretenses of upholding amateur standards they should investigate."[1]

Nonetheless the 1919 season continued, though the Canton Bulldogs' next game with the Toledo Maroons had to be cancelled due to a traction workers strike in Toledo, leaving fans with no way to get to the park for the game.

On November 16, the first Canton vs. Massillon game since 1917 was played. The Bulldogs won a decisive victory over the Tigers, 23–0. Jim Thorpe played a fine game, plunging over the goal line for a touchdown, kicking two extra points and a field goal, and punting the ball 63 yards on one attempt. But he was hardly the only star of the game. Cecil Gregg returned a Massillon punt for a 45-yard touchdown, and Joe Guyon caught a pass from Thorpe and ran 82 yards for a score.

The next week found Canton playing the Akron Indians. The Akron squad had brought in a couple of college ringers using assumed names for the game, but it hardly mattered as the Bulldogs won, 14–0. Jim Thorpe kept himself out of the game until the fourth quarter.

On Thanksgiving Day, November 27, 1919, once again 10,000 fans packed the Cubs park in Chicago to watch the second battle of the year between Hammond and Canton with a touch of snow on the field. The Hammond Bobcats had beefed up their squad for the second Canton game. They added Paddy Driscoll, a former Northwestern star who was a great kicker and a great breakaway runner, and Paul Meyers, one of the greatest ends in Wisconsin football history. Meyers had just closed out his collegiate career the week before in the University of Chicago game.

The only score of the game occurred following the Canton kickoff. Paddy Driscoll took the ball, but immediately three Bulldogs hit him hard, causing him to lose the ball. Howard "Horse" Edwards, Canton's 207-pound guard from Notre Dame, fell on it at the Hammond 20-yard line. Jim Thorpe ran the ball straight ahead for six yards. Then Pete Calac added six yards for a first down. On the next play Thorpe ran through left tackle and crashed into the end zone for the touchdown. Thorpe kicked the extra point, making the score Canton 7, Hammond 0.

As the game continued Hammond fought back hard, but the Bulldogs stopped two drives with goal-line stands. Each was followed by booming punts by Thorpe to move the ball downfield. In the fourth quarter, Hammond's George Halas suffered a fractured collarbone and was taken to the hospital. Canton withstood the Hammond challenge and remained undefeated going into their second game with Massillon.

Going into the second Canton game, Massillon was having a disappointing season with a record of 5–2–1. After winning their first five games, Massillon lost to the Cleveland Tigers, 3–0, when former second team All-American Roscoe "Skip" Gougler, from Pitt, missed five field goals, including one from within the 20-yard line. Then the Tigers lost to the Canton Bulldogs, 23–0, and the game with the powerful Dayton Triangles ended in a 0–0 tie. On the other hand, Canton stood at 8–0–1 going into the game. So a victory for Massillon would salvage their season and might just give the Tigers a partial claim to the so-called Ohio League championship.

The game was played on November 30 and Massillon showed up in Canton with a huge squad. Some were advancing the notion that the Tigers had signed as many players as possible to keep them from signing with the Bulldogs.

The first half ended in a 0–0 tie. Massillon had made several strong drives only to be stopped by a determined Canton defense. Jim Thorpe was playing with a bad back. In the third quarter a strong wind suddenly began to blow at the back of the Bulldogs. So Thorpe attempted to kick two long field goals and missed. However, on his third attempt, from the 40-yard line with Pete Calac holding, Thorpe's field goal made the score 3–0 Canton. Massillon kicker Skip Gougler attempted to tie the score with a field goal from the Tigers' 45-yard line but strong gusts carried the ball out of bounds on the 15-yard line. With time running out Massillon drove Canton deep in its own territory. With their goal line behind their backs, the Bulldogs decided to punt. Thorpe, aided by the strong wind, boomed a long punt. The ball kept rolling when it hit the ground, all the way to the Massillon 5-yard line — a 95-yard punt. The Canton Bulldogs won the game, 3–0, and once again laid full claim to the so-called Ohio League championship.

In Illinois Walter H. Flanigan had put together a first-class team for 1919, the Rock Island Independents. He upgraded his schedule from previous campaigns to include teams from Indiana and Ohio. Although he lost to the $20,000 Hammond Bobcats squad, 12–7, the game drew 7,000 fans to Douglas Park in Rock Island. Following that loss and a scoreless tie against the Pine Village A. C. from Indiana, the Rock Island Independents went undefeated the rest of the 1919 season, closing it out with a 17–0 victory over the Akron Indians. Rock Island quarterback Rube Ursella, formerly of Minnesota, scored 99 points during the season.

Walter Flanigan challenged the Canton Bulldogs to play a game for the national championship of professional football. He even offered Canton a $5,000 guarantee. But the game was turned down by Jim Thorpe, who told Flanigan that the Bulldogs had already disbanded for the year.

While Canton once again had a great season, the team lost money and the future of professional football in Ohio was in doubt. The Bulldogs games against Pitcairn and Columbus had only drawn 2,000 fans. While the first Massillon game had drawn 10,000, the second had only attracted 7,000.

The Massillon team had lost money too, so much in fact that Jack Donahue and his partner announced they would not field a team for the 1920 season. Youngstown was also done with pro football.

It was apparent to everyone connected with professional football that sweeping changes to operations, salaries and scheduling would have to come about if the game was to survive. Most importantly, the regionalization of pro football had to come to an abrupt end. In 1919 there were 241 teams scattered across the United States that were considered professional. They existed in every city and town from Bridgeport to Philadelphia to Flint to Dubuque and beyond. In Chicago alone there were 28 teams. Informal leagues without any structure existed in several states such as New York, Pennsylvania, Ohio, Indiana and Illinois. The answer to the dilemma facing the sport seemed to be the formation of a national league.

17

The NFL Is Born

In the spring of 1920 no major league team offered Jim Thorpe a contract. So he signed with Akron of the International League and had his finest ever year in professional baseball, hitting .360 with 188 hits, including 16 home runs.

As the fall of 1920 approached, it was still uncertain what the status of professional football would be. The game was being played by a hodgepodge of company teams and town teams, agreeing to play each other on short notice with a set of ad hoc rules. Although nearly everyone connected had come to the conclusion that organization was necessary, everything about professional football was still happening by mere chance. George Halas said later, "You often didn't know whom you were playing the next Sunday. We had to make sure the teams would show up on the dates scheduled."[1]

On Sunday, August 20, 1920, a meeting was held in Canton, Ohio, to discuss the rapidly approaching season. Jim Thorpe was still playing minor league baseball in nearby Akron and attended, representing Canton at the meeting. Also attending were Carl Stork of Dayton, Stanley Cofall of Cleveland, and Fred Ranney of Akron. The four men decided to organize another Ohio league for the coming football season.

They also voted unanimously not to seek the services of any college players in the coming season. The hiring of college players who were padding their bank accounts and playing under assumed names had brought the wrath of intercollegiate heads down on the professional game to a point where it had becoming threatening.

Ralph Hay, who owned the Canton Bulldogs, loved the game. He believed that pro football had a far greater future than just organizing another Ohio league. So he arranged another meeting to further discuss the matter of the coming season.

At 8:15 P.M. on the evening of September 17, 1920, a group of players, coaches and managers, men who were visionaries as much as entrepreneurs, representing 11 professional football teams, met in the showroom of Ralph

Hay's Hupmobile Auto Agency in the Odds Fellows building in Canton, Ohio. Little did anyone know at that time, as these men sat on running boards of the automobiles — because there were not enough chairs — and sipped beer, that they would be the founders of the most popular sports business in American history. No one could have ever predicted that evening that the behemoth of professional football that had its humble genesis in this unassuming meeting would attain popularity of astonishing proportions.

Ninety years later, on Sunday, February 7, 2010, 106,500,000 professional football fans would sit down in front of television sets to watch the New Orleans Saints defeat the Indianapolis Colts, 31–17, in Super Bowl XLIV (44) in Miami, Florida. The game would be broadcast in 232 countries and territories, and fans would spend an estimated $8.868 billion on game-related merchandise, apparel and snacks.

That evening in 1920 in Canton, Ralph Hay chaired the meeting and A.F. Ranney of the Akron Professional Football Team kept the minutes. Both Jim Thorpe and George Halas were among the assembled representatives that evening. The meeting started with Hay announcing that there was only one item to address under "Old Business." Massillon had withdrawn from professional football for the 1920 season.

Then the meeting progressed to address the first item on the agenda under "New Business." The following 19 words as stated in the minutes would change the sporting world forever. "It was moved and seconded that a permanent organization be formed to be known as American Professional Football Association."[2] The motion was carried.

Next Jim Thorpe was elected president of the Association, Stanley Cofall vice president, and A. F. Ranney secretary and treasurer.

Ralph Hay had first been nominated for president, but he declined, citing Thorpe's prominence in the game and knowing that the league would have a far greater chance of achieving legitimacy if it was identified with him. However, Thorpe's election as president would be mostly ceremonial and he would have no real administrative duties. There was little difference between Jim Thorpe's election as president of the first professional football league and his signing a major league contract with the New York Giants. Regardless of how much he would play or didn't play, his association with the league would attract fans to the games.

With an organizational structure in place for the Association, the members acted to formalize it by moving the following motions:

1. A fee of $100 should be charged for membership in the Association.
2. Jim Thorpe as president should appoint a committee to work in

conjunction with an attorney to draft a constitution, bylaws and rules for the Association.

3. All Clubs should mail to the secretary by January 1, 1921, a list of players used by them during the preceding season, so that the secretary could furnish all Clubs with duplicate copies of the same, so that each Club would have first choice in services for 1921 of his team of this season.

4. All Clubs would have printed on their stationery, "Member of American Professional Football Association."

5. It was acknowledged that Mr. Marshall of the Brunswick-Dalke Collender Company, Tire Division, had presented a silver loving cup to be given the team, awarded the championship of the Association. Any team winning the cup three times should be adjudged the owner.

With those humble beginnings professional football as we know it today was born.

The charter member teams in the American Professional Football Association were the following:

Canton Bulldogs
Cleveland Indians
Dayton Triangles
Akron Professionals
Rochester (NY) Jeffersons
Rock Island Independents
Muncie Flyers
Chicago Cardinals
Hammond Pros
Decatur Staleys
*Massillon Tigers (withdrew and did not play in the APFA)

By the beginning of the season four other teams would join the league, the Buffalo All-Americans, Chicago Tigers, Columbus Panhandles and Detroit Heralds.

George Halas was the player-manager of the Decatur Staleys. Halas was born February 2, 1895, and raised on Chicago's west side. He was a graduate of Crane Technical High School and the University of Illinois, where he played football, basketball and baseball. While Halas only played one full season of football (his senior year) at Illinois due to injuries, he played three years of varsity baseball and had a batting average of .350.

Following graduation in 1918, George Halas went into the U.S. Navy.

On January 1, 1919, Halas was a member of the Great Lakes team that won the Rose Bowl. The Rose Bowl was played by service teams that year and the Great Lakes Navy team defeated Mare Island United States Marine Corps, 17–0, with 27,000 in attendance. George Halas caught a 45-yard touchdown pass from Paddy Driscoll, rushed for 34 yards, and drop-kicked a 30-yard field goal. He also averaged 43.5 yards for six punts and returned nine punts for 115 yards.

During the 1919 baseball season, after being injured in a spring training game, George Halas played in only 12 games for the New York Yankees before he was optioned to the St. Paul club in the American Association because he was having a difficult time hitting a major league curve ball.

George Halas (Sports Story Reprints).

Halas didn't report for spring training in 1920, preferring to keep his $55 a week job working for the Chicago, Burlington and Quincy Railroad designing bridges, and focusing on football.

Later in 1920 Halas went to work for the Staley Starch Works in Decatur, Illinois. A. E. Staley, the company president, was very enthusiastic about sports and had already fielded a very strong semi-professional baseball team managed by former major league pitcher "Iron Man" Joe McGinnity. During the summer of 1920 George Halas played outfield on the Staley baseball team.

Now the company wanted to organize a pro football team, and that fall George Halas was selected to both play on the team and coach it. Subsequently, Halas was dispatched to the historic meeting at Ralph Hay's auto agency in Canton in September 1920.

In 1920, the start-up Staleys would finish their first professional football season with a record of 10–2–2. Each player on George Halas' Decatur Staleys team would be paid $1,781 for the season, which was more than any member of the Canton Bulldogs team except Jim Thorpe.

Jim Thorpe was paid $2,500 for the 1920 season plus a part of the gate. While he received no salary for serving as president of the league, this did not preclude Ralph Hay from rewarding Thorpe with bonus money.

Although a formal league had been organized, the APFA teams continued to schedule games outside of it, often referring to them as exhibitions. The first game played featuring a team from American Professional Football Association took place at Douglas Park in Rock Island, Illinois, as the Independents defeated the St. Paul Ideals, 48–0.

One week later the first game played between two of the APFA teams was played. The Dayton Triangles defeated the Columbus Panhandles, 14–0.

The Akron Pros (Professionals) would be crowned the league's first champions, finishing with a record of 8–0–3.

The Canton Bulldogs finished their 1920 season with a 4–3–1 record. On December 4, 1920, a landmark game for the APFA was played in New York involving Jim Thorpe's Bulldogs. At the Polo Grounds in New York, 10,000 fans saw the Buffalo All-Americans defeat the Bulldogs, 7–3. It was the first professional football game played in New York in several years and was considered a showcase game for professional football. In the third quarter Jim Thorpe kicked a field goal from placement to give the Bulldogs a 3–0 lead. However, a few minutes later "Swede" Youngstrom, the great Buffalo right guard from Dartmouth, picked up a blocked punt by Thorpe and ran into the end zone for Buffalo's winning touchdown.

Although the league survived intact for the 1920 season, the APFA was on shaky grounds throughout it and in some respects very bush league in its organization. There were even instances when a visiting team had to worry about getting out of town with its share of the gate.

George Halas recalled that when his Decatur Staleys played at Rock Island, they incurred the wrath of the fans after the Staleys' George Trafton made a hard tackle on Rock Island halfback Joe Chicken, breaking his leg. Following the game, the Rock Island fans made serious menacing gestures toward Trafton. Halas immediately decided to hand an envelope to Trafton containing $3,500, which was the Staleys' split for the game. According to Halas, "I figured if they started something, I'd have nothing to run for except the $3,500. Trafton would be running for his life."[3]

During the 1921 baseball season Jim Thorpe, now 33 years old, played for Toledo in the American Association. No one was accusing him of not being able to hit curve balls any longer. In 1921 Thorpe hit .358 with 181 hits, including nine home runs. On July 13, 1921, Thorpe had perhaps his finest day in organized baseball as he hit three home runs for Toledo vs. Milwaukee. All three home runs would have been out of any major league park.

However, Thorpe had to share the minor league headlines, because that same day Bunny Brief hit three home runs playing for Kansas City in the American Association. Previously, Brief played four years in the major leagues (1912-1913 St. Louis Browns, 1915 Chicago White Sox, and 1917 Pittsburgh Pirates). In 569 at-bats in the big leagues Brief hit only five home runs.

The Chicago Tigers became the first American Professional Football Association team to fold following the 1920 season. As the APFA approached its second season, it was apparent to everyone that in order to survive, the league could not stand on formalities and had to develop a strong business plan. So on April 30, 1921, team owners led by George Halas voted to replace Jim Thorpe as president with Joe Carr.

Not only was Joe Carr president and founder of the Columbus Panhandles professional football team, he was an experienced sports executive and former sports editor of the *Ohio State Journal*. He was also president of the Ohio State Baseball League. Later Carr would serve three years as the leader of the American Basketball Association. He would leave the ABA in 1928 to become the director of promotions for the National Association. Under Carr's leadership, baseball's minor leagues would grow from 12 leagues in 1933 to 41 in 1939, the year that he died.

A. E. Staley came to the conclusion that, due to the financial loses his football team incurred during the 1920 season, he could not field a team in 1921. So Staley gave George Halas $5,000 and told him to move the team to Chicago. The only stipulation that Staley placed on the deal was that the team would retain the name The Staleys for one year. So Halas took the club to the big city and rented the Cubs park where the Chicago Tigers had played their games.

The APFA expanded to 21 teams for the 1921 season, adding ten teams, although some of them, like the Cincinnati Celts and Detroit Tigers, a new version of the Detroit Heralds, would only last one season. The added teams included: Evansville Crimson Giants, Washington Senators, Cincinnati Celts, Minneapolis Marines, Detroit Tigers, Louisville Brecks, New York Brickley Giants, Tonawanda Kardex and Green Bay Packers.

The Green Bay Packers had been organized by George Calhoun and Earl "Curly" Lambeau, who succeeded in convincing the heads of the Indian Packing Company to put up $500 for uniforms and equipment for the team. In the 1919 season the Packers had achieved a record of 10–1, outscoring their opponents, 565–18. What was most remarkable was that the Green Bay players had literally played the schedule for fun. At the end of the season the club's profits after expenses were divided among the players, netting each player a salary of $16 for the season or $1.45 a game.

For the 1921 season Jim Thorpe left Canton and became the player-coach of the Cleveland Indians. The team was hard hit financially and finished with record of 3–5–0. Thorpe played in just five games and scored only one touchdown.

As the season got under way, Thorpe asked Jack Cusack to come from Oklahoma to help him manage the team's finances. When Cusack arrived in Cleveland what he found was blatant graft being carried out in the team's accounting process. On two separate occasions, Cusack found large discrepancies between the numbers of complimentary tickets allowed, ranging from $900 to $1,000.

On December 3, following the game at New York's Polo Grounds with the New York Brickley Giants, the Cleveland treasurer accepted a check for the Indians' share of $3,750, which was about $250 short, and left the hotel without paying the players or their expenses. When a bellhop came to Cusack's room with a bill for his and Thorpe's expenses, he realized that something had gone wrong. Cusack and Thorpe immediately pursued the Cleveland treasurer, tracking him down at Pennsylvania Station, and demanded that he pay the players. When the treasurer said that he would mail the players checks from Cleveland, Thorpe and Cusack enlisted the services of two New York City Police Department detectives stationed in the lobby. The whole matter was resolved when the dispute was moved to a police station and the team treasurer, accompanied by his lawyer, agreed to return to the hotel, sign over the check to Cusack, and pay the players. The difference was then given to the treasurer.

Following two additional exhibition games, the Cleveland Indians football team was disbanded.

In the 1922 baseball season Jim Thorpe continued to play minor league ball. While he hurt his arm sliding in a spring training game, he still hit .308, playing in 35 games for Portland in the Pacific Coast League. Then Thorpe was traded to Hartford-Waterbury of the Eastern League, where he hit .344 in 96 games with 131 hits, including nine home runs. It would be the last year that Jim Thorpe would play professional baseball.

On June 24, 1922, the American Professional Football Association changed its name to the National Football League.

Also, beginning in the 1922 season the restrictive covenant was lifted on the Staleys' team name. So George Halas, a staunch Cubs fan, renamed his

Chicago football team the Bears. It would be many years before Halas started to be identified with the moniker "Papa Bear."

The NFL consisted of 20 teams for the 1922 season. One of the new teams was the Oorang Indians. Walter Lingo had purchased the NFL franchise for $100 at the league's June meeting. Lingo also put up the NFL's obligatory $1,000 as a guarantee that he would not employ college players with remaining eligibility on his team.

Walter Lingo was one of the most eccentric but colorful persons ever to own a professional football team. Lingo loved dogs. He was the owner and operator of the Oorang Kennels, breeders of Airedales and a particular breed of Airedale, the King Oorang, that Lingo had produced by bringing in and breeding many great Airedales from all over the world. The Oorang Kennels was a booming canine enterprise. Lingo's kennels were spread over several acres of his land and he had an army of trainers, night watchmen, kennel attendants, hunters and clerks on his payroll. Lingo even sold Airedales by mail order.

Besides loving Airedales, Walter Lingo also loved Indians. He had grown up in La Rue, Ohio, site of an old Wyandotte Indian village, and had read Indian tales extensively. Lingo believed that a spiritual bond existed between Airedales and Indians. To showcase his Airedales, Lingo devised a plan to field an all–Indian professional football team. So he hired Jim Thorpe to organize the Oorang Indians, representing Marion, Ohio, in the NFL. Marion had been put on the map as the home of President Warren G. Harding.

Walter Lingo never really cared much about football, and his ownership of a professional football team was simply a marketing campaign to have the football team make his dogs look good. Lingo was convinced that his dogs could learn something special from Indians that they could not learn from white hunters. To raise money, the Oorang Indians trained hunting dogs and sold them. According to Lingo, he placed Jim Thorpe in charge of the team for express purpose of advertising his Oorang Airedales.

Joe Carr, the NFL president, had received a complaint from the man who owned the field where Oorang played its games, complaining that Walter Lingo had located the cage where he kept a bear for training the dogs very near the field. The owner told Carr if the cage, which was emitting obnoxious odors, was not cleaned up, he would evict the team.

Lingo and the Indians players used the bear in the training of the dogs. The bear was kept in a cage with two compartments separated by a sliding door. Carr was in Marion when the owner complained and witnessed Thorpe getting into the cage after the team was unable to move the bear by poking it with a stick. Thorpe simply shouldered the bear the way he would a tackler into the adjoining compartment.

The first order of business in organizing the Oorang Indians football team for Jim Thorpe was to recruit an all–Indian team. Thorpe began to contact former Carlisle players and was able to recruit some first-class and well-coached Indian players such as Lo Boutwell, Elmer Busch, Big Bear, Pete Calac, Xavier Downwind, Joe Guyon (an All-American at Georgia Tech), Eagle Feather, Stillwell Sanooke, Joe Little Twig and Bill Winneschick.

But to round out his squad Thorpe had to have tryouts, and they attracted Indian players from all over the country, many ranging in age from 30 to 50 years old. Nonetheless Thorpe found some talent. He was able to recruit from the Ojibwe reservation in Wisconsin, George Vettermack, Alex Bobidosh and Ted St. Germaine, a very good tackle who had played at Dickinson College. St. Germaine, who was 37 years old, also had a law degree from Yale. Reggie Attache was a Mission Indian with high school experience from California. There was also Horatio Jones from the Haskell Indian Nations University, Baptiste Thunder, a Chippewa, Ed Nason, another Indian without any college football experience, and Ted Lone Wolf, a player with high school experience from Flandreau, South Dakota.

With his squad assembled, Thorpe began to whip them into shape. During the month of September each day Thorpe held practice sessions. In the evenings he took the Indians on long runs behind packs of Walter Lingo's dogs.

Jim Thorpe and the Oorang Indians began the 1922 NFL season on Sunday, October 1, 1922 at Dayton, Ohio. However the Dayton Triangles massacred the Indians, 36–0. Thorpe remained on the sideline and never played in the game. It is doubtful if even the great Jim Thorpe could have made any difference in the outcome of the game. Dayton took the opening kickoff and drove right downfield for a touchdown with ease. At halftime, Oorang was behind, 16–0. Everything that could go wrong that day seemed to go wrong. In the fourth quarter the Indians punted, but instead of running with the ball, the Dayton player who caught the football kicked it right back to the Indians. One of the Oorang players barely touched the ball before the Triangles' Glenn Tidd scooped it and dashed downfield for a touchdown.

Viewed through the prism of twenty-first century political correctness, the Oorang Indians were an exploitation of Native American athletes and their culture. However, in 1922 Walter Lingo's all–Indian professional football team was as much about marketing as athletics. The Oorang pre-game and halftime shows were a spectacle as popular as the football game. Entertainment was provided by both the dogs and the players. Lingo's Airedales retrieved targets, did tricks and even trailed the bear, causing it to become treed, while his Indian players performed exhibitions of tribal dances, tomahawk and knife throwing contests, among other gaudy spectacles.

The following week, on Sunday, October 8, at Marion, Ohio, the Oorang Indians played their only home game of the 1922 season, defeating the Columbus Panhandles, 20–6. The Indians were led by Joe Guyon, who scored two touchdowns, one a 55-yard run.

Next the Oorang Indians lost to the Canton Bulldogs, 14–0. Then, in a non-league game played in a snowstorm at Indianapolis, the Oorang Indians beat the Indianapolis Belmonts, 33–0. While Oorang made $2,000, there was considerable controversy about the game as the crowd felt that Coach Thorpe ran up the score by playing his first team players throughout the game against a much weaker Belmonts team.

The following week the shoe was on the other foot as Oorang, once again playing an NFL opponent, was crushed by the Akron Pros, 62–0.

The Minneapolis Marines were next on the Oorang schedule. The game was played at Minneapolis as an early winter storm began to descend upon the Twin Cities, and saw the Marines come from behind to win, 13–6. The Indians were ahead 6–0 at the half. However, the Marines took the lead 7–6 in the third quarter. At this point Jim Thorpe made his first appearance in a game during the season. His entry into the hard-fought defensive battle provided little in the way of a rallying cry as the Marines scored another touchdown in the fourth quarter and won the game.

At that point the Oorang Indians had a record of 2–3 and headed to Chicago to play the Bears. Although Jim Thorpe played the entire second half and scored a touchdown on a short plunge, the more powerful Bears won the rain-soaked game, 33–6.

It was now mid–November in the NFL's inaugural season and the Oorang Indians were in Wisconsin to play the Milwaukee Badgers, led by former Centre College All-American Bo McMillin. A crowd numbering about 6,500 turned out for the game and saw the Badgers defeat the Indians, 13–0. However, it was not McMillin who was the star of the game, but rather former Rutgers star Paul Robeson, one of the first African Americans to play professional football, who scored two touchdowns for Milwaukee. Robeson was playing professional football to assist him in attending Columbia Law School. For Oorang, Jim Thorpe played and provided what little offense the Indians could muster.

The following week at Buffalo, Jim Thorpe was once again a force to be reckoned with on the gridiron. The Oorang Indians defeated the Buffalo All-Americans, 19–7, as Thorpe ran for two touchdowns, passed to Joe Guyon for an extra point and then late in the fourth quarter passed to Guyon for 30-yard touchdown.

The Oorang Indians concluded their 1922 NFL schedule on November

30 by once again defeating the Columbus Panhandles, 18–6, at Columbus. For the NFL games on their schedule, the Indians finished in 11th place with a record of 3–6–0, scoring 69 points while allowing 190.

On December 3, the Oorang Indians concluded the 1922 season by playing their second non-league game at Durant, Michigan, losing to the Durant All-Stars, 29–0.

While the season had been a success for Walter Lingo and his kennels, the football played by the Oorang Indians was mediocre. While six NFL teams had not won as many games as the Indians, the failure of the Oorang Indians as a professional team, according to Ed Healey, Chicago Bears Hall of Fame tackle, was due in part to the fact that Jim Thorpe was not a very good coach. Thorpe did not instill discipline in the team. One of the more well-known stories involving the off-field antics of the Oorang Indians took place in Chicago. The bartender wanted to close the saloon for the night and a few of the Oorang players tossed him into a telephone booth and turned it upside down, then proceeded to drink until early morning. The next afternoon the Indians were easily beaten by the Bears. It is only fair to question, with all the pre-game and half-time shenanigans involving the Oorang players in tomahawk throwing, etc., if it was possible for them to take the game seriously.

Lou Boutwell, the Oorang Indians' Chippewa quarterback, said that because people had a misconception about Indian players, thinking they were a bunch of wild men even though most of them were college educated, they had an opportunity to exploit that jaded thinking. "It was a dandy excuse to raise hell and get away with it when the mood struck us. Since we were Indians, we could get away with things the whites couldn't. Don't think we didn't take advantage of it."[4]

FINAL NFL STANDINGS 1922

Team	Won	Lost	Tied
Canton Bulldogs	10	0	2
Chicago Bears	9	3	0
Chicago Cardinals	8	3	0
Toledo Maroons	5	2	2
Rock Island Independents	4	2	1
Racine Legion	6	4	1
Dayton Triangles	4	3	1
Buffalo All-Americans	5	4	1
Green Bay Packers	4	3	3
Akron Pros	3	5	2
Milwaukee Badgers	2	4	3

Team	Won	Lost	Tied
Oorang Indians	3	6	0
Louisville Brecks	1	3	0
Minneapolis Marines	1	3	0
Rochester Jeffersons	0	4	1
Hammond Pros	0	5	1
Columbus Panhandles	0	8	0
Evansville Crimson Giants	0	3	0

The NFL began its second season in 1923 with 20 teams. The 1923 edition of the Oorang Indians would be a miserable football team. Outscored by their NFL opponents, 235–24, along the way to a 1–9–0 season, the Indians were defeated by the Minneapolis Marines, 23–0, Buffalo All-Americans, 57–0, Cleveland Indians, 27–0 and Canton Bulldogs, 41–0. In fact the Oorang Indians would not score their first touchdown of the season until the seventh game, against the St. Louis All-Stars who defeated them, 14–7, at Sportsman's Park.

On November 11, 1923, at Cubs' Park in Chicago, the Bears beat the Oorang Indians, 26–0. George Halas recovered a Jim Thorpe fumble, then ran 98 yards for a touchdown with Thorpe chasing him all the way. Halas' touchdown run would remain an NFL record until 1972.

The 1923 Oorang Indians would finish in 18th place in the NFL, defeating only the last-place Louisville Brecks, 12–0, in the final game of the season.

Jim Thorpe scored 3 points in the 1923 season, kicking a field goal to prevent the Indians from being held scoreless by the Columbus Tigers, 27–3, on November 25. In the fourth quarter of the game Thorpe was injured and missed the Oorang Indians' final three games of the season.

The off-field antics of the Oorang Indians continued with regularity during 1923. The night before the St. Louis game, the team was out frolicking late in a speakeasy. After getting on a trolley, they discovered it was headed in the wrong direction. So the Oorang players got off the trolley and lifted it off the tracks, then positioned it in the opposite direction.

The Oorang Indians franchise folded after the 1923 season. The novelty of an all–Indian team was no longer a drawing card. Walter Lingo's marketing campaign for his Airedales using Indians and professional football had run its course.

However, Jim Thorpe, despite being 35 years old in 1923, was still adding episodes to his gridiron legend. After the Oorang Indians folded, Thorpe joined the Toledo Maroons for a couple of post-season exhibition games.

Toledo was playing the Oklahoma All-Stars, who had just signed Steve

Owen, a talented rookie 230-pound tackle out of Phillips University who would go on to become a great player in the NFL and coach the New York Giants from 1930 to 1952. On the first play from scrimmage, Owen found himself face-to-face with Jim Thorpe, who was blocking for the runner. Owen smashed into Thorpe with a hand flying in his face, knocking him down. The same thing happened on the second play. As Thorpe was lying on the ground, Owen looked down at Thorpe and said, "Old Jim has slowed up, I guess. He doesn't care for this blocking business anymore."[5] On the third snap Owen ignored Thorpe and went straight for the ball carrier. All at once, Owen found himself on the ground with a thumping feeling in his head, stunned and shaken. A teammate advised him to keep an eye on the old Indian.

One of the longest running facts vs. myths on the professional football career of Jim Thorpe originates from the 1923 NFL season. Thorpe long maintained that he kicked a 99-yard punt in a game during the 1923 season. That feat may be apocryphal. There is, however, substantial documentation that Thorpe did kick a 95-yard punt in the second Canton vs. Massillon game in 1919.

Added grist for the mill in regard to Thorpe's punting ability was provided by the comments of Thorpe's former Carlisle Indians and Canton Bulldogs teammate, Joe Guyon. In 1935 Guyon was coaching football at St. Xavier High School in Louisville, Kentucky. In a speech at the school, Guyon claimed that he had once witnessed Thorpe punt a football 107 yards. According to Guyon, Canton was playing the Chicago Bears and the ball was on the Canton one-yard line, forcing the Bulldogs to punt. The field was wet and sloppy, so Jim Thorpe asked George Halas if he could borrow ten yards to get firmer turf. Halas declined. Thorpe punted the ball out of his end zone over the head of Bears safety Joe "Dutch" Sternaman to the 3-yard line.

Regardless, the official NFL record for the longest punt is given to Steve O'Neal, who booted the ball 98 yards for the New York Jets vs. the Denver Broncos on September 21, 1969.

18

A Fading Star

Although he had been paying income tax for several years, in 1924 Jim Thorpe became a citizen of the United States, officially giving up his status as an Indian ward of the government. Although Thorpe's best days on the gridiron were behind him, he continued to play, both for the love of the game and because it provided a living. He had once been the greatest fullback in the game. He continued to play hard as he could but now all the defenses were keying on him and Thorpe took a real beating in the games. But he never complained.

In the fall of 1924 Jim Thorpe played football for the Rock Island Independents, who finished fifth in the NFL with a record of 5–2–2. While Thorpe made appearances in all nine games, he only scored seven points, all with his foot, one extra point and two field goals.

In 1925 Tim Mara and Will Gibson purchased the New York NFL franchise for somewhere between $500 and $2,500. Neither Mara nor Gibson was sure of the amount. According to Mara, who knew little about football, "I figure an exclusive franchise for anything in New York is worth what I paid."[1] On October 18, 1925, the advent of professional football in New York was greeted by 20,000 fans at the Polo Grounds as the Giants defeated the Ben Franklin Yellowjackets of Philadelphia (later the Eagles), 14–0.

Jim Thorpe attempted to continue his professional football career by joining the newly formed New York Giants in the NFL. However, he failed to get in shape and played so poorly in the Giants' second game against Philadelphia that he had to be pulled from the game. Although he was playing on an injured knee, on October 28, 1925, the Giants dropped him. His contract then reverted back to Rock Island.

In 1923 Thorpe was separated from his wife Ida. The marriage ended in divorce the following year in Oklahoma on the grounds of desertion.

In late October 1925, Thorpe married Freeda Kirkpatrick, a woman of Scotch-Irish descent from Endicott, West Virginia. With Thorpe kicked off the New York Giants, the couple began a honeymoon in the west. The marriage would end in divorce in 1943 with Freeda charging Thorpe with "excessive drinking." However, Thorpe's wanderlust was a contributing factor to the divorce. Freeda got custody of the couple's four sons by the marriage, Carl Phillip, William, Richard and John.

Professional football was still a risky business in 1925. Newspapers refused to legitimize professional football by giving its games much space on the sports pages, and a lot of college football coaches and influential alumni were still advancing the notion that the pro game was out to kill college football.

But at the University of Illinois a player named of Harold "Red" Grange, also known as the "Galloping Ghost," was wrapping up a remarkable college career and would soon lead the NFL to solid ground in the professional sports business. Red Grange was the most celebrated college player since Jim Thorpe, and he would bring the NFL what it had been seeking since it was formed — headlines. George Halas stated that prior to Grange joining the Bears, he would look each day for some mention of the Bears in the newspapers and if he found just a two-inch item, the Bears front office would be delighted. Even when he found articles in two foreign language newspapers in Chicago, everyone was ecstatic.

In his college career Red Grange, playing for legendary Illinois coach Robert C. Zuppke, had scored 31 touchdowns, rushed for 3,362 yards and passed for another 571 yards. Zuppke, like Pop Warner, knew how to get the most out of his players. A legend on the University of Illinois campus has it that prior to the 1922 Iowa game Zuppke told Grange and the rest of the "Fighting Illini" squad, "This is a game that calls for men of supreme courage. Men of Iron! There will be no substitutions in this game. The only man who comes out of that lineup will be a DEAD MAN!"[2]

Red Grange played his last college game on November 21, 1925, against Ohio State. In the game won by the Fighting Illini 14–9, Grange showed his versatility as he gained 115 yards on the

Red Grange (Sports Story Reprints).

ground, including one 25-yard touchdown run, and gained another 43 yards on intercepted passes, returned kicks and punts for 26 yards and kicked one punt for 34 yards.

The following day, Red Grange signed a professional football contract with George Halas and the Chicago Bears for $100,000. The amount of Grange's contract was due in part to the fact that he became the first professional football player to hire an agent, C. C. Pyle, to represent him in negotiations.

George Halas maintained that when he signed Red Grange, it was the turning point in professional football. After signing Grange, Halas announced that the Bears would play the Chicago Cardinals on Thanksgiving Day, and people lined the streets to buy tickets. On November 26, 1925, 35,000 fans jammed Cubs park to witness Red Grange's first professional game. While the game ended in 0–0 tie, Grange gained 92 yards rushing and modern professional football was born.

Following the 1925 NFL season the Chicago Bears began a grueling exhibition trip, playing 18 games, eight in one 12-day period. Games were played in St. Louis, Philadelphia and Washington. The exhibition series is credited with establishing the legitimacy of professional football as well as saving the New York Giants franchise. The Bears vs. Giants exhibition game at the Polo Grounds attracted 73,000 fans. The Bears beat the Giants 19–7, and the player that most of the fans came to see, Red Grange, didn't disappoint them, intercepting a pass in the fourth quarter and scoring a 30-yard touchdown.

While Red Grange was presented with a check for $50,000 for playing in the game, George Halas took the opportunity to endorse products. Though he refused a cigarette ad because he didn't smoke, Halas did endorse products ranging from sweaters, shoes, caps, a doll and a soft drink, for the tidy sum of $35,000.

As the exhibition schedule continued the Bears lost to the Providence Steamrollers in Boston, 9–6. In the game Red Grange hurt his left arm. Then, as the Bears were getting beaten in Pittsburgh by an All-Star team, 21–0, Grange broke a blood vessel in his injured arm. By the time the Bears arrived in Detroit, a blood clot had formed in Grange's arm and he was unable to play. So the Bears paid out $9,000 in refunds to fans.

When the Bears and Giants played a rematch game in Chicago on December 13, Grange was still unable to play. Still the Bears beat the Giants, 9–0.

On New Year's Day, January 1, 1926, the Bears played the Tampa Cardinals, a barnstorming team that included Jim Thorpe and several of his former teammates from the Rock Island Independents. It was the first professional football game ever played in Tampa. The game played at Plant Field was billed on the game program as the "Grange Game," the clash of the old (Jim Thorpe) vs. the new (Red Grange).

Following the kickoff, on the second play, a Jim Thorpe fumble led to a speedy field goal by the Bears and a 3–0 lead. Red Grange played only 20 minutes but was the star of the game, running for a 70-yard touchdown to cap a 17–3 Bears victory. The newspapers were not kind to Jim Thorpe in reporting his game performance. One paper stated that Thorpe spent a terrible afternoon attempting to move his huge bulk, with its old-time speed, under a blazing Florida sun.

The following day the Bears defeated Jacksonville, 19–6.

The exhibition tour moved on to New Orleans where the Bears won, 14–0, with Red Grange rushing for 136 yards on 16 carries and one touchdown.

When the exhibition tour reached the Los Angeles Coliseum on January 16, 1926, another huge crowd of 75,000 fans witnessed the game as the Bears defeated the Tigers, 17–7, with a rejuvenated Grange scoring two touchdowns. The 14-week tour concluded with games in San Francisco, Portland and Seattle.

The NFL continued to expand and contract during the mid–1920s and at times appeared on shaky economic grounds over the next few years. However, the Chicago Bears exhibition tour had been highly successful and gave the league exactly what it needed at that moment in time, a signature team from a big city with the most famous player in the professional game.

Even though the Chicago Bears had put together a grueling exhibition schedule, the following year it would be eclipsed by the Duluth Eskimos, who played in the NFL from 1923 to 1927. Following the 1926 NFL season the Eskimos owner got in touch with Stanford All-American fullback Ernie Nevers and asked him to play for Duluth for a salary of $15,000 and a percentage of the gate. While Nevers agreed, he never asked how long the tour would be. As it turned out, it was a marathon 29-game exhibition tour that lasted 112 days, starting in Portland, Maine, and ending in San Francisco. Amazingly, the Eskimos made the tour with a 13-man squad.

Following the 1923 college football season Glenn "Pop" Warner left the University of Pittsburgh, where he had won three national titles, and became head coach of Stanford. It was at Stanford that Warner, with Nevers in his backfield, would win another national championship in 1926. Stanford also beat Notre Dame, coached by Knute Rockne, in the 1925 Rose Bowl (27–10). The Notre Dame backfield featured the legendary "Four Horsemen" (Harry Stuhldreher, Don Miller, Jim Crowley and Elmer Layden), so named by *New York Herald* sportswriter Grantland Rice. However, in the 1925 Rose Bowl, Ernie Nevers rushed for 114 yards on 34 carries, more than the Four Horsemen combined.

Later Pop Warner, completely ignoring Jim Thorpe, told Arthur Daley of the *New York Times* that Ernie Nevers was the greatest player he ever coached. He said Nevers was more conscientious and dependable. Warner also stated in an interview with Grantland Rice, "Nevers was a great team player, giving his best all the time. Thorpe never gave more than forty percent of his best."[3]

As far as Ernie Nevers was concerned, his relationship with Pop Warner was mutual admiration. "He was the greatest. He could fix a brace better than a doctor; he had more psychology than the trainer; he had more energy than the student manager — and as for football, no one knew as much as Pop,"[4] said Nevers.

For his praise of Nevers and slight of Thorpe, Pop Warner received some terse criticism from fans of Jim Thorpe. They felt that Warner had ridden to fame on the back of Thorpe's athletic achievements and if he had backed Thorpe up, he would have never lost his Olympic medals.

Glenn "Pop" Scobey Warner (Cumberland County Historical Society).

The Pandora's Box that Warner had opened in the Nevers vs. Thorpe controversy refused to die. In the 1940's, at a football luncheon with both Warner and Thorpe in attendance, Warner tried to put a new spin on the controversy he had created. He told the assembled crowd that Jim Thorpe was his best half back and Ernie Nevers was his best fullback he ever coached.

Ernie Nevers, like Jim Thorpe, also played major league baseball, pitching for the St. Louis Browns for three seasons, 1926–1928, finishing with a career won-lost record of 6–12. Nevers also had the distinction of serving up two home runs to Babe Ruth in 1927 as the "Sultan of Swat" was setting the all-time season record of 60 round trippers that would stand until 1961. While Ernie could boast that he once hit a double off Walter Johnson, Jim Thorpe had a better career batting average (.252) than Nevers (.200).

In the 1926 football season Jim Thorpe struggled to remain part of the game that he had done so much to advance, and he returned to Canton for one last season. Then he decided to sit out the 1927 football season and try a new sporting venue. In the winter of 1927-1928, Thorpe barnstormed, playing professional basketball with his team "Jim Thorpe and His World-Famous Indians."

Other than playing on the Haskell Indian School basketball team in 1907, Jim Thorpe had little experience at the game. However, still fresh in his mind were Walter Lingo's marketing skills he had observed during his tenure with the Oorang Indians. So in the winter of 1927-1928, Thorpe put together an all–Indian basketball team and went out on a 45-game barnstorming tour of New York, Pennsylvania and Marion, Ohio. When Thorpe's all–Indian basketball team arrived in Carlisle, Pennsylvania, there were close to 3,000 fans at the station. The reception was nearly as large as the one the town had given him on his return from the 1912 Olympics.

Over time, Thorpe's basketball enterprise was forgotten. Then, in 2005, a fellow named Anthony in Jamestown, New York, bought an old book, *Jesse James and His Greatest Hauls*, at an auction in Pennsylvania. When Anthony took the book home and began leafing through the pages, he discovered a big red ticket. It was for a basketball game between Jim Thorpe and His World-Famous Indians and the Clothes shop, to be played at the Y.M.C.A. Gym on Tuesday, March 1, 1927. After attempting to do research on the ticket and coming up with very little, Anthony contacted the PBS series *History Detectives.*

Wes Cowan of *History Detectives* was dispatched to Jamestown and began to research the matter. While Cowan didn't find out very much about the ticket, it was nonetheless a direct connection with a forgotten part of the Jim Thorpe saga. The search for the ticket's history was chronicled on *History Detectives* Episode 10 in 2005.

Wes Cowan did, however, speak with Thorpe's grandson, Mike Koehler. Koehler was unable to provide any historical detail on his grandfather's basketball team or the 1927-1928 tour. Instead he offered a philosophical response. Koehler told Cowan that while his grandfather had firmly established his identity as an athlete, it didn't leave much room for Jim Thorpe the father, the husband or the grandfather. "All the athletic teams he got involved with from Carlisle to the pros to teams such as this one, he was able to find the sense of family that he didn't experience throughout much of his life."[5]

Since the discovery of the ticket, little detail on the tour has been brought to light. With a historical void in the Jim Thorpe story recently discovered, many writers have felt a need to fill that void with rhetoric similar to Thorpe's grandson's.

But attempting to attach a philosophical reasoning to Thorpe's semi-pro basketball team is a useless exercise when it is so apparent that the tour of the team during the winter of 1926-1927 was simply a bread and butter exercise. Thorpe was aging and up until this time in his life, professional sports had provided him and his family with a livelihood. With his skills diminished and his star fading, Thorpe needed to reinvent himself and forge on. Forming an all–Indian basketball team seemed like a logical answer to providing necessary income. Perhaps in some respects it was a sideshow, but it was a common practice for professional sports teams and professional athletes of the time to tour for the dollar in the off-season.

In fact the practice of professional sports barnstorming and exhibitions had been going on for decades. Even Babe Ruth, who made $80,000 a year playing for the New York Yankees, barnstormed in the off-season during the 1920s. With no television coverage and radio in its infancy, fans across America were left with the daily newspapers to chronicle the professional sporting events and heroics of the athletes. After having to use their imaginations to conjure up an image of these titans, the opportunity to see them in the flesh in barnstorming exhibitions was a huge thrill for the fans and profitable for the participants.

As the baseball season approached, on April 13, 1928, Jim Thorpe, a month shy of turning 40 years old, sent a telegram to Dick Rudolph, his former teammate, pitcher and coach of the Boston Braves, who by then was managing the Waterbury minor league team. He asked Rudolf for a job. But Rudolf informed Thorpe that the club had nothing to offer him. It had not been that long ago that having the chance to sign Jim Thorpe for your minor league club would have been a huge advantage at the gate. But now Thorpe was considered done.

On December 10, 1928, Thorpe played in his final professional football game for the Chicago Cardinals. The Chicago Bears beat the Cardinals 34–0. Thorpe played so badly that he was removed from the game and then retired. Thorpe had played professional football for 12 years with 13 teams.

JIM THORPE'S PROFESSIONAL FOOTBALL EXPERIENCE

Year	Team
1915	Canton Bulldogs
1916	Canton Bulldogs

Year	Team
1917	Canton Bulldogs
1919	Canton Bulldogs
1920	Canton Bulldogs (APFA)
1921	Cleveland Indians (APFA)
1922	Oorang Indians (NFL)
1923	Oorang Indians (NFL)
1923	Toledo Maroons (NFL)
1924	Rock Island Independents (NFL)
1925	New York Giants (NFL)
1926	Canton Bulldogs (NFL)
1928	Chicago Cardinals (NFL)

19

Thorpe Goes to Hollywood

Around 1920 Jim Thorpe had an estate with an estimated value at $100,000 which included farms in Oklahoma, city real estate and negotiables. But by 1930 Thorpe was 42 years old, retired from football and baseball, and broke. Someone suggested that he should go to California. So Thorpe, along with his second wife and young sons Carl and Bill (two other sons, Dick and Jack, would be born later in the 1930s), made their way to the Golden State and settled in Hawthorne.

The Great Depression had set in and nearly 25 percent of the American population was unemployed. Jobs were hard to come by, even for the greatest athlete in the world. So Thorpe did what he could. He became the master of ceremonies for C.C. Pyle's cross-country marathon, known as the "bunion derby." When the program went bankrupt, Thorpe had to sue Pyle for his $50 paycheck. Then Thorpe took a job as a painter. He finally settled in working as a day laborer in Los Angeles, using a pick and shovel for $4 a day, excavating a site for a new hospital. But Jim Thorpe was still newsworthy, and newspapers never missed an opportunity to snap pictures of him with his shovel and run articles on his demise. It was unbelievable humiliation for Thorpe, but he never complained.

While drinking had been part of the cause for Thorpe's economic demise, it also gave him the courage to communicate openly with his sons. Thorpe's oldest son Carl said, "When he was drinking was the time he'd really talk to us. He'd say, 'I really screwed up my life drinking. Don't ever drink.' He'd say it so many times, so many ways. 'You've seen what I've done with my life. Don't do the same things.'"[1] According to Carl, his father's whiskey-laced rhetoric was his way of apologizing for not spending more time with the family.

When Thorpe was not drinking he was not so apologetic or sentimental, but a rather stern disciplinarian who would have a switch out in an instant to whip his sons. Thorpe also could not tolerate bragging. Thorpe never kept newspaper clippings or scrapbooks on his athletic heroics around the house and never spent any time reminiscing about them with his sons. Carl Thorpe said the kids at school would ask him questions about his father, but he just couldn't answer any of them.

Some movie scouts found Thorpe and his family living in a frame cottage in Hawthorne near some oil wells and truck farms. So they offered him work. Soon Thorpe began a new career playing bit parts in Hollywood Class B westerns for $7.50 a day.

In 1931 Jim Thorpe would appear as Swift Arrow in the movie *Battling with Buffalo Bill*, staring Tom Tyler. It would be the first role for Thorpe, both credited and uncredited, in a total of 64 movies over the next 20 years.

Immediately the film studios started sending out more photos of Thorpe than their stars and profited from the human interest copy. Thorpe would sit around all day giving interviews. But he was still only getting an extra's day's pay. Thorpe said that he didn't resent the situation at first, because he was looking ahead, believing that the studios would offer him something more substantial. He would soon realize that he was being exploited by the Hollywood moguls. The kind of interviews that were printed were distasteful. The often pictured him as a pathetic, broken or futile character. One article even stated that the rugs in his home were of cheap quality, but that his wife, being a great housekeeper, kept them clean.

That same year, Thorpe, desperately needing money, sold the movie rights to his life story to MGM for $1,500. However, the movie would not be made until the early 1950s after Warner Brothers bought the rights from MGM.

On July 30, 1932, the Olympic Games (X Olympiad) began in Los Angeles with opening ceremonies. Jim Thorpe, down on his luck, was so broke he didn't have enough money for a ticket to the games. But when his plight became public, thousands of sympathetic people offered their tickets to him.

The Vice President of the United States, Charles W. Curtis, who had been born on the Kansa/Kaw Indian–allotted land which later became part of North Topeka, Kansas, and was $1/8$ Indian himself, invited Thorpe to sit with him in the presidential box and gave him his pass for the entire games. As Thorpe was announced and rose to his feet in the presidential box, the crowd of 100,000 gave him a thunderous standing ovation.

As the games continued, Thorpe would show up daily at the Coliseum and look down on the games from his lofty perch. It prompted columnist Westbrook Pegler to write, "Old Jim, he just sits around. Some days he sits in two or three of the boxes reserved for royalty and nobility of the amateur sports business. Once he sat in the governor's box. He is a privileged character. Slightly pathetic, but privileged."[2]

One of the American athletes that Thorpe was keenly interested in watching was Jim Bausch, a.k.a. "Jarrin' Jim," a former bruising 210-pound All-American fullback from the University of Kansas who was competing in the decathlon. Although Bausch was in fifth place after the first day, his performances in the discus and pole vault were so daunting that they lifted him to a world record 8462 points in winning the gold medal.

Although the point values had been changed in the decathlon since the 1912 Olympics, Bausch would have still beaten Jim Thorpe using the old scoring system. However, Thorpe's record in the pentathlon would never be broken because the event was dropped after the 1924 Olympics.

At the time of the Olympics, Jim Thorpe had attempted to reignite his athletic star by publishing a ghost-written book titled *Jim Thorpe's History of the Olympics*. But the book sold very few copies. Meanwhile Thorpe continued to earn a living through the next few years of the Depression by playing insignificant parts in movies and giving lectures on his athletic career. Despite his precarious financial condition, Thorpe never asked to be paid for his personal appearances.

In 1932 Thorpe played an uncredited role in "Hold 'Em Jail" starring Bert Wheeler and Robert Woolsey, featuring 16-year-old Betty Grable. The film, set in a prison, climaxes with a zany football game in which Thorpe has a bit part.

Thorpe also found time in the fall of 1932 to return to the Haskell Institute where as a student his interest in football had begun after watching Chauncey Archiquette play fullback. During halftime of a Haskell football game, Thorpe put on a kicking demonstration. Standing at the 50-yard line, he proceeded to kick the ball over the goal posts, first at one end of the field and then the other.

By early 1933 there were about a thousand Indians in and around Hollywood who were seeking bit parts in the movies. The Indians were becoming disgruntled with the fact that often the movie studios would hire Arabs, Hawaiians, Mexicans, Negroes and even Chinese to play the parts of Indians in the movies. So Jim Thorpe and a Blackfoot Indian actor known as Chief Many Treaties decided to do something about it. They organized a band of 250 Indians representing 18 tribes to protest.

According to Chief Many Treaties, a real Indian couldn't get a job in the movies any longer. He had previously spoken with Sol Rosenblatt, the national administrator for the movie code, and was threatening to take his case to President Roosevelt.

Jim Thorpe asserted that Indians were not very aggressive, so he had decided to do something about getting work for them. Thorpe felt that most directors were ignorant of tribal dress. Thorpe said that on one occasion he had to argue for a half-hour to convince a director that Indians did not wear war paint and carry tomahawks to a peace conference. Thorpe also had to point out that Indians never wore mustaches.

"It isn't my idea to tell directors how to cast their pictures," Jim explained, "but I think they should use bona fide Indians as extras and in atmosphere scenes. For a long time, almost every nationality has represented us, often to the discredit of the Indian on the screen."[3]

Soon after he and Chief Many Treaties began their campaign for obtaining film bits for Indians with the casting bureau, Jim Thorpe was put in charge of all Indian extras in Hollywood.

In June, 1933, Thorpe filed suit against Columbia Pictures Corporation for $100,000 over the use of his name and picture in the film *The White Eagle.* While Jim Thorpe did not appear in the movie, the studio claimed that he had agreed to appear in the film, then backed out. Therefore Columbia alleged that it was too late to recall the advance advertising for the film that had occurred nation-wide. Thorpe lost the suit.

In August 1933, Thorpe, an excellent rider who as a youth in Oklahoma had saddled and ridden unbroken colts, was severely injured with numerous lacerations, bruises and a wrenched shoulder when he was thrown from a bucking horse while working as an extra in the Warner-First National film *The Telegraph Trail,* starring John Wayne. Thorpe had been attempting to ride the horse Indian style without a saddle when the horse began bucking.

Earlier in the year Thorpe's 16-year-old daughter Gail had nearly died in a fire attempting to escape from her dormitory room at the Chilocco Indian School in Arkansas City, Kansas.

Although Thorpe was not making much money, he was enjoying his Hollywood experience. He hung out with Western stars Tom Mix and Buck Jones. A close friend and drinking buddy of Thorpe's was Wallace Beery. After drinking all night until 3:00 A.M., the two would arrive at the Thorpe Spanish stucco house and continue to raise a ruckus until dawn, despite the fact that his wife and kids were attempting to sleep.

Thorpe kept making bit part appearance in movies. During the summer of 1934 his football skills were called upon when he worked as the technical advisor to University of Southern California coach Sam Berry on scenes for *College Rhythm.*

The year 1935 was a banner year for Jim Thorpe in Hollywood. He appeared in 18 credited and uncredited roles. Thorpe even got to play a couple of uncredited sports roles, one as a major league baseball player in *Alibi Ike* and another as a football player from Carlisle in *Fighting Youth.* He also played in *Barbary Coast,* starring Edward G. Robinson and Miriam Hopkins. His first major part took place that year with Helen Gahagan and Randolph Scott in *She*.

Helen Gahagan was married to actor Melvin Douglas. In 1944 Helen Gahagan Douglas was elected to the U.S. House of Representatives from California. In 1950 she ran unsuccessfully for the U.S. Senate against Richard M. Nixon in a campaign filled with considerable mud slinging, so much in fact that she tagged Nixon with the nickname of "Tricky Dick." However, many elite Democrats considered Helen Gahagan Douglas an extremist and backed Nixon in the election, including former Ambassador Joseph P. Kennedy. In fact, Congressman John F. Kennedy even delivered a campaign contribution of $1,000 from his father to Nixon in his Congressional office.

The 1916 Olympic Games had been awarded by the I.O.C. to Germany but were cancelled due to World War One. In 1931 the I.O.C. awarded the 1936 Olympic Games to Germany. This award of the games came two years before Adolf Hitler and the Nazis took control of Germany. Subsequently, as the goose-stepping Nazis launched their anti–Semitic policies and the start of the 1936 games approached, Hitler announced that only members of the Aryan race would be permitted to compete on the German Olympic team. The result was immediate outrage in the United States. The banning of non–Aryans from Germany's Olympic team was viewed as a violation of the Olympic code.

Avery Brundage, head of the American Olympic Committee, called for an American boycott of the games. However, the Nazis brought Brundage to Germany and smoothed things over with a guided tour of pristine Olympic training facilities. The Nazis assured Brundage that the facilities were for use by German Jews and gave him the VIP treatment. Consequently, Brundage changed his stance.

However, the A.A.U. and its eloquent, outspoken

Jim Thorpe circa 1935.

leader, Jeremiah Maloney, continued to support a boycott of the games, as did New York Governor Al Smith, 41 college presidents and nearly all of America's trade unions. Maloney advanced the belief that participating in the games in Berlin was giving American moral and financial support to the Nazi regime.

In December 1935, as the controversy increased over the possible boycott of the 1936 Olympic Games in Berlin, Jim Thorpe was on the set of *Treachery Rides the Range* in Tujunga Canyon. Reporters caught up with him in a break between scenes and asked him for his opinion of the possible American boycott of the Olympic Games.

Jim Thorpe advanced an opinion that the American team should compete and that the Olympics should not be mixed with politics. "Personally, I would be deeply disappointed — in fact, I think it would be almost a disgrace — if the United States were out of the eleventh Olympiad. Let's keep out of old world affairs; religious, political and every other sort, and especially out of affairs that might lead to bad feeling."[4]

The Nazis, feeling immense pressure not only from the United States but also from various countries in Europe, modified their anti–Jewish participation policy in the Olympics. They allowed a part–Jewish athlete, Helene Mayer, a fencer who had won a gold medal at the 1928 Games, to become a member of the German Olympic team. In addition the Nazis also permitted Theodor Lewald to act as an advisor to the German Olympic Organizing Committee.

Eventually the 1936 Olympic Games took place and the American team did compete, although some Jewish-American athletes, including Harvard track star Milton Green, chose to boycott the Games. The American team consisted of 312 athletes, and Jesse Owens, a black man, would win four gold medals for the U.S.A.

As Jesse Owens won the 100 meters, the 200, the long jump and anchored the 400-meter relay team to victory, a stone-faced Adolf Hitler watched coldly from his box. As "The Star Spangled Banner" was played and Jesse Owens stepped forward to receive his medals, Hitler looked the other way. Once he strode out of his box.

By 1937 Jim Thorpe, now 49 years old, had ballooned to 235 pounds and was attempting to sell automobiles in Pasadena. He soon returned to the movie lots. In August, Thorpe was paid $25 to play a Mongol guard wearing steel chain-mail armor in the film *The Adventures of Marco Polo*.

However, one thing had changed. Thorpe now refused to give interviews to studio publicity men or newspaper reporters without being paid. He said that he had been photographed hundreds of times and the talking and posing were of no advantage for him. Furthermore, he felt that all the writers wanted to do was talk about old things that stirred up unhappy feelings for him.

It was also in 1937 that Thorpe returned to Oklahoma to help his Sac and Fox people rescind their vote on a new tribal constitution. Using his own scarce money, he also urged them to vote to abolish the United States Bureau of Indian Affairs. However, the agency prevailed in Congress.

An often told story involving Jim Thorpe and his Hollywood experience involves an incident that took place in 1938, although some question where it happened. The story goes that Thorpe was working in Utah as an extra on the set of *Northwest Passage*. One day on the set, while dressed as an Indian Chief for his bit part, Thorpe was passing by a group of college boys who were working as extras in the same movie. To pass the time between shoots, the boys were fooling around, playing games that demonstrated their individual athletic ability. They were also making winner-takes-all bets on these games. One of the athletic feats they were participating in was a broad jump that had progressed to ten feet.

William "Bill" Frawley, who later played Fred Mertz on the hugely popular television series *I Love Lucy*, was aware of the true identity of the Indian Chief on the set. So Frawley bet all takers that the out-of-shape old man playing the Indian Chief could beat all the college boys in the broad jump. Bets were covered totaling $100 when the books closed. Then Jim Thorpe, a.k.a. the Indian Chief, made a few stretch movements and proceeded to leap an amazing ten feet eight inches. While Thorpe's broad jump was not quite his Pentathlon leap of 23 feet 2 and $7/10$ inches in the 1912 Olympics, it was good enough to beat all the competition that day.

On August 23, 1939, Thorpe was in New York working on the lecture circuit, telling youngsters about his feats in the Olympic games of 1912 and his football career at Carlisle, while promoting youth fitness. Although his relationship with John McGraw had been stormy, over the years since his playing days ended, Thorpe had remained a New York Giants baseball fan. So he went to the Polo Grounds for the first time since 1933. When members of the New York press discovered that Thorpe was in the ball park, they invited him into the press box to watch the game and converged upon him.

The older, more sophisticated Jim Thorpe was cordial with the reporters. He told them he didn't do his best work with the Giants. He said he tried too hard to make good for John McGraw. He played better ball after he left the Giants. Although he had only hit seven home runs in his big league career, Thorpe stated that with a live ball like they were currently using in the majors, he would have hit about 15–20 home runs a year. Furthermore, he believed that his batting average would have been 30–40 points higher.

But Thorpe raised some eyebrows when he decided to put a little spin on his football playing days in New York. Thorpe said that he played some good football in New York and believed he was better with the New York football Giants than he had been at Carlisle.

When asked about his preferences for sports, Thorpe remarked that he preferred track. He said that he used to get $750 a game playing football and never made more than $7,500 in a season playing baseball. "You don't last long enough and you come out of it all crippled up. The best sport from the health standpoint is track."⁵

As Thorpe watched the game it was pure nostalgia for him. He said that Giants center fielder Frank Demaree, because of his speed, reminded him of George Burns. Then he asked the reporters what was going on with Mel Ott. "He moves like a fellow going to the showers after a game with the old Massillon Tigers," said Thorpe. The reporters explained that Ott was suffering from a bad Charley horse. As he watched 210-pound Zeke Bonura run out a triple, Thorpe remarked, "He is really put together. Yes, he should be in football. It would be fun to see him running through tacklers."⁶

Thorpe left before the game was over and the Giants had lost to the Chicago Cubs, 8–3. "I don't like to see the Giants lose," said Thorpe. "They're still my team."⁷

By 1940, Jim Thorpe had become so skilled at public speaking that the same lecture bureau which handled speaking assignments for First Lady Eleanor Roosevelt signed him to a contract and he began making national appearances. The speakers bureau brought structure to Thorpe's presentations and developed a menu of four standard speeches for organizations to choose from.

The first was "Jim Thorpe Views the Sports Season," where he would speak on current sporting topics. Although the International Rotary Club had begun a campaign to get Thorpe's Olympic medals back, he was reticent to speak out on the issue. However, Thorpe never forgot about what he considered his unfair treatment at the hands of the A.A.U. in 1912. So he felt compelled to speak out against the organization when he perceived that a further injustice was being brought forth to a current athlete.

In particular in late 1940, Jim Thorpe was concerned about the threats of the A.A.U. that all college football players who chose to participate in the 1941 East-West Shrine benefit game in San Francisco on New Year's Day and compete with or against Tom Harmon would be declared professionals. Tom Harmon was an All-American halfback from the University of Michigan and the leading college rusher and Heisman Trophy winner for 1940. The problem, according to the A.A.U., was that Harmon had cashed in on his reputation by appearing on the Eddie Cantor radio show for $900 and therefore was a professional. While the A.A.U. had no jurisdiction over college football, it was threatening the players who played with or against Harmon in the East-West Shrine game with loss of amateur status in other sports it supervised such as basketball, track and boxing.

Consequently, on January 1, 1941, 42 of 43 players who played in the game with Harmon lost their eligibility in A.A.U.–controlled collegiate sports. Only Rice's Fred Hartman was spared because he applied for dispensation to play.

"If the American Athletic Union was made up of businessmen," said Thorpe, "there probably wouldn't have been any trouble with Harmon, or Eleanor Holm (suspended from the 1936 Olympics team by Avery Brundage after she had attended a cocktail party on the transatlantic cruise ship taking her to Germany) in the last Olympics, or about me." Thorpe stated that there was no sense in the ruling of the A.A.U. in the Harmon case, in view of some of their other rulings. As a case in point, Thorpe singled out the West Coast football players. "Whenever the movies want football scenes, they put them to work. They're the type. Nothing is ever said about it."[8]

The second Thorpe canned address was "Until Now, or Thirty Years an Athlete," in which he would tell about his own experiences in sports, tales about the New York Giants, the Carlisle Indians and the Canton Bulldogs.

Thorpe would pepper his address with humorous anecdotes such as the one about the student at Carlisle who had gone out for the football team six years without getting his letter. Thorpe would sigh and say, "it was a sad thing, long time, no C."

The third was "An Hour with Jim Thorpe," which was a sort of inspirational talk on the significance of sports in modern life. The target audience for this talk was primarily young groups, high schools and athletic organizations.

The fourth was "The American Indian Today." In this talk Thorpe would appear in full Sac and Fox Indian regalia complete with headdress and would espouse his views on the state of Indian affairs in the country.

Thorpe would tell his audience, "Indians are Americans, and yet for the most part, they rank as aliens. They are eligible for the draft, but even if they are called they do not become citizens. The Indians who fought in the last war were not granted citizenship until after it was over. Personally, I don't see any sense in it."[9]

The year 1940 was a busy one for Thorpe in Hollywood. He appeared in three movies, including a role as Gray Cloud in *Arizona Frontier* with Tex Ritter, which received favorable reviews. In the film, Ritter played Tex White-deer, a white boy raised by Gray Cloud (Thorpe). Tex's ancestry becomes a problem when as a government agent he is charged with making the decision of where the east and west branches of the railroad meet. The song "Red River Valley" was also introduced in the film.

That same year Thorpe's son Carl Phillip, 13, appeared in a movie based on the life of Knute Rockne.

The following year Thorpe was out on the lecture circuit when he learned on April 1, 1941, that his wife Freeda had filed for divorce in Los Angeles, charging him with cruelty. On October, 29, 1941, Freeda Thorpe was granted a divorce and was awarded custody of their four children. Freeda allegedly had a difficult time adjusting to Thorpe's long absences from home throughout their 15-year marriage. She stated that at times, unannounced, Thorpe would hit the road for three weeks or more. She also was concerned with his drinking. Later his son Carl attempted to downplay his father's frequent absences from home by rationalizing his sojourns as part of his Indian heritage, a throwback to the days when Indians would leave the tribe for long hunting trips. Nonetheless, Jim Thorpe was completely distraught by the divorce and the following few years would be some of the darkest in his life.

When the United States entered World War II, Thorpe wanted to be part of the war effort. However, he was 53 years old and the U.S. Government didn't really have an assignment for him.

So in March 1942, Jim Thorpe moved to Romulus, Michigan, and began working as a security guard at the Ford Rouge plant in Dearborn where the G.P. (or "jeep") vehicle was being produced for the U.S. military. However on February 11, 1943, Thorpe suffered a heart attack and was taken to Henry Ford Hospital in Detroit.

After recovering, Thorpe returned to Oklahoma in October 1943, and settled down in Tulsa. There were rumors circulating that he might be offered a coaching job at the Bacone Indian College at Muskogee, Oklahoma. Thorpe was also considering entering his four sons in Chilocco Indian School in Chilocco, Oklahoma.

However, by November Thorpe had failed to land the coaching job, so he packed up, moved back to California and began working in a war plant in Oxnard.

Thorpe was very proud of the fact that in July 1943, his oldest daughter Grace graduated from the recruiting school at the Third Women's Army Corps Training Center at Ft. Oglethorpe, GA. Grace Thorpe was assigned to recruiting duty in the Ninth Service Command with headquarters at Ft. Douglas, Utah. Later she was awarded a bronze star for her actions in the Battle for New Guinea. After the Japanese surrender, Grace Thorpe served as a personnel interviewer for General Douglas MacArthur at his headquarters in Tokyo during the occupation of Japan.

In January 1944, Jim Thorpe returned to Detroit and resumed working in the Ford plant. But before long it was back to Hollywood as Thorpe signed a contract with Paramount Pictures to play to a rough gold miner in the film *Road to Utopia* starring Bing Crosby, Bob Hope and Dorothy Lamour. The picture was released in 1946.

Thorpe also appeared in two other films in 1944, having an uncredited bit part in *Outlaws of Santa Fe* and as Henchmen Spike in *Outlaw Trail* starring Hoot Gibson.

Still not satisfied with his contribution to the war effort, in 1945 and well past the age of acceptance for the Army and Navy, Thorpe joined the Merchant Marines and served on an ammunition ship, the *U.S.S. Southwest Victory*, before the war ended. The ship supplied ammunition to American and British troops on the fronts of India.

After a chance meeting in Lomita, California, on June 2, 1945, Thorpe married for a third time. Thorpe's new wife was Patricia Gladys Askew, whom he had first met about 30 years previously while he was playing professional football for the Rock Island Independents. At the time Patricia, a native of Louisville, Kentucky, was running a bar in San Pedro, California.

Now Jim Thorpe not only had a new wife, he had a business agent. Patricia had very good business sense and immediately made sure that he was paid for his personal appearances. In fact, she set the standard rate for his future appearances at $500.

However, Patricia was not particularly liked by the Thorpe children. Although Patricia had been deceased for 12 years in 1982, Jack Thorpe told *Sports Illustrated* magazine, "Truthfully, I can't say one good word about her."[10]

Carl Thorpe said that Patricia was a very assertive person; she recognized the Thorpe brand and arranged for his father to get money from his personal appearances. Prior to this, Thorpe had continued making a lot of personal appearances for free, even when he had little money to spare. But Carl Thorpe also maintained that the money his father brought in was being used to provide Patricia with extravagant gifts such as diamond rings and furs. According to Carl, as long as his father had a buck for the next day, he was fine. Patricia, or Patsy as she was known, wasn't like that.

Late in 1945, Thorpe was working as the bartender in Patricia's tavern in San Pedro, now known as "Jim Thorpe's All-American Supper Club." While the establishment didn't have the location or allure of other former sports heroes' eateries such as former heavyweight champion Jack Dempsey's neat little two-room Italian-American Restaurant on Broadway between 49th and 50th streets in New York, at the time it was a living.

One day, 21-year-old Bill Thourlby entered the dimly lit bar of the restaurant. There was a "For Sale" sign in the window and Thorpe was the only person in the place. Thourlby asked Thorpe how business was. Thorpe replied that there wasn't much of it. From this point forward Thorpe would have a lasting relationship with Thourlby for the rest of his life and refer to him as Buddy, his adopted son.

Thourlby was the drifter son of a wealthy St. Clair, Michigan, industrialist. He had attended two colleges, served in the armed services and was currently working as an extra in the movie *Rhubarb* starring Ray Milland.

But with a stake from his father, Thourlby bought into the business. The business still failed. According to Thourlby, the generosity of Thorpe helped sink it. "Every broken down athlete would come in needing a free meal and a drink, and Jim saw that they got it,"[12] said Thourlby.

Jack Dempsey had known Jim Thorpe for years. It was Dempsey's opinion that Thorpe's restaurant and bar failed because he didn't have any experience in the industry and he lacked a good business partner.

Thorpe's love of booze was not a factor in the collapse of the business. Thourlby maintained that, by this time in his life, Jim Thorpe was really not that much of a drinker any more, because he couldn't handle it. One or two drinks would have his head spinning.

Out of the restaurant business, Thorpe and Thourlby began making the daily casting rounds of the movie studios in Hollywood. When Thorpe introduced Thourlby to executives at Paramount, he stated that he wanted them to meet "my buddy." When Paramount decided to sign Thourlby, they brought out a contract made out to "Buddy Thorpe." From that time going forward, Bill Thourlby would use the name of Buddy Thorpe informally. Thourlby would go on to appear in 20 credited and un-credited roles in movies and television, including playing Max Schmeling in the 1953 film *The Joe Louis Story*. He would also be the producer of two films.

According to Thourlby, Thorpe was not very tidy in his personal affairs. He went to the police station one day to pay a parking ticket for him and found out that Thorpe had 300 filed against him.

Promoters were always attempting to cash in on Thorpe's fame. One wanted Thorpe to enter professional wrestling but he would have nothing to do with it. Thourlby maintained that all Jim Thorpe wanted was to have a place in football. Any assistant coaching job would have suited him fine. It is ironic that the same fate was inflicted upon Babe Ruth. Claire Ruth had stated that after the Babe retired as a player, he got up every morning until the day he died and waited by the phone for a call offering him a job as a manager. It is just so incredible that two of the most iconic athletes of the twentieth century, Thorpe and Ruth, were ignored by the sporting establishment following their playing days, unless their fame could be exploited.

Thourlby believes his close relationship with Thorpe was a factor in his first two marriages not being successful. Thorpe was never close to any of his children and found his relationship with Thourlby a substitute of his choosing. By the mid–1970s Thourlby owned a men's clothing store in Atlanta. Hanging on the wall of his Peachtree Street store was a picture of Thorpe that had the inscription, "To my son Buddy, from your dad, Jim Thorpe—1951."[12]

In 1948 Jim Thorpe, now 60 years old, was hired by the Chicago Park District. As a supervisor of recreation, his duties included giving talks on athletics, training, living a clean life and staying out of trouble. Thorpe also made an appearance at an Old Timers' game in August 1948 at Wrigley Field in Chicago and hit a 348-foot home run off former Chicago White Sox great Urban "Red" Faber. Later that year Thorpe briefly returned to the gridiron. Wearing jersey number 68, Thorpe put on a field goal kicking exhibition during halftime of a San Francisco 49ers game at Kezar Stadium, kicking a few from mid-field.

The following year, in 1949, Thorpe and his third wife Patricia returned to Los Angeles and took up residence in a hotel. Thorpe tried his hand at operating and managing a girls' softball team called the Jim Thorpe Thunderbirds, playing in the National Softball Congress that toured the nation.

Thorpe was also back in the movies in 1949, appearing in an uncredited role in *White Heat* with James Cagney. Thorpe played one of the message passers in the prison mess hall scene where Cagney goes berserk.

In August 1949, Warner Brothers, which had bought the rights to Jim Thorpe's life story from MGM for $35,000, began filming his biography. The studio hired Thorpe as a technical adviser. However, the job was more ceremonial than practical and mostly he just sat around on the set watching his life story being exaggerated and filmed.

Burt Lancaster, chosen to play the part of Jim Thorpe, underwent weeks of strenuous physical training to prepare for the role. Thorpe taught Lancaster how to kick a football, and the actor worked out for several weeks with players from USC and UCLA in order to learn the fundamentals of the game. For the track scenes, Lancaster was coached by former USC track coach Jess Hill. For the actual track events in the film, Lancaster was doubled by Al Lawrence, who later would win a bronze medal for Australia in the 10,000 meter run at the 1956 Olympic Games in Melbourne.

Charles Bickford was selected to play Pop Warner and Phyllis Thayer played Thorpe's first wife, Iva. The film was directed by Michael Curtiz.

Also Warner Brothers would make an unsuccessful attempt to reclaim Jim Thorpe's Olympic medals as part of an advertising campaign prior to the release of film.

While Jim Thorpe had been searching for recognition for the past quarter century, it finally came his way in a flurry of accolades beginning in January 1950. That month 391 sports writers and broadcasters voted in a poll to determine the greatest football player for the first half of the twentieth century. Jim Thorpe won hands down.

Player	College	Votes
James Thorpe	Carlisle	170
Harold (Red) Grange	Illinois	138
Bronko Nagurski	Minnesota	38
Ernie Nevers	Stanford	7
Sammy Baugh	Texas Christian	7
Don Hutson	Alabama	6
George Gipp	Notre Dame	4
Charles Trippi	Georgia	3

*Four players received two votes each and ten players received one vote each.

That same year Jim Thorpe was named the most outstanding male athlete of the half-century in the Associated Press mid-century poll of the nation's sportswriters and sportscasters, beating other sports greats such as Babe Ruth, Bobby Jones, Jack Dempsey, Ty Cobb and Joe Louis. Of 393 voters, 252 (64 percent) named Thorpe first, 45 named him second and 29 third. Babe Ruth drew only 86 first-place votes, Jack Dempsey 19 and Ty Cobb just 11 first-place votes.

However, while Thorpe was named the number one football player of the period 1900–1949, in track Thorpe was voted second behind Jesse Owens.

In 1950 Jim Thorpe would make the last of his 64 appearances in a feature film, playing a Navajo in *Wagon Master*, starring Ben Johnson and Ward Bond, directed by John Ford.

In 1951 Warner Brothers released the dramatized film of Thorpe's life, *Jim Thorpe—All-American*, starring Burt Lancaster. A producer asked Thorpe to get a face-lift in order to travel about as an advance man promoting the film. Halfway through the face-lift, Thorpe walked out. He just considered it all nonsense.

The film premiered on August 24, 1951, in Carlisle, Pennsylvania, and Oklahoma City, simultaneously at the request of Thorpe. In Carlisle 15,000 people turned out and a marker in Thorpe's honor was placed on the court-house lawn on Public Square.

The week before, Thorpe had been inducted into the National College Football Hall of Fame in New York.

In an interview about the film with Hollywood gossip columnist Hedda Hopper, Burt Lancaster was quite cavalier about the movie. "In 'Jim Thorpe' we didn't beat people over the head with the Indian problem. Thorpe had his bad breaks, but they weren't due to the fact that he was an Indian. As he realized in later life, his downfall as an athlete was largely brought on by weakness in his own nature — a feeling that the world was against him, unreasonable stubbornness, and the failure to understand the necessity for working as the member of a team"[13]

Burt Lancaster's statement in regard to the Native American aspects of the film was an understatement. The film completely ignored Jim Thorpe's considerable advocacy to increase Indian visibility in Hollywood and his tireless quest to increase the quality of life for Native Americans.

Later in 1951, after an infection on his lower lip failed to heal, Thorpe entered a Philadelphia hospital as a charity patient for an operation for lip cancer.

As soon as Thorpe was released from the hospital, with a bandage on his lower lip, he headed straight for New York to help hype a bit part his friend Bill Thourlby, a.k.a. Buddy Thorpe, had in a movie.

With *Jim Thorpe — All-American*, being highly successful at the box office, reporters were appalled at the fact that Thorpe was broke and not receiving a dime. Arthur Daley of the *New York Times* asked Thorpe about the situation. "Back in 1931, I sold the story of my life to M.G.M. for $1,500. I never did read the contract, especially the fine print. Although I'd been led to believe that I'd receive $20,000, I've received nothing."[14]

To assist Thorpe with his medical bills, professional baseball and other groups held fundraisers, some raising thousands of dollars. On January 30, 1952, a fundraiser for Thorpe was held in Canton, Ohio, and 703 people attended. The featured speaker was Branch Rickey, general manager of the Pittsburgh Pirates, who called for the return of Thorpe's Olympic medals. Thorpe was present and was presented with a check for $1,000 and a wrist watch.

Always attempting to find another way to use his fame as his meal ticket, Thorpe created yet another enterprise, "Jim Thorpe's All-American Thunderbirds," a group of a half-dozen Indians with a song and dance show, and took them out on tour. To some observers it was a pathetic spectacle to see the man who 40 years ago had been called "the world's greatest athlete," by the King of Sweden, nearly penniless and reduced to performing in an aborigine side show.

U.S. Representative Frank Bow of Ohio (Canton) had been in attendance at the Thorpe fundraiser where Branch Rickey had raised the issue of restoration of Thorpe's Olympic medals. So in February, 1952, a subcommittee in Congress led by Representative Bow began a campaign to get Avery Brundage, president of the U.S. Olympic Committee (U.S.O.C.), to use his influence to restore Thorpe's medals to him. However, by now Brundage had acquired a somewhat aristocratic stance on the matter and the attempt by Bow failed.

Patricia Thorpe was always concerned that if her husband and Brundage met face-to-face on the matter, Thorpe would hang one on him. But at this stage in his life, Jim Thorpe was more mellow than antagonistic. "Sure he could get those things back for me, but so far he's just played shut-mouth," said Thorpe. "He's stubborn and opinionated."[15]

As the year passed and the Indian group tour was completed, Thorpe and his third wife Patricia began operating a bar in Henderson, Nevada. There, on August 9, 1952, Thorpe suffered his second heart attack. Although he had arrived at the hospital unconscious, after three days Jim Thorpe was on his feet and demanded to be released. All that the doctors could do was to tell him to take it easy.

20

The Battle for Thorpe's
Medals and Remains

On March 28, 1953, Jim Thorpe was eating dinner with his wife in his auto trailer at Lomita, California, outside Los Angeles when he suffered a third heart attack. Patricia Thorpe's screams brought a neighbor, Colby Bradshaw, rushing to their trailer. Bradshaw administered artificial respiration on Thorpe for nearly a half-hour before the county fire rescue squad arrived and took over. Thorpe was momentarily revived and recognized people around him. However, he soon suffered a relapse and died. Thorpe was 64 years old. He had been living in the trailer not because of his economic situation, but because he liked the mobility of it.

The Indian Leader of the Haskell Institute wrote in its obituary, "The Great Spirit has taken Jim Thorpe's life. Will He ever replace him?"[1]

Tom Eagleman was born on the Crow Creek Sioux reservation at Fort Thompson, South Dakota. He had received eight years of schooling before attending Carlisle. By 1965, Eagleman was the only living football teammate of Jim Thorpe's from his days at Carlisle. Eagleman was a senior at Carlisle when Jim Thorpe was a freshman. He played football with Thorpe and later played on the same minor league baseball team with him. He was also Thorpe's roommate for one year.

In 1965, Eagleman gave the Associated Press his recollections of Jim Thorpe. A reporter asked Eagleman if Thorpe was as great as they claim. Eagleman stated that as a broken field runner, Thorpe was unmatched. He said not even Jim Brown of the Cleveland Browns was Thorpe's equal. "Brown isn't fast enough like Jim — maybe through the line he is as good, but he's not fast enough to get around the outside."[2]

For many athletes who achieve some degree of fame during their lifetime, their death is the end of their story. The death of Jim Thorpe would ignite a posthumous firestorm of activities surrounding his final resting place and the restoration of his Olympic medals. In fact, the Jim Thorpe saga continues until this very day. It is doubtful that the legacy of any other sports icon in American history has endured a postscript drama like that following the death of Jim Thorpe.

Following his death, Thorpe's body lay in state at Malloy's mortuary in California for 50 hours as mourners filed past his body. But soon his remains would begin an odyssey taking him from one burial spot to another to another to yet another. It seemed that in death as in life, Jim Thorpe was constantly wandering across the vast expanse of the American continent.

From California Thorpe's body was taken to Shawnee, Oklahoma. The night before his burial, six of his children and many relatives from the Thunderbird Clan of the Sac and Fox tribe held a session of secret rites of prayer and feasting. However, before the ritual had concluded, Patricia Thorpe, who had limited sensitivity toward Native American cultural affairs, arrived in a hearse and took Jim's body away to another cemetery.

On April 13, 1953 Jim Thorpe was laid to rest in a mausoleum at Garden Grove Cemetery. He was buried following the reading of requiem high mass in the shadow of an athletic stadium that bears his name. However, this burial would only be temporary. As Patricia Thorpe was unable to pay for the crypt rent, she moved Jim Thorpe's corpse to Tulsa, Oklahoma.

The Thorpe children had wanted to bury their father in Oklahoma and build a memorial there, a 21-foot-high marble statue of Thorpe depicting him as a Carlisle Indian football player. Lacking the necessary funds, Patricia Thorpe asked the State of Oklahoma to fund his burial. State officials did appropriate $25,000 for a memorial to Thorpe, but Governor William H. Murray refused to sign a spending bill authorizing the funds to build the monument. Ross Porter, the general manager-editor of the *Shawnee News-Star*, who headed up the memorial committee, accused the governor of double-crossing the committee.

At the moment it seemed that the great Jim Thorpe was coming ever closer to being buried in a pauper's grave. To most observers outside the family, the logical place for Jim Thorpe to be buried would in Carlisle. During the filming of *Jim Thorpe—All-American*, a local committee had attempted to gain an agreement on a burial site for Thorpe in Carlisle. The committee had even selected a site near the field where Thorpe played football. But according to John B. Fowler, who was a member of the committee, "Pat just wanted too much money. We felt like we were getting in a bidding war."[3] Fowler said they tried again after Thorpe died, but Patricia's price was still way too high.

A few months later, as the battle ensued over where Jim Thorpe should be buried and who should pay for it, Patricia Thorpe was in New York. One night she and Bill Thourlby were watching a documentary on television about an old, but quaint, little Pennsylvania coal mining town nestled in the Pocono Mountains about 70 miles from Philadelphia name called Mauch (pronounced Mock) Chunk, that had fallen on hard times. The situation in Mauch Chunk had become so bleak that even the young people were leaving town as soon as they graduated from high school. According to Thourlby, Patricia Thorpe liked the appearance of the town. She sat up in her chair and told Thourlby, "I've got an idea."[4]

Although Jim Thorpe had never laid eyes on the town, Patricia Thorpe told Thourlby that she intended to call the mayor of Mauch Chunk and arrange a meeting. She intended to tell the mayor that if the town changed its name to Jim Thorpe, Pennsylvania, she would move his remains there for burial. It just might be a stimulus for tourism which could save the town. So Patricia Thorpe called the mayor of Mauch Chunk and drove out to the town the following day.

Mauch Chunk, Pennsylvania, was first settled in 1818 when 400 acres were cleared and 40 buildings constructed. Josiah White and his business partner Erskine Hazzard installed "bear trap locks" which permitted coal boats to travel from Mauch Chunk to Easton, Pennsylvania. The town's name of Mauch Chunk is the Lenni Lenope words *macht tschunk* meaning "sleeping bear." In 1827, the Mauch Chunk Railroad, which became known as the Switchback Gravity Railroad, was opened to transport coal from Summit Hill to Mauch Chunk.

In 1855 the Lehigh Valley Railroad, founded by Asa Packer, began freight and passenger service between Mauch Chunk and Easton.

A disastrous flood occurred in 1862, damaging the canal and wiping out many of the early buildings. But Mauch Chunk recovered and rebuilt. With the canal severely damaged by the flood, in 1868 the Lehigh and Susquehanna Railroad was extended from Mauch Chunk to Easton.

Soon the busy but humble coal town began to gain a reputation as an excursion destination. As more and more millionaires built permanent or vacation residences in Mauch Chunk, it became known as the "Switzerland of America." Thousands of tourists were soon to follow. John Jacob Astor and his bride honeymooned in Mauch Chunk. By 1882, to accommodate the cultural tastes of its upper crust residents and tourists, Mauch Chunk built the Wahnetah Hotel, a fine resort hotel and an opera house. Small German breweries also dotted the landscape to serve miners, tourists and millionaires alike.

However, following World War One, Mauch Chunk started an economic decline as anthracite coal began to lose its competitive edge as fuel. By 1932,

Mauch Chunk was fast falling on hard times as the last shipment of coal was sent down the Lehigh Canal from Laury's Station to Bristol. Four years later the rails and cars of the Switchback Railroad were sold at auction for scrap. Suddenly the stark contrast of the town's past between coal miners and railroad barons started to fade away.

Old Mauch Chunk Station.

By the early 1950s Mauch Chunk was attempting to hang on as a community and continue with its boom and bust economy by either attracting industry or tourism. Actually the community was made up of two towns — Mauch Chunk and East Mauch Chunk, separated by a deep gorge in which the Lehigh River flowed, with a total population of about 6,000. For some reason a rather fierce rivalry existed between the two towns and they had separate school districts and municipal services.

Joe Boyle, the former editor and co-publisher of the *Mauch Chunk Times-News*, had been organizing a "nickel a week" fund to bring industry to the town. Donations from the townsfolk had grown to about $17,000 when Patricia Thorpe contacted the town in September 1953.

Local citizens liked Patricia Thorpe's idea of bringing her husband's remains to their community for burial. They thought that merging and renaming the towns would end sectional rivalry and provide positive impetus for change and economic growth. So at the May primary election in 1953, the residents believed that with talk of a 400-bed hospital, a museum and benefit football games, there was very little to lose. So they voted by a 10–1 margin to merge the towns and become The Borough of Jim Thorpe, Pennsylvania. Subsequently, $12,500 was diverted from the industrial fund to pay for most of the $17,000, 20-ton mausoleum for Thorpe's burial that was erected in his honor along Route 903.

Jim Thorpe had been dead for 11 months when his body was brought to the town named for him on February 8, 1954. However, his memorial was not yet ready, so he was temporarily buried in a crypt at Evergreen Cemetery. Then a most distasteful incident occurred. One of the pallbearers who had carried the casket containing Thorpe into the cemetery became convinced that the town had been duped, that the coffin was too heavy and therefore it had to be filled with rocks.

The controversy spread across the town like a brush fire. So Joe Boyle took it upon himself to prove to all that the coffin did indeed contain the remains of James Francis Thorpe. With the assistance of two morticians, Boyle had the body exhumed and the coffin opened. Inside was Thorpe.

The official dedication of Thorpe's memorial took place on Memorial Day of 1957. Thorpe's three daughters attended along with Pennsylvania's senators and legislators, as well as several former Carlisle Indians teammates including Joe Guyon and Pete Calac. Al Schacht, who had played minor league baseball with Thorpe in Jersey City, was the master of ceremonies. The crowd was estimated to be about 15,000.

The residents made sure that Thorpe's final resting place would not become a souvenir stand. His monument stands in a very quiet, well-groomed

Jim Thorpe Memorial, Jim Thorpe, PA.

and peaceful preserved spot of land on a hill above the town. Carved into the centerpiece of the memorial is the appraisal of King Gustav of Sweden following Thorpe's Olympic heroics in the 1912 games.

"SIR, YOU ARE THE GREATEST ATHLETE
IN THE WORLD"
KING GUSTAV STOCKHOLM, SWEDEN
1912 OLYMPICS
1888   JIM THORPE   1953

In honor of Thorpe's heritage and his athletic achievements, the Thorpe Memorial Mausoleum Committee brought earth from his birthplace in Prague, Oklahoma, additional soil from Saupula, Oklahoma, the Polo Grounds in New York, the Indian Field at Carlisle Indian School and the Olympic Stadium in Stockholm, Sweden.

When the Mauch Chunk communities merged and changed their names to Jim Thorpe, Pennsylvania, Bert Bell, former president of the Philadelphia Eagles, was the commissioner of the NFL and was the national chairman for the town's efforts. Following Bell's death in 1959 from a heart attack suffered during a game at Franklin Field in Philadelphia, plans for fund raising, including a benefit football game and the possibility of a hospital specializing in cancer and cardiac conditions, faded. For a while there was even talk about establishing the professional football hall of fame in Jim Thorpe, Pennsylvania, which eventually went to Canton, Ohio, in 1962. The unfortunate fact was that Bert Bell's "Jim Thorpe Foundation" had only raised $1,000 at the time of his death in 1959. Furthermore, no one in the NFL, including George Halas, rushed to take Bell's place in the effort.

The tourism envisioned by the town did not happen overnight. Consequently, by 1964 some residents were seeking to restore the old name of the town, Mauch Chunk. One resident, speaking with the UPI about the deal made with Patricia Thorpe, was absolutely cynical, "All we got was a dead Indian."[5]

What Patricia Thorpe got in the deal to bring Jim Thorpe's remains to the town has never been revealed. Joe Boyle would remain eternally mum on the subject. It is well known that initially Patricia had plans to open a motel in Jim Thorpe, Pennsylvania. However, Bob Knappenberger, who worked at the American Hotel in Mauch Chunk when Patricia first came to town, says he handed her a check that officially ended her association with the town after Thorpe's remains were received. It was for no more than about $500—basically to get her out of town.

Jim Thorpe was honored in many ways by the town. Mauch Chunk High School was renamed Jim Thorpe High School. The Mauch Chunk National Bank became the Jim Thorpe National Bank and the fire department became the Jim Thorpe Fire Department.

The town's coal mining past came back to life when Hollywood descended on and around Jim Thorpe, Pennsylvania, to film the 1970 movie *The Molly Maguires*, starring Richard Harris and Sean Connery. The old Mauch Chunk Jail was where more than 20 of the "Molly Maguires" were held during a labor dispute after being charged with conspiracy and murder. They were convicted on several of the charges on the testimony of a corrupt Pinkerton infiltrator played by Harris, which resulted in four of them being hanged in the prison's courtyard. The old jail was in use from 1871 to 1995. Today the jail is a museum.

Today residents in Jim Thorpe, Pennsylvania, are still of mixed thoughts about the economic progress that has been made since Thorpe's remains were received. But the reality is that, nearly 60 years after Jim Thorpe's remains came east, the merged communities of Mauch Chunk and East Mauch Chunk have become a vibrant town, bustling with tourists, bikers, artists, musicians and young entrepreneurs.

While the Jim Thorpe memorial located up on a hillside just outside town on Route 903 is a bit of a side attraction, the town of Jim Thorpe, Pennsylvania, thrives with bed and breakfast establishments, a hotel, a museum, shops and trendy restaurants. There is a steam locomotive that pulls tourists in passenger cars from Old Mauch Chunk station into the mountains along the Lehigh River Gorge. Three miles from downtown, whitewater rafting takes place. The town even has several festivals each year celebrating such events such as St. Patrick's Parade Weekend, Earth Day and the Jim Thorpe Birthday Celebration, the third weekend in May each year, along with several others.

However, most of Jim Thorpe's children and grandchildren have never accepted Pennsylvania as the final resting place for their father and grandfather. The exception and staunchest supporter of keeping her father's remains in Jim Thorpe, Pennsylvania, was Grace Thorpe. On April 7, 2008, she died at the age of 86 at the Claremore Veterans Center in Claremore, Oklahoma. The passing of Grace opened a window of opportunity for Jack Thorpe to renew the battle for his father's remains without strong family opposition.

In January 2001, Thorpe's three sons, led by Jack Thorpe, 64 years old and the youngest of Thorpe's five living children, asked the Borough of Jim Thorpe, Pennsylvania, to return his father's remains to the family for proper Indian burial in his native Oklahoma. According to Jack, Patricia Thorpe effectively auctioned off his father's name and body to the town. "We offered to work with them to help them succeed, but they don't need the bones of my father to succeed,"[6] said Jack.

Considering the contempt that the Thorpe children demonstrated towards their father's third wife over the ensuing decades since his demise, it seems a bit suspect that a rallying cry would come from the family for the transport of Thorpe's remains back to Oklahoma when the state flatly rejected his burial at the time of his death. It seems that the Thorpe children have never come to realize that all that Patricia Thorpe did was find a respectful and dignified burial plot for their father in Mauch Chunk, when no one else wanted him.

On September 7, 1954, Glenn "Pop" Warner died of throat cancer at the age of 83 at Palo Alto, California. He was buried in Springdale, New York, in a family plot in Maple Wood Cemetery. Ernest Sutton and John Waterman, who played for Warner at Carlisle, were honorary pallbearers.

Regardless of the feelings of the Thorpe children toward Patricia Thorpe, the fact was that she was fiercely loyal to the legacy of her husband. Rather than eulogize Warner, Patricia Thorpe stated that he really had crossed her husband up on the Olympics scandal. She said it was too bad considering that Warner rode to fame on Jim's ability.

On April 6, 1975, Patricia Thorpe died of a heart attack at age 76 in Hesperia, California. At the time of her death, she had been operating a nursing home and carrying out the fight to return Jim Thorpe's Olympic medals.

For now the remains of Jim Thorpe continue entombed in the Pennsylvania town named for him. Back in 2001, Mayor Ron Confer told the *Philadelphia Inquirer* that he would never unilaterally agree to give up the body. "That's really up to the voters. I'd say today we're content the way things are."[7]

The final chapter in Jim Thorpe's story is still being played out. On June 24, 2010, Jack Thorpe, now 72 years old, filed suit in Scranton, Pennsylvania, to have his father's remains returned to Oklahoma under a federal law designed to give Native American artifacts back to their tribal homelands. Addressing the defendants that include several current and former town officials, Thorpe said, "The bones of my father do not make or break your town. I resent using my father as a tourist attraction."[8] Thorpe said that he waited to file the suit until the last of his half-sisters, meaning Grace Thorpe, died, to avoid a family conflict over the lawsuit.

The issue of changing the town's name of Jim Thorpe back to Mauch Chunk has appeared twice on the ballot, being defeated both times in 1964 and 1965. Even today, from time to time the issue of the town being named for Jim Thorpe is resurrected. The issue was epitomized about 20 years ago, when one resident used to ride around town with a sign in his Chevrolet that read "JIM CHUNK."

The Pro Football Hall of Fame was established in Canton, Ohio in 1963. On September 7, 1963, the first 17 players were enshrined. They included:

Sammy Baugh	Don Hutson
Bert Bell	Earl (Curly) Lambeau
Joe Carr	Tim Mara
Earl (Dutch) Clark	George Preston Marshall
Harold (Red) Grange	John (Blood) McNally
George Halas	Bronko Nagurski
Mel Hein	Ernie Nevers
Wilbur (Pete) Henry	Jim Thorpe
Robert (Cal) Hubbard	

Jim Thorpe had been dead for ten years, but he kept winning awards and being selected to all-time lists. In 1955 the NFL established the Jim Thorpe Trophy to honor its MVP. With each acknowledgement came renewed calls for justice from the International Olympic Committee in restoring Thorpe's Olympic medals and records.

By the late 1960s Thorpe's oldest daughter Grace and the Junior Chamber of Commerce at Carlisle were leading campaigns. When Avery Brundage, who was still serving as president of the IOC, was informed of the latest effort

Jim Thorpe statue, Jim Thorpe, PA.

to have Thorpe's Olympic achievements reinstated, he said, "Oh, no! Not again. Can't you let sleeping dogs lie?"[9] Brundage maintained until the day he died that Thorpe had violated the rules in the 1912 Olympic Games and was not an amateur when he won in Stockholm.

One of the ironies in Brundage's response was that he personally benefited from the expulsion of Jim Thorpe's 1912 Olympic records. When the AAU declared Thorpe a professional, his Olympic records were erased. Therefore the revised records for the 1912 games showed F. R. Bie of Norway as the winner of the pentathlon and Hugo Wieslander of Sweden the winner of the decathlon. In the revised records, the removal of Thorpe moved Avery Brundage of the United States up to fifth place in the pentathlon.

Following the 1972 Summer Olympics in Munich, Avery Brundage retired as president of the IOC. Brundage's legacy is not, however, his rigid stance on the return of Jim Thorpe's Olympic medals and records. He will be best remembered for his controversial decision during the 1972 Olympic Games to permit the games to continue after a Palestinian terrorist group's attack on September 5 which killed 11 Israeli athletes. Brundage was replaced as president of the IOC in 1972 by Michael Morris (a.k.a. Lord Killanin) of Ireland.

For many years the bronze trophy, a 200-pound bust of King Gustav V of Sweden that had been given to Thorpe at the 1912 Olympic Games, had seemed to be missing. In 1972, E. Donald Sterner of Colts Neck, New Jersey, who played tackle on Thorpe's professional Canton Bulldogs for several years, found the bust in the IOC museum at Lausanne, Switzerland.

Meanwhile, the struggle for reinstatement and return of the Thorpe medals and records continued on many fronts. Haskell Junior College in Lawrence, Kansas, was starting an American Indian Hall of Fame to honor athletes of at least one-fourth American Indian or Alaskan native heritage. One of the prime goals of the Hall was to fight for the restoration of Jim Thorpe's Olympic medals.

In Oklahoma, the Thorpe children incorporated a nonprofit Jim Thorpe Foundation in July 1973, to control the use of their father's name and the distribution of his medals and belongings. Profits from the foundation were targeted to assist other Indians.

Also in Carlisle, Pennsylvania, the local Jaycees began a petition drive, hoping to obtain 10,000 signatures and enlist the help of President Richard Nixon and the Congress in petitioning the IOC.

Finally on October 12, 1973, at its national convention in West Yellowstone, Montana, the AAU restored Thorpe's amateur status for the period of 1909–1912. The move cleared the way for the United States Olympic Committee to petition the IOC for the restoration of Thorpe's medals and records.

By 1976 Thorpe's oldest daughter by his first marriage, Grace, was taking up the banner of her father's cause for reinstatement. Grace Thorpe had been an activist for Indian affairs for several years. In 1972 she had been one of a band of Indians to occupy Alcatraz Island in San Francisco Bay, claiming that when the Federal government vacated the island it should have been returned to the Indians as a part of treaty made with the Sioux that dictated that any unused lands should be returned to them.

Grace stated that the enormity of her father's fame never hit her until his death. "The family received a telegram from President Eisenhower and Dad's enormous popularity and fame must have hit me for the first time. I'm determined to fight for Dad's reputation until his records are restored."[10]

In early summer 1975, the U.S. Olympic Committee urged the IOC to return Jim Thorpe's two gold medals.

Now bolstered with favorable decisions on her father's circumstances by the AAU and the USOC, Grace Thorpe took the case for her father's Olympic medals to Washington. She had recently received a paralegal degree from Antioch (Ohio) College and came to Washington to work in an internship for the Senate Subcommittee on Indian Affairs in the office of Senator James G. Abourezk of South Dakota.

Suddenly, the United States Congress became involved in the struggle for the return of Thorpe's medals. Senator Abourezk was chairman of the Senate Subcommittee on Indian Affairs and introduced Senate Resolution 144 (co-sponsored by Senator Quentin Burdick of North Dakota), calling for the restoration of Jim Thorpe's amateur status as an athlete in an attempt to aid his legacy by restoring his Olympic medals.

President Gerald Ford, a former football player at the University of Michigan, got involved too. The President wrote a letter as a private citizen with a lifetime interest in sports to Lord Killanin, president of the IOC, endorsing the decision by the USOC. to restore Thorpe's two gold medals.

"The White House
Washington, August 8, 1975
Lord Michael Killanin,
President, International Olympic Committee,
Chateau de Vidy Lausanne, Switzerland,
Dear Lord Killanin:
    It has come to may attention that the Amateur Athletic Union, the governing body for the United States in international competition in athletics, has requested from your Committee favorable consideration of the reinstatement of James P. Thorpe as an amateur athlete in good standing for the period of 1909 through 1912.
    Together with the United States Olympic Committee and the Amateur

Athletic Union, I hope the reinstatement of Jim Thorpe's amateur status can be achieved. Throughout my life and my active participation in sports, the name of Jim Thorpe has represented excellence, dedication, pride and competitive zeal. Jim Thorpe was one of the greatest athletes the world has known. He has become a legend in this country.

To Americans of Indian heritage, Mr. Thorpe has meant much more. He is a hero and in the American Indian's struggle for human dignity and freedom, Jim Thorpe represents a man who was able to contribute significantly to American Society while retaining the values of his cultural ties with the past.

For this reason, I urge you, and your Committee to consider the A.A.U.'s request.

I say this as a private citizen with a lifetime interest in sports. This decision is clearly up to you and the Committee your represent under the rules of the International Olympic Committee, by which the Unites States abides. I also recognize that under the letter of the present day rules of the Committee, a favorable decision may be difficult to reach, but I hope the Committee will consider this request and act with a sense of equity in the light of history and of the contribution that Jim Thorpe has made to the world of sport.

With warm regards,
Gerald R. Ford."[11]

While President Ford's letter did not move the IOC to action on the Jim Thorpe matter, the endless stream of acknowledgments continued. That same year Thorpe was inducted into the National Track and Field Hall of Fame at Charleston, West Virginia.

On July 20, 1976, the International Olympic Committee decided to take no action on restoring Thorpe's Olympic medals. The IOC's meeting took place the week before the start of the Olympic Games at Montreal, and it had an agenda inundated with pending problems, including a dispute over the Taiwanese teams that were being shut out of Canada for political reasons and a boycott threat by Africans. Consequently, the matter of Jim Thorpe was passed over.

The issue of what constituted amateur status had raised its ugly head prior to the start of the XI Winter Olympic Games in February 1976, at Sapporo, Japan. Austrian skier Karl Schranz, who had won a silver medal at the Olympic Games at Innsbruck in 1964, was disqualified from the Games by the IOC. The charge against Schranz was that he had lent his name and picture to advertising for financial gains.

On September 26, 1979, the U.S. House of Representatives passed a resolution by a voice vote asking the IOC to reinstate the records of Jim Thorpe to the official Olympic books. The U.S. Senate had passed the resolution on September 11.

Following the Congressional resolutions and with the approach of the

Winter Olympic Games to begin in Lake Placid, New York, in February 1980, the movement to restore Jim Thorpe's Olympic medals really began to pick up widespread support.

Robert W. Wheeler, who had written a 1975 biography of Jim Thorpe, banded together with Thorpe's second-oldest son Bill and Bill Olsen, spokesman for the Southwestern Historical Society Wax Museum in Grand Prairie, Texas. The trio began a Jim Thorpe exhibit in the museum featuring a life-size picture of Thorpe along with several mementos. Alongside the Thorpe exhibit was a petition in which there were 20,000 signatures collected. So Wheeler approached the Ohio Jaycees with the idea of a national petition drive.

In late 1979, the Ohio Jaycees, led by special projects chairman Jack Cracium, began an intensive national petition drive to restore Thorpe's medals. He gathered 50,000 signatures in Ohio alone. Cracium's next move was to have the international Jaycees organization meet in Sweden and inform the IOC of what they were doing.

The Thorpe case also got international help in 1980 from Paul Ohl, a French-Canadian writer who also served as president of the International Committee for the Reinstatement of James Frances Thorpe. In 1978 Ohl met with Grace Thorpe and was given access to her personal letters and clippings in regard to the Thorpe case. The information became the basis for Ohl's book, *"Le Dieu Sauvage"* (The Savage God), which made a strong case for Thorpe's reinstatement.

By 1982 Robert W. Wheeler and Florence Redlon had established the Jim Thorpe Foundation in Washington and began gaining further support of Congress. The ultimate goal was to argue the Thorpe case with the IOC.

Two of the IOC members most adamant about not changing their positions on Thorpe were Americans, Douglas F. Roby and Julian K. Roosevelt. Roby's reluctance was based in part on his conviction that the motivation of the Thorpe family in seeking the reinstatement of the medals was economic — that they were going to open a museum.

However, Roosevelt, a yachtsman and semi-retired investment banker from Oyster Bay, New York, simply was not well informed on the matter. In fact, he was not even aware that the AAU and the USOC had reversed themselves on Thorpe's amateur status. In regard to Robert W. Wheeler's petition drive, Roosevelt stated that he didn't care how many signatures had been collected on a petition — they were just spinning their wheels.

The long struggle to restore Jim Thorpe's Olympic medals finally came to an end on October 13, 1982, when William E. Simon, president of the USOC, met with IOC president Juan Antonio Samaranch and was successful at restoring Thorpe's medals posthumously. While the IOC agreed to add the name of "Jim Thorpe" to the list of athletes who were crowned Olympic Champions at the 1912 Olympic Games, it did not agree to modify the official report of the Games.

So while Thorpe's gold medals in the pentathlon and decathlon have been restored, the official records of the 1912 Olympic Games still show Ferdinand Bie of Norway as the pentathlon winner and Hugo Wieslander of Sweden as the winner of the decathlon. While the IOC had no intention of asking the heirs of Ferdinand Bie or Hugo Wieslander to surrender their gold medals, it would have been a futile request. According to Bie's family, his 1912 Olympic gold medal for the pentathlon had been stolen many years ago. As for Wieslander's gold medal, it was on display in the Swedish Hall of Fame in Stockholm.

Both Douglas Roby and Julian Roosevelt reversed their positions and voted for the return of the medals. In 1984 the USOC would censure Roosevelt, one of two Americans serving on the 88-member IOC, for missing too many USOC meetings and for his lack of support for USOC policies. According to William E. Simon, Roosevelt had repeatedly voted in the IOC counter to the USOC stance on issues.

When asked why it had taken so long for the IOC to change Thorpe's status, President Samaranch stated, "I don't know. For the first time since I became president we studied this problem, and we solved it in two hours."[12]

William E. Simon had served both Presidents Nixon and Ford in the Treasury Department and knew how to make political deals. Whether Simon made any extraordinary concessions or agreed to any future favors to the IOC in return for the restoration of Jim Thorpe's Olympic medals is not known.

The exact reasons the IOC suddenly reversed itself on the Jim Thorpe medals are subject to speculation. Perhaps seeing that hundreds of thousands of signatures were collected in a petition drive favoring Thorpe may have led the IOC to realize that the Jaycees could also collect millions of dollars for legal actions on the matter. The IOC is a very conservative organization that is rich with television contract money from the winter and summer Olympic Games. It may have come to the conclusion that to carry on a 70-year fight over the Thorpe medals no longer made any sense, or that legal action could seriously damage the IOC's image and become unsettling to the status quo.

Robert W. Wheeler had also brought to the attention of the IOC that Jim Thorpe was a ward of the U.S. Government in 1913 and therefore should have been provided legal counsel. Thorpe faced the charges alone, and not even his mentor Glenn S. "Pop" Warner rose to defend him. According to Wheeler, although he denied it, Pop Warner had arranged for Thorpe to play summer baseball. Wheeler claimed that he had statements from Warner's secretary and other associates that he had sent Thorpe and two other Carlisle students to North Carolina to play baseball under the school's "outing" system.

All this was coming to light just as the IOC's stance on professional competitors not being permitted to compete in the Olympic Games was starting to ease. In some ways the Thorpe case may have been perceived as a moot issue, not worthy of an agenda item.

Furthermore Wheeler was prepared to inform the IOC that the rules of the 1912 Olympic Games (or V Olympiad) had been violated in regard to objections to the qualification of a competitor. According to Wheeler, the rules stated that objections to a competitor "must be accompanied by a deposit of 20 Swedish kroner and received by the Swedish Olympic committee before the lapse of 30 days from the distribution of prizes."[13] The action taken against Thorpe had occurred in January 1913, six months after the 1912 Olympic Games were completed.

While Grace Thorpe was an important player in the ultimate decision of the IOC in the decision to return Jim Thorpe's gold medals, the most persistent of the Thorpe children in the fight had been his second-born daughter, Charlotte. Sometimes fighting the IOC alone, she had put $8,000 of her own money into the battle and also fought with her siblings who she felt had an ulterior motive of making money off the restoration of her father's Olympic medals.

For Charlotte Thorpe, the restoration of her father's amateur status and the return of his medals was an incomplete victory. She felt her father will always be viewed as a victim rather than a victor. "I just kept on pushing," said Charlotte. "The IOC hated me. That's all right, I couldn't care less. But after all the effort and all the years I've put into this, I'd call it a lost cause."[14]

Grace Thorpe felt her sister Charlotte was a bit emotional and difficult to talk with. "She's just a little contrary, it doesn't mean she's wrong. But she is wrong in feeling she did all the work,"[15] said Grace.

It may be perceived as half a loaf, but justice had finally been done for Jim Thorpe. Unfortunately it came 29 years after his death. On January 18, 1983, in Los Angeles, Juan Antonio Samaranch, president of the IOC, presented new gold medals to two of Jim Thorpe's children, oldest daughter Gail (pentathlon medal) and oldest son Bill (decathlon medal). Present for the ceremonies were six of Jim Thorpe's seven children, 13 grandchildren and 16 great-grandchildren.

The Thorpe medals eventually found a resting place in an exhibit in the Oklahoma State Capitol, having been donated by the Thorpe children. But

15 years after the medals were restored, they were stolen from the exhibit. They were recovered when an 18-year-old janitor, Terry D. Anderson, turned himself in to the Oklahoma Highway Patrol on September 24, 1998.

Today the legacy of Jim Thorpe is still being rebuilt, but as a sports legend he has no equal. On December 11, 2004, at a sports memorabilia auction, Jim Thorpe's Canton Bulldogs football jersey sold for $284,350. The jersey, from 1916-1917 with a tan Canton "C" knit into the fabric, had been preserved by Thorpe's third wife, Patricia.

Although his Olympic medals have been returned and the somewhat macabre battle for his remains continues, the truth about Jim Thorpe, All-American, Olympic Champion and major leaguer, is that he is still a big draw at the gate.

Chapter Notes

Chapter 1

1. "I am no more proud of...," Jim Thorpe with Maxwell Stiles, "This Is My Story," *Sports World,* September 1949, 43.

Chapter 2

1. "have viewed the land as a...," Frank Waters, "The Changing and Unchangeable West," from Clarus Backes, editor. *Growing Up Western* (New York: Harper Perennial, 1989).
2. Ibid.
3. "I wanted him to go and...," Jack Newcombe, review of "The Best of the Athletic Boys," *Sporting News,* January 24, 1976.
4. "When we begin to give our Indians the same...," R. H. Pratt, October 14, 1916, from documents in the archives of the Cumberland County Historical Association and The Hamilton Library Association, Carlisle, PA.
5. "There is as much hope of educating the Apache...," O. B. Super, "Indian Education at Carlisle," *New England Magazine,* April 1895, 32.
6. "miserable state of cultural dislocation...," Jane Yu, "Carlisle Indian School," *The Pennsylvania Center for the Book,* Spring 2009. www.libraries.psu.edu/palitmap/CarlisleIndian School.htm.

Chapter 3

1. "hotly contested resulting in a victory for us...," from "The Chicago Trip — Game with the Wisconsin University," *The Indian Helper,* A Weekly Letter, from the Indian Industrial School, Carlisle, PA 12, no. 12 (December 25, 1896): 2.
2. "My boys have gone into the foot-ball craze...," O. B. Super, "Indian Education at Carlisle," *New England Magazine,* April 1895, 33.
3. "Irregular playing was resorted to by Cornell...," from "The Cornell Game — Rank Umpiring," *Carlisle Daily Herald,* published in *The Indian Helper,* October 14, 1898. http://home.epix.net/~landis/hudson.html.
4. "The Art Department at Carlisle had been...," Sarah McAnulty, "Angel DeCora: American Artist and Educator," www.tfaoi.com/aa/4aa27b.htm.
5. "since the track and field seem more adapted...," Jeffrey Powers-Beck, *The American Integration of Baseball* (Lincoln: University of Nebraska Press, 2004): 42.

Chapter 4

1. "Are those the clothes you had on...," Jim Thorpe with Maxwell Stiles, "This Is My Story," *Sports World,* Vol. I, September 1949, 68.

2. Ibid.

3. "Most of the times the games...," James A. Peterson, "Thorpe of Carlisle," from the 19th annual Hinckley & Schmitt Football Luncheon, from the archives of the Pro Football Hall of Fame, Canton, OH.

4. "The Indian loves football better...," Walter H. Eckersall, "Football, the Indian Game," *Chicago Tribune,* 12 November 1907, 12.

5. "There is no reason why the Carlisle students," Dr. Carlos Montezuma, "Carlisle's Athletic Policy Criticized by Dr. Montezuma," *Chicago Tribune,* 24 November 1907, C2.

6. "The contracts are coming in...," Jeffrey Powers-Beck, *The American Integration of Baseball* (Lincoln: University of Nebraska Press, 2004): 36.

7. "What for...," from "Out of Jim Thorpe's Past," *Harrisburg Patriot,* 21 January 1969, 21.

Chapter 5

1. "Here it is...," Jim Thorpe with Maxwell Stiles, "This Is My Story," *Sports World,* Vol. I, September 1949, 69.

2. "You don't think you can beat me...," Arthur Daley, "Painting the Lily Again," *New York Times,* 20 December 1938.

3. "All of us had been warned...," Harold Sauerbrol, "Thorpe Was So Powerful That He Even Beat Tide of Atlantic Ocean, Ex-Teammate Recalls," *Cleveland Plain Dealer,* date unknown, from the archives of the Pro Football Hall of Fame, Canton, OH.

4. Ibid.

5. "To say Thorpe is the whole team...," Jim Thorpe with Maxwell Stiles, "This Is My Story," *Sports World,* Vol. I, September 1949, 69.

Chapter 6

1. "Thorpe showed his all round...," from "Jim Thorpe Wins Pentathlon Tryout," May 1912, in Thorpe file at the National Baseball Hall of Fame library, Cooperstown, NY.

2. "There is no denying...," Jim Thorpe with Maxwell Stiles, "This Is My Story," *Sports World,* Vol. I, September 1949, 70.

3. "You, sir, are the most...," from article by Robert Edgren in *News Tribune,* 20 July 1912, in Thorpe file at the National Baseball Hall of Fame library, Cooperstown, NY.

4. "Pittsburg has never tried to...," from "Jimmy Thorpe Likes The Sox," *Boston Post,* 12 August 1912, 7.

5. "His people, the Hopi Tribe of Arizona...," from "Spectacular Parade of Military and Civic Organizations" *The Carlisle Arrow* 9, no. 2, 13 September 1912.

6. Ibid.

7. Ibid.

8. "sat alone in an automobile...," from "New York Honors Athletes," *Chicago Daily Tribune,* 25 August 1912, C3.

Chapter 7

1. "Dunno." from Wonderful Indian Thorpe, an article in the Pittsburgh Gazette, October 20, 1912.

2. "as we came up to the Army game...," Jim Thorpe with Maxwell Stiles, "This Is My Story, *Sports World,* Vol. I, September 1949, 70.

3. "I guess that was the longest run...," Gene Schoor, *The Jim Thorpe Story: America's Greatest Athlete* (New York: Simon & Schuster, 1976): 5.

4. "Thorpe went through the West Point line...," from "Thorpe's Indians Crush West Point," *New York Times,* 10 November 1912.

Chapter 8

1. "Jim Thorpe who in the Olympic...," from Sports Observatory Snapshots, an article by Edward Moss, published in an unknown source, January 1913, in the archives of the National Baseball Hall of Fame and Museum, Cooperstown, NY.

2. "I never saw Thorpe...," Sam Weller, "'Cal' Would Sign Thorpe for Sox," *Chicago Daily Tribune*, 29 January 29 1913, 14.

3. "Thorpe Apology Offered," source unknown, Thorpe file at the National Baseball Hall of Fame Library, Cooperstown, NY.

4. Ibid.

5. "Olympic Prizes Lost: Thorpe No Amateur," *New York Times*, 28 January 1913, 3.

6. "Amateur rules don't make...," Harvey T. Woodruff, *Chicago Daily Tribune*, 16 February 1913, C4.

7. "The 'crime' for which Thorpe has...," from "Mr. Thorpe's Case," *The Sporting News*, 6 February 1913, 1.

Chapter 9

1. "Football is fine...," from a clipping dated April 11, 1940, in the Thorpe file at the National Baseball Hall of Fame Library, Cooperstown, NY.

2. "If I had one, I have had a dozen...," from *Chicago Daily Tribune*, 7 February 7 1913, 18.

3. "Had I known you wanted him...," from a letter by P. T. Powers to Garry Herrmann, 1 February 1912, in Thorpe file at the National Baseball Hall of Fame Library, Cooperstown, NY.

4. "I want to say for Thorpe...," from "Thorpe Dealt Fair," *The Sporting News*, 13 February 1913, 3.

5. "I am not going to count anything...," from "Big Crowd Sees Thorpe Sign Contract with Giants," source unknown, in Thorpe file at the National Baseball Hall of Fame library, Cooperstown, NY.

6. "Abner Davis before he shipped...," Ty Cooke, 6 February 1913, clipping in Thorpe file at the National Baseball Hall of Fame Library, Cooperstown, NY.

7. "That's the hardest ball...," Jim Thorpe, as told to Irving Wallace, "It's Mister Umpire," *American Legion Magazine*, 1940, 19.

8. "It keeps one guessing...," Hugh Fullerton, *Chicago Daily Tribune*, March 13, 1913, 10.

9. "The idea that a good many people...," from "Thorpe in Giant War Paint," *The Sporting News*, 16 March 1913, 2.

10. "You know Chief...," Lawrence S. Ritter, *The Glory of Their Times—The Story of the Early Days of Baseball Told by the Men Who Played It* (New York: Macmillan, 1966), 75.

11. "He has a lot to learn about baseball...," John J. McGraw, "Jim Thorpe Is Fine Prospect; He Will Stick The Season," *Atlanta Constitution*, 6 April 6 1913.

12. Ibid.

13. "In another month or so...," from "Jim Thorpe's Future Is Assured," *Sporting Life*, 19 July 1913.

14. "Besides no Indian knows how to drink...," Jeffrey Powers-Beck, *The American Integration of Baseball* (Lincoln: University of Nebraska Press, 2004): 92.

15. . "Jim was a horse for work...," Arthur Daley, "Pop Warner Discusses Jim Thorpe," *New York Times*, 20 November 1947.

16. "I am convinced that nothing helps a young man...," John J. McGraw, *My Thirty Years in Baseball* (New York: Boni and Liveright, 1923): 257.

Chapter 10

1. "Say John, what do you think...," John J. McGraw, *My Thirty Years in Baseball* (New York: Boni and Liveright, 1923): 242.

2. Ibid.

Chapter 11

1. "I am pretty sure that Mr. Friedman...," Fred Bruce, letter to Mark Griffen, 18 November 1913, from the archives of the Cumberland County Historical Association and The Hamilton Library Association, Carlisle, PA.

2. "an unwholesome and unsatisfactory condition...," Mark Griffen, letter to Cato Sells, 24 November 24 1913, from the archives of the Cumberland County Historical Association and the Hamilton Library Association, Carlisle, PA.

3. Ibid.

4. "There are some other matters...," from an article in the *Adams County News*, Gettysburg, PA, 14 February 1914, from http://home.epix.net/~landis/investigation.html.

5. "Have any loans or advances been...," from Carlisle Indian School, Hearings Before the Joint Commission of the Congress of the United States, Sixty-Third Congress, Second Session, to Investigate Indian Affairs, February 6, 7, 8, and March 25, 1914. Washington, Government Printing Office, 1914.

Chapter 12

1. "This is the year Jim gets...," Damon Runyon, "Th' Mornin's Mornin'," March 1915, in Thorpe file at the National Baseball Hall of Fame Library, Cooperstown, NY.

Chapter 13

1. "one fellow lost his barber shop...," from an article in the *Los Angeles Evening Herald*, 14 December 1939, pg. 13, from the archives of the Pro Football Hall of Fame, Canton, OH.

2. "that any player crossing the goal line...," from "Jack Cusack, Pioneer in Pro Football," from the archives of the Pro Football Hall of Fame, Canton, OH.

3. "Sunday night a side bet of...," from the Canton *Evening Repository*, 29 November 29 1915, 6.

4. "I had thirty dollars bet on that game...," from "Jack Cusack, Pioneer in Pro Football," from the archives of the Pro Football Hall of Fame, Canton, OH.

5. "You shouldn't do that Sonny...," from an article by the Professional Football Researchers Association (re: 1915), www.profootballresearchers.org.

6. "It was the most powerful line...," from "Nash Hands Bulldogs Credit," Canton *Evening Repository*, 4 December 1916, 7.

7. "After a decade and a half and oft-time...," from "At Last Canton Can Boast Clear Title to 'Pro' Championship," Canton *Evening Repository*, 4 December 1916, 7.

Chapter 14

1. Letter from H. N. Hempstead to August Herrmann, 24 April 1917, from the August Herrmann Papers, 1877–1938, in the archives of the National Baseball Hall of Fame Library, Cooperstown, NY.

2. "The aborigine comes for a...," from "Gossip of the Game," *Cincinnati Commercial Tribune*, 24 April 24, 3.

3. "Hell we ain't even got a hit...," Arthur Daley, "Of Historical Importance," *New York Times*, 30 April 1967, in Thorpe file at the National Baseball Hall of Fame Library, Cooperstown, NY.

4. "It seemed to be right in front...," W. A. Phelon, "Red and Cub Hurlers Were in Wonderful Form, and Their Work was Equal Until The Tenth Inning — Chicago Fans Applauded Both Men," *Cincinnati Times-Star*, 3 May 1917, 3.

5. "No sir, Mr. McGraw...," from "A deep-seated urge to get in the ring with a real fighter," *Sports Illustrated*, 17 October 1977, http://sportsillustrated.cnn.com.

6. "You know Jim...," from "Canton Wins Again —1917," Professional Football Researchers Association, www.profootballresearchers.org.

7. "Pro football in the days of Jim Thorpe...," from "We Remember Jim Thorpe," in the archives of the Pro Football Hall of Fame, Canton, OH.

Chapter 15

1. "He has heard so often...," Frank Graham, *McGraw of the Giants — An Informal Biography* (New York: G.P. Putnam's Sons, 1944): 125.

2. Ibid.

3. "Most of time we were on our own...," Lawrence S. Ritter, *The Glory of Their Times — The Story of the Early Days of Baseball Told by the Men Who Played It* (New York: Macmillan, 1966), 93.

4. Ibid, 92.

5. "What do you think you would do...," Ted Williams, "Jousting with the Knights of the Keyboard," in John Thorn, ed., *The Complete Armchair of Baseball* (New York: Galahad, 1997), 425–427.

Chapter 16

1. "In the east it is a common occurrence...," Walter Eckersall, "Pro Football Looms as Danger to Great College Game," *Chicago Daily Tribune*, 26 November 1919, 15.

Chapter 17

1. "You often didn't know whom...," Associated Press Sports Staff, *A Century of Sports* (Plimpton Press, 1971): 2.

2. "It was moved and seconded...," from the minutes of the American Professional Football Association, 17 September 1920, from the archives of the Pro Football Hall of Fame, Canton, OH.

3. "I figured if they started something...," Associated Press Sports Staff, *A Century of Sports* (The Plimpton Press, 1971): 6.

4. "It was a dandy excuse to raise hell...," from Oorang Indians Media Guide, 1922-1923, Professional Football Researchers Association, 1981, from the archives of the Pro Football Hall of Fame, Canton, OH.

5. "Old Jim has slowed up...," Associated Press Sports Staff, *A Century of Sports* (The Plimpton Press, 1971): 6.

Chapter 18

1. "I figure an exclusive franchise for...," Associated Press Sports Staff, *A Century of Sports* (Plimpton Press, 1971): 6.

2. "This is a game that calls for men...," Dan Kennedy, "Men of Iron — A Salute to the 100th Anniversary of Football at Illinois," *Illinois Quarterly* 2, No. 3 (Fall 1990): 8.

3. "Nevers was a great team player...," Kyle Crichton, "Good King Jim," *Collier's*, 14 November 1942, 42.

4. "He was the greatest...," Associated Press, "Grid Men Mourn Warner," *The Home News,* 8 September 1954, 38.

5. "All the athletic teams he got...," from "History Detectives," Episode 10, 2005: "Jim Thorpe Ticket," Jamestown, New York. Oregon Public Broadcasting, www.pbs.org/history-dectectives.

Chapter 19

1. "When he was drinking...," Paul Zimmerman, "Calling Signals," *Weekend Kickoff,* 25 October 1974: 2.

2. "Old Jim, he just sits around...," Westbrook Pegler, "Whata Man Was Thorpe, but Whata Man IS Jim Bausch," *Chicago Daily Tribune,* 8 August 1932, 17.

3. "It isn't my idea to tell directors...," from "Casting Bureau to Obtain Film Bits for Indians," *Chicago Daily Tribune,* 19 March 19 1933, W7.

4. "Personally, I would be deeply...," George Schafer, "Add Jim Thorpe to Voters for U.S. in Olympics," *Chicago Daily Tribune,* 7 December 1935, 29.

5. "You don't last long enough...," Stanley Frank, "You Can't Give Giants Back to This Old Injun," unknown source, 24 August 1939, in Thorpe file at the National Baseball Hall of Fame Library, Cooperstown, NY.

6. "He moves like a fellow going to...," Will Wedge, "Thorpe Inspects the Giants," unknown source, 24 August 1939, in Thorpe file at the National Baseball Hall of Fame Library, Cooperstown, NY.

7. "I don't like to see the Giants lose...," Stanley Frank, "You Can't Give Giants Back to This Old Injun," unknown source, 24 August 1939, in Thorpe file at the National Baseball Hall of Fame Library, Cooperstown, NY.

8. "If the American Athletic Union was made up...," Stanley Woodward, "A visit with Jim Thorpe," *New York Tribune,* 23 December 1940.

9. Ibid.

10. "Truthfully, I can't say one good...," Jack McCallum, "The Rebuilding of a Legend," *Sports Illustrated,* 25 October 1982: 65.

11. "Every broken down athlete...," Furman Bisher, *Atlanta Constitution,* 19 March 1972, 31.

12. Ibid.

13. "In 'Jim Thorpe' we didn't...," Hedda Hopper, "Burly Burt Has a Brain," *Chicago Daily Tribune,* 12 August 1951, F4.

14. "Back in 1931...," Arthur Daley, "A Visit with Jim Thorpe," *New York Times,* 11 November 1951.

15. "Sure he could get those things back...," James A. Bruchard, "Thorpe Wants Trophies He Won in 1912 Olympics," unknown source, in Thorpe file at the National Baseball Hall of Fame Library, Cooperstown, NY.

Chapter 20

1. "The Great Spirit...," from "Jim Thorpe Dies," *The Indian Leader,* Haskell Institute, 10 April 1953, 7.

2. "Brown isn't fast enough like...," Associated Press, "Thorpe Teammate Recalls Jim," *Chicago Tribune,* 15 August 1965, C5.

3. "Pat just wanted too much money...," Jack McCallum, "The Rebuilding of a Legend," *Sports Illustrated,* 25 October 1982: 62.

4. "I've got an idea...," Furman Bisher, *Atlanta Constitution,* 19 March 1972, 31.

5. "All we got was a dead Indian...," United Press International, "Carlisle Is Keeping Thorpe in Dignity," unknown source, 6 September 1981, in Thorpe file at the National Baseball Hall of Fame Library, Cooperstown, N Y.

6. "We offered to work with them...," Jonathan Poet, "Jim Thorpe's Son Seeks to Move Body from Pa.," *Philadelphia Inquirer,* 19 August 2001.

7. Ibid.

8. "The bones of my father...," from "AP Newsbreak: Thorpe's Son Seeks Return of Remains," KGO-AM 810, San Francisco, 24 June 2010, http://hosted2.ap.org/KGOAM.

9. "Oh, no...," C. C. Johnson Spink, "We Believe," *The Sporting News,* 14 June 1969.

10. "The family received a telegram...," from "Justice for Jim Thorpe," *Congressional Record— Senate,* S 10230, 10 June 1975.

11. From "Jim Thorpe," *Congressional Record*— Senate, S 18137, 9 October 1975.

12. "I don't know...," Jack McCallum, "The Rebuilding of a Legend," *Sports Illustrated,* 25 October 1982: 52.

13. "must be accompanied by...," Bob McCoy, "The Thorpe Case," unknown source, 10 June 1983, in Thorpe file at the National Baseball Hall of Fame library, Cooperstown, NY.

14. "I just kept on pushing...," Dave Anderson, "Jim Thorpe's Family Feud," *New York Times*, 7 February 1983, C4.

15. Ibid.

Bibliography

Books

Allen, Lee. *Cooperstown Corner: Columns from* The Sporting News *1962–1969.* Cleveland, OH: SABR.

Anderson, Lars. *Carlisle vs. Army: Jim Thorpe, Dwight Eisenhower, Pop Warner and the Forgotten Story of Football's Greatest Battle.* New York: Random House, 2007.

Associated Press Sports Staff, Supervising Editor: Will Grimsley, Photo Editor: Thomas V. diLustro. *A Century of Sports.* Norwood, MA: Plimpton Press, 1971.

Bernotas, Bob. *Jim Thorpe: Sac and Fox Athlete (North American Indians of Achievement).* New York: Chelsea House Publishers, 1992.

Crawford, Bill. *All American: The Rise and Fall of Jim Thorpe,* Hoboken, NJ: John Wiley & Sons, 2005.

Dellinger, Susan. *Red Legs and Black Sox: Edd Roush and the Untold Story of the 1919 World Series,* Cincinnati, OH: Emmis Books, 2006.

Elfers, James E. *The Tour to End All Tours: The Story of Major League Baseball's 1913-1914 World Tour.* Lincoln: University of Nebraska, 2003.

Graham, Frank. *McGraw of the Giants, an Informal Biography.* New York: G. P. Putnam's Sons, 1944.

Jenkins, Sally. *The Real All Americans: The Team That Changed a Game, a People, a Nation.* New York: Doubleday, 2007.

Johnson, Lloyd. *Baseball's Book of Firsts.* Philadelphia, PA: Courage Books, 1999.

McGraw, John J. *My Thirty Years in Baseball,* New York: Boni and Liveright, 1923.

Neft, David S., Richard M. Cohen and Michael L. Neft. *The Sports Encyclopedia: Baseball 2000,* New York: St. Martin's Griffin, 2000.

Oorang Indians Media Guide 1922-1923, compiled, written and edited by Bob Braunwart, Bob Carrol and Joe Horrigan. Warminster, PA: Professional Football Researchers Association, 1981.

Powers-Beck, Jeffrey. *The American Indian Integration of Baseball.* Lincoln: University of Nebraska, 2004.

Reichler, Joseph L., editor. *The Baseball Encyclopedia: The Complete and Official Record of Major League Baseball,* 7th Edition. New York: MacMillan, 1988.

Ritter, Lawrence S. *The Glory of Their Times: The Story of the Early Days of Baseball Told by the Men Who Played It.* New York: Macmillan, 1966.

Schoor, Gene, *The Jim Thorpe Story: America's Greatest Athlete.* New York: Pocket Books, 1976.

Waters, Frank. *"The Changing and Unchangeable West," in Growing Up Western,* edited by Clarus Backes. New York: Harper, 1989.

Wheeler, Robert W. *Jim Thorpe: World's Greatest Athlete,* Norman: University of Oklahoma Press, 1975.

Williams, Ted. *Jousting with the Knights of the Keyboard, from the Complete Armchair Book of Baseball,* edited by John Thorn. New York: Galahad Books, 1997.

Special Collections

The August "Garry" Herrmann Papers 1877–1938, at the National Baseball Hall of Fame Library & Archive.

Magazines

Crichton, Kyle. "Good King Jim." *Collier's.* November 14, 1942.
Kennedy, Dan. "Men of Iron: A Salute to the 100th Anniversary of Football at Illinois." *Illinois Quarterly,* 2, no. 3 (Fall 1990).
McCallum, Jack. "The Rebuilding of a Legend." *Sports Illustrated,* October 25, 1982.
Super, O.B. "Indian Education at Carlisle." *New England Magazine,* April 1895.
Thorpe, Jim. "This Is My Story," *Sports World,* 1, No. 4, September 1949.

Newspapers

Atlanta Journal & Constitution
Boston Daily Globe
Boston Post
Canton Daily News
Canton Evening Repository
Chicago Tribune
Cincinnati Commercial Tribune
Cincinnati Enquirer
Cincinnati Post
New York Times
Sporting News

Websites

www.arlingtoncemetery.com
www.bolding.com/BSR/Nation.htm
www.hailtopurple.com
www.historyplace.com/worldwar2/triumph/tr-olympics.htm
http://home.epix.net/~landis/investigation.html
www.leatherhelmetillus.com/v
www.mmbolding.com
www.newyorkhistoryreview.com/football.html
www.nytimes.com
www.pabook.libraries.psu.edu/palitmap/CarlisleIndianSchool.html
www.profootballhof.com.
www.profootballresearch.com
www.tfaoi.com/aa/4aa/4//276b.htm
www.thediamondangle.com/archive/jan03/1913tour.html
www.time.com

Libraries

Boston Public Library
New York Public Library

North Brunswick (NJ) Public Library
The Public Library of Cincinnati and Hamilton County

Archives

Cumberland County Historical Society — Carlisle, Pennsylvania
Pro Football Hall of Fame — Canton, Ohio
The National Baseball Hall of Fame & Museum — Cooperstown, New York

Index